Sheila Hamilton Macdonald is a sole practitioner barrister based in the Midlands. She specialises in family property cases, including disputes between cohabitees, ancillary relief on divorce, inheritance issues and contested probate. She also has a particular interest in mental health issues and their connection to property matters. As well as taking instructions via solicitors, she is also able to take instructions by direct or licensed access, and she is available for consultation by appointment in London and Leeds. Her website is www.sheilamacdonaldbarrister.com.

A Practical Guide to Inheritance Act Claims by Adult Children Post-Ilott v Blue Cross

A Practical Guide to Inheritance Act Claims by Adult Children Post-Ilott v Blue Cross

Sheila Hamilton Macdonald
Barrister
Gothic House, Barkergate, Nottingham
0115 784 2768
shm@familyproperty.org.uk

Law Brief Publishing

Published 2017 by Law Brief Publishing, an imprint of Law Brief Publishing Ltd
30 The Parks
Minehead
Somerset
TA24 8BT

www.lawbriefpublishing.com

Paperback: 978-1-911035-23-7

For Carrie, with love

PREFACE

I am deeply indebted to the wisdom, common sense and companionship of all of the clients that I have had the good fortune to represent in Inheritance Act matters over my career.

It would also have been impossible to write this book without the efficient and supportive clerking of Kate Brown and her colleagues Emma and Hannah, who kept the practice wheels turning while I wrote. Many thanks for all that you do.

Thanks to my enormously supportive editors and publishers Tim Kevan and Garry Wright, who stuck with this book through a period that was eventful, to put it mildly.

Finally, my deep gratitude to Sidney Ross, who guided me through my first steps in this difficult field with patience and unstinting generosity, both of his time and his knowledge.

This first edition of the book states the law as it is on 1st November 2017.

Sheila Hamilton Macdonald
November 2017

TABLE OF CASES

Re A (Child of the Family) [1998] 1 FLR 347

Re A (A Minor: Paternity: Refusal of blood test) [1994] 2 FLR 463

Ames v Jones BAILII [2016] EW Misc B67 (CC)

B v IB [2013] EWHC 3755 (Fam)

B v Nugent Care Society [2010] 1 WLR 516

Ball & Ors v Ball & Ors [2017] EWHC 1750 (Ch)

Barrett v Bem [2012] EWCA Civ 52; [2012] Ch. 573

Baynes v Hedger [2009] EWCA Civ 374

Re Beaney [1978] 1 WLR 770

Beckett v McMillan [2015] NI Ch 8

Berger v Berger [2013] EWCA Civ 1305

Bosworthick v Bosworthick [1927] P. 64

Brooks v Brooks [1996] A.C. 375; [1995] 3 W.L.R. 141; [1995] 3 All E.R. 257; [1995] 2 F.L.R. 13

Re Bunning [1984] Ch. 480; [1984] 3 W.L.R. 265

Re Callaghan [1985] Fam 1

Cameron v Treasury Solicitor [1996] 2 F.L.R. 716; [1997] 1 F.C.R. 188

Carapeto v Good [2002] EWHC 640 (Ch)

Carr v Beavan [2008] EWHC 2582 (Ch)

Challinor v Challinor [2009] EWHC 180 (Ch); [2009] W.T.L.R. 931

Re Collins Deceased [1990] Fam 56

Re Coventry (Deceased) [1980] Ch 461

Cunliffe v Fielden [2005] EWCA Civ 1508; [2006] Ch. 361

Re Debenham [1986] 1 F.L.R. 404; [1986] Fam. Law 101

Dellal v Dellal [2015] EWHC 907 (Fam)

Re Dennis Deceased [1981] 2 All ER 140

Dingmar v Dingmar [2006] EWCA Civ 942; [2007] Ch. 109; [2006] 3 W.L.R. 1183; [2007] 2 All E.R. 382; [2007] 1 F.L.R. 210; [2006] 2 F.C.R. 595; [2006] W.T.L.R. 1171

Dixit v Dixit & Ors (1983) [Unreported: 1988 WL 1608577]

Re Duranceau [1952] 3 DLR 714

E v E, [1966] 1 WLR 709; [1966] 2 All ER 44

Re Edwards [2007] EWHC 119

Escritt v Escritt (1982) 3 FLR 747

Espinosa v Bourke [1999] 1 F.L.R. 747; [1999] 3 F.C.R. 76; [1999] Fam. Law 210

F & S v TH [2016] EWHC 1605 (QB)

Ford v GKR Construction [2000] 1 WLR 1397

Re Freeman Deceased [1984] 1 WLR 1419

Re G (Parentage: Blood Sample) [1997] 1 FLR 360

Re Garland [2007] EWHC 2 (Ch); [2007] 2 F.L.R. 528; [2007] W.T.L.R. 797

Goenka v Goenka [2014] EWHC 2966 (Ch); [2016] Ch. 267

Re Gulbenkian's Settlement Trusts (No. 1) [1970] A.C. 508; [1968] 3 W.L.R. 1127

Guney v Kingsley Napley [2016] EWHC 2349 (QB)

Hanbury v Hanbury [1999] 2 F.L.R. 255; [1999] 3 F.C.R. 217

Re Hancock (Deceased) [1998] 2 FLR 346

Harrington v Gill (Estate of Frederick Bailey Deceased) (1983) 4 F.L.R. 265

Hunter v Butler [1996] RTR 396

Ilott v The Blue Cross and Others [2017] UKSC 17

Iqbal v Ahmed [2011] EWCA Civ 900

Janion v Janion [1929] P. 237

Jelley v Iliffe [1981] Fam 128

Re Jennings [1994] Ch. 286; [1994] 3 W.L.R. 67; [1994] 3 All E.R. 27

Kebbeh v Farmer [2015] EWHC 3827 (Ch)

Re Kennedy Deceased [1980] CLY 2820

Key v Key [2010] EWHC 408 (Ch); [2010] 1 W.L.R. 2020

King v Dubrey [2015] EWCA Civ 581

Re Leach [1986] Ch. 226; [1985] 3 W.L.R. 413

Lewis v Warner [2016] EWHC 1787 (Ch); [2017] Ch. 13; [2016] 3 W.L.R. 1545; [2017] 2 F.L.R. 133; [2016] W.T.L.R. 1399

Lilleyman v Lilleyman (Costs) [2012] EWHC 1056 (Ch)

Lim v Walia [2014] EWCA Civ 1076

M v S [HC ChD, unreported, 16 July 2001]

McNulty v McNulty [2002] EWHC 123 (Ch); [2002] W.T.L.R. 737

Musa v Holliday [2012] EWCA Civ 1268; [2013] 1 F.L.R. 806

Myers v Myers [2004] EWHC 1944

Nahajec v Fowle [2017] EW Misc 11

Negus v Bahouse [2008] EWCA Civ 1002; [2012] W.T.L.R. 1117

Palmer v Lawrence [2011] EWHC 3961 (Ch)

Parnall v Hurst [2003] WTLR 997

Piglowska v Piglowski [1999] 1 WLR 1360

Pinnock v Rochester [2011] EWHC 4049 (Ch)

Prinsep v Prinsep (No. 2) [1930] P 35

Robinson v Bird [2003] EWHC 30 (Ch); [2003] W.T.L.R. 529

Re Salmon Deceased [1981] Ch 167

Sandhu v Gill [2006] Ch 456

Seals v Williams [2015] EWHC 1829 (Ch)

Sen v Headley [1991] Ch. 425; [1991] 2 W.L.R. 1308

Smith v Smith & Others [2011] EWHC 2133

Spencer v Anderson [2016] EWHC 851 (Fam)

Stack v Dowden [2007] 2 AC 432 House of Lords

Stead v Stead [1985] FLR 16, [1985] Fam Law 154

Stephanides v Cohen [2002] EWHC 1869 (Fam); [2002] W.T.L.R. 1373

Stock v Brown [1994] 1 FLR 840

Suggitt v Suggitt [2012] EWCA Civ 1140; [2012] W.T.L.R. 1607

Taylor v Bell [BAILII Citation [2015] EW Misc B3 (CC)]

Thomas v Jeffery [2012] EWCA Civ 693

W(RJ) v W(SJ) [1972] Fam 152

Re Watson [1999] 1 F.L.R. 878; [1999] 3 F.C.R. 595; [1999] Fam. Law 211

Watts v Watts [2014] EWHC 668

Williams v Johns [1988] 2 FLR 475

Williams v Seals [2014] EWHC 3708 (Ch); [2015] W.T.L.R. 339

Wingrove v. Wingrove (1885) 1 PD 81

Wodzicki v Wodzicki [2017] EWCA Civ 95

Wooldridge v Wooldridge [2016] Fam. Law 451

W*right v Waters* [2014] EWHC 3614 (Ch); [2015] W.T.L.R. 353

Zarrinkhat v Kamal [2013] W.T.L.R. 1477

ABBREVIATIONS

AC		Adult child
DP		Deceased parent
Ilott	CA-Q	Ilott Court of Appeal Quantum
Ilott	SC	Ilott Supreme Court

CONTENTS

Chapter One	Introduction	1
Chapter Two	History and Overview	7
	The Ilott Case in the Supreme Court	7
	History	10
Chapter Three	Before You Start	13
	Preliminary	13
	Disputes About Parentage	15
	Domicile	19
	Limitation	20
	Costs	24
	The Settlement Imperative	26
	Proportionality	27
Chapter Four	The Machinery of the Act	31
	What the Act Does, and What It Doesn't	31
	Eligibility: The Portal	38
	The Threshold: Stage 1	44
	Making Provision: Stage 2	50
	The Maintenance Standard	59
	Starting the Balancing Exercise Under Section 3	67
Chapter Five	Taking Instructions: The Form E Exercise	71
	Form E General Approach	71
	General Points on Completing the Forms	75
	Inheritance Act Specific Form: Section 1 Completion Guidance	76
	Form E Completion Guidance: Overview	79
	Form E Part 4: Other Information	85
Chapter Six	Specially Significant Section 3 Factors in Adult Child Claims	91
	Overview of Section 3	91
	Section 3(1)(e): The Size and Nature of the Net Estate	92
	Section 3(1)(a): AC's Financial Resources and Needs	101

	Sections 3(1)(c) and (d) Any Obligations Which D Had Either Towards AC, or to Any Other Beneficiaries, or to Any Other Claimants	110
	Sections 3(1)(b) and (c): Resources and Needs of Other Beneficiaries and Claimants	118
	Section 3(1)(f): Health and Disability	126
	Section 3(1)(g): 'Sweeper' Section	124
	Section 3(3): Assumed Responsibility	133
	Section 3(6): Earning Capacity and AC's Own Obligations	136
Chapter Seven	Completing the Balancing Exercise for Stage 1	137
	Value Judgment	137
	Balancing	138
	Espinosa v Bourke: A Classic Example From Practice	141
Chapter Eight	The Court's Powers, and Completing Stage 2	143
	Overview of the Court's Powers	143
	Powers Under Section 2: Property in the Estate	144
	Property in the Hands of Third Parties: Section 2(4)(a)	158
	Property Held in a Joint Tenancy: Section 9	158
	Voidable Dispositions: Section 10	160
	Completing the Balancing Exercise for Stage 2	162
	A Real-Life Example of Stage 2: Espinosa Again	164
	Over-Provision and Ambitious Claims	165
Chapter Nine	Other Legal Claims on the Estate by Adult Children	167
	Overview	167
	Probate Challenges	168
	Other Challenges	172
	Claims Under the Trusts of Land and Appointment of Trustees Act [TLATA] 1996	175
Chapter Ten	Practice and Procedure	177
	Appropriate Court	177
	Early Neutral Evaluation (ENE)	178
	Early Disclosure	178

	Settlement	181
	Urgent and Interim Applications	183
Coda	A Final Word on Client Care	185
Appendix I	Inheritance (Provision for Family and Dependants) Act 1975	187
Appendix II	Inheritance Act Instruction for Use With Form E: Section 1	225
Appendix III	Further Reading	229

CHAPTER ONE
INTRODUCTION

1.1 The purpose of this book is to guide you through how to put together a claim in a 1975 Act application by an adult child. While it concentrates on claimants, it should also be of assistance to those defending a claim, whether they are executors/administrators or beneficiaries. It is intended to be helpful to legal practitioners without specific experience in this area of the law, but I hope it will also be helpful to potential claimants or defendants who are considering acting in person.

1.2 This is not a textbook, but a practical guide. It does not discuss the law in detail, but points out the areas of danger, doubt and uncertainty, and directs you onward to practitioner textbooks that will help with specific issues in your client's case.

1.3 The focus is on case preparation and not on litigation. There is very little in this book about procedure, and I have recommended further textbooks for those aspects of your case. It does, however, deal in detail with the question of making settlement offers and of attempting to settle via mediation. The litigation costs of an Inheritance Act claim are extremely high, and many claims are simply not cost-effective to litigate. Apart from the general duty on all parties to attempt to settle at the earliest possible stage under the Civil Procedure Rules, it can be negligent to advise a client to bring or defend a claim where the estate will certainly be exhausted long before the matter has reached trial.

1.4 You will come to see right away that Inheritance Act cases require considerable preparation work at the beginning of your instructions if costs and time are not to be wasted: in other words, that they are front-loaded. It is extremely risky to enter into litigation, or even into negotiations with the other side, without a realistic and reasonable idea of what your client is likely to achieve, and how she can achieve it. But extensive preparation work at an early stage is inevitably expensive, so I have suggested various ways in which you can be sure that you concentrate on what is relevant and do not get sidetracked into factors which are not relevant. The main tactic is to structure your instructions, which I have based in this book on the Form E exercise.

1.5 There are two factors that need to be borne in mind in preparing an adult child claim since the Supreme Court decision in *Ilott.* The first, which has been important since the Act was first passed, is the necessity of looking at **all** of the factors under section 3 of the Act when deciding whether or not reasonable provision has been made. The second, which has been confirmed by *Ilott SC*, is that the section 3 exercise is, in every case and at both of its stages, a value judgment by the trial Judge. These two factors taken together mean that you must put together the most complete case available and make as dispassionate a judgment as you can about your client's prospects, because it is likely to become increasingly difficult to challenge the first-instance value judgment. This book therefore goes through the matters you will need to consider so as to get your claim in good order as early as possible.

1.6 I start by highlighting at Chapter 3 some matters that you need to consider at the very early stage, including questions of whether your client is eligible to make a claim. We will then look at how the Act works in Chapter 4, and clear up some common misconceptions about its purpose.

1.7 In Chapter 5, I will suggest a way of getting the best instructions possible from your client by using a modified Form E from the matrimonial jurisdiction, with suggestions for a substituted Section 1 which sets out matters more relevant to an Inheritance Act claim. I have provided links to the Form that I have created for these extra questions, which is included in this book at Appendix 2 and also available on my website. We will work through the amended Form E, setting out the matters upon which you may need further instructions or follow-up in the case of an adult child.

1.8 Then in Chapter 6 we will apply the facts that you now have from those instructions to the factors that the Court must consider under section 3 of the Act, with a special emphasis on how these factors have impacted on adult child claims in the past and may be significant in your case. Many of these factors apply to all claimants but there are some matters at section 3(3) which are specific to child claims, including the claims of adult children, and we will look at these.

1.10 At Chapter 7, we will look at how the section 3 balancing exercise, or value judgment, has been carried out in the past, and I will suggest the factors to look out for when making a "stage 1" assessment in your adult child case, namely whether or not the disposition of the estate has made reasonable provision for your client.

1.11 Chapter 8 deals with the considerable powers that the Court has to redistribute the deceased parent's estate where it is appropriate to do so. We will look at those powers, and then consider how they have been used in the "stage 2" assessment, namely how the Court orders reasonable provision to be made for the adult child. We will look in particular at the firm re-statement in *Ilott* SC that the relevant standard is **reasonable maintenance** and in particular that the award is not intended to provide the claimant with capital.

1.12 Inheritance Act claims are often combined with other claims, particularly challenges to the Will, proprietary estoppel, or claims to a beneficial interest in a trust, and I have given a brief guide to these in Chapter 9.

1.13 Finally, although this is not a procedural guide, I deal with some early stage procedural issues at Chapter 10, particularly the questions of settlement, early neutral evaluation and financial dispute resolution (FDR) hearings.

1.14 I make no apologies for the fact that the focus of this book is also on client care. More than most other areas of the law, this is an area where the adviser is often faced with deep grievances which are now impossible to resolve. Nobody looking through the case law can fail to be struck by how often long-standing grudges are played out with the Inheritance Act as the background, and long-forgotten family feuds are re-ignited. It is not enough to be satisfied that you have got the law right; you can get the law right and still give the client a bad or indifferent service. An adult child who has been left nothing under a parent's Will or intestacy usually has a double grief: not just the death of a parent, but an agonising and unanswerable question about why s/he was not thought of at the last. That grief can be channelled into using litigation to fight old family battles, including attempts to impose blame for DP's death on other family members by punishing them financially. Cases involving second families can be particularly fraught. One of the biggest challenges for a practitioner is to explain to an emotional client, convinced that the Will is not "fair", that the 1975 Act is not, in fact, about fairness.

1.15 I have tried to point out where appropriate the stages of the case where insensitivity to the client's needs and failure to explain the law adequately can have harmful and even disastrous costs consequences. It is very common when representing the estate, for example, to receive initial instructions not to yield by a millimetre or cede one penny. They may be sensible instructions, but they are more likely to be instructions given under the pressure of intense emotion and therefore not properly or fully informed. Your difficult task as the legal adviser is to make it clear that you understand that pressure, while at the same time spelling out how the law can, and cannot, assist.

1.16 I gratefully adopt and adapt the words of Hughes LJ in *Ilott SC* itself, where at [4] he said "*some of the factors inevitably dealt with ... may apply also to types of case other than those of adult children living separately from the deceased, but there is no occasion ... to attempt to meet every difficulty to which claims for family provision may arise*". This is specifically a book about adult child claims and it does not deal with family provision claims more generally. All Inheritance Act claimants will have to consider the s.3 factors in their particular case, for example, but in this book I am only commenting on the factors that will be of particular relevance to "AC".

1.17 Finally, a few words about naming and the tangles that can arise. I was reminded while writing this book of David Hockney's remark about the pre-eminent master of post-Impressionism that "*some people refer to him as Van Hoch, some as Van Goff and some as Van Go, so I'm just going to call him Vincent*". Although abbreviating the Inheritance (Provision for Family and Dependants) Act 1975 to "the Inheritance Act" risks some very minimal confusion with the earlier Act of 1938, it is to my mind better than constant repetition of "the I(PFD)A 1975", which is awkward and unwieldy, and avoids confusion with the Insolvency Act 1986, which is often referred to as the "IA". Accordingly, therefore, the Act is referred to as "the Inheritance Act" throughout.

1.18 In an effort to keep the language of this book as inclusive and gender-neutral as possible, I have called the adult child claimant "AC" throughout, and the deceased parent "DP". I have used the feminine pronoun for AC and DP throughout except where a male is clearly being referred to – in relation to paternity, for instance. However, where I am dealing with the author of a Will, I have preferred to use the words “testator” and “executor” to the (to my mind) over-fussy “testatrix” and “executrix”.

1.19 The case law on Inheritance Act claims by adult children does not reflect all of the issues which are likely to arise in practice, and it is more than helpful to look at how the Courts have dealt with those issues when the claim has been made for example by a widow or an infant child. I have tried to make the class of claimant clear in every case. The one big difference to bear in mind when looking at surviving spouse cases is that the maintenance standard is higher, and I have tried in all appropriate examples to indicate where I believe an AC would do less well under similar circumstances.

1.20 For further information, discussions and updates on Inheritance Act claims by adult children, including reports of new cases as they appear, please visit my website at http://familyproperty.org.uk/inheritance-act-book/ where you can also join my mailing list and an adult children Inheritance Act practitioners' forum.

CHAPTER TWO
HISTORY AND OVERVIEW

2.1 The Ilott Case in the Supreme Court
2.2 History

2.1 The Ilott Case in the Supreme Court

2.1.1 The Supreme Court decision in *Ilott v The Blue Cross and Others* [2017] UKSC 17 (which from now on I will refer to as *Ilott SC* to distinguish it from the Ilott cases in the lower courts) is a pivotal point in the development of adult children to make claims against the estate of their deceased parents. For the first time, the highest court in the land looked at the Inheritance (Provision for Family and Dependants) Act 1975 and analysed how the Act is working -- with a particular focus on adult child claimants.

2.1.2 It is not by chance that the first ever Inheritance Act case to reach the Supreme Court is one brought by an adult child. Although there have been other points of doubt and conflict surrounding the 1975 Act -- the position of cohabitees, for example, or the degree to which an applicant under section 1(e) was being maintained by the deceased -- it is the rights of adult children to make claims under section 1(1)(c) and 1(1)(d) of the Act that have caused the most controversy, and many of the practical difficulties. As Hale B points out in her judgment in *Ilott SC*, the general public have definite, but often contradictory, views about how far an adult child should be able to claim an inheritance from her parent.

2.1.3 Testamentary freedom, or the absolute right to leave one's property as one wishes, appears to have surprisingly broad support in the UK. There is a strong sentiment that a testator should not be obliged to leave property to family members who have disappointed or wronged her in some way, but is completely free to leave property to those outside the family for whom she feels ties of gratitude or simply affection. The less appreciated difficulty with total testamentary freedom however is that it is also the freedom to be cruel; to be spiteful;

to be prejudiced; and to be unreasonable or unjust. As we will see, the Inheritance Act does not prevent testators being any of these things; the Act's machinery will only operate when the objective result of the spite or injustice is not to make reasonable provision for AC.

2.1.4 Ilott SC preserves the principle of testamentary freedom in two main ways: first, by re-emphasising that the relevant standard is the maintenance standard, and that any changes in the disposition of the estate must be closely linked to that standard. It also re-emphasises that weight **must** be given to the testator's wishes, even where, as in *Ilott* itself, the testator's expressed wish that the charities should benefit had been, as the original trial judge found, "harsh and unreasonable" towards her only child.

2.1.5 Two members of the Supreme Court give judgements in *Ilott SC.* Hughes LJ, with whom all of the other members of the Court agree, sets out the Court's decision on the facts of the *Ilott* case and gives guidance on the correct approach for future cases. Hale B's judgement sets out the societal background to the 1975 Act legislation, including the attitudes expressed to adult child inheritance in recent studies, and then identifies significant inadequacies within the Act which make the Court's decision more difficult. It is noteworthy that this section of the judgment was not unanimous, so the observations made by Hale B did not have total support.

2.1.6 The judgment is therefore split between what we can call the practical and the theoretical. Both are of considerable interest, but for the purposes of this book we are going to concentrate on Hughes LJ's judgment because it is the one which is of most practical and immediate relevance to us as practitioners.

2.1.7 The Supreme Court decision in *Ilott* is not revolutionary; on the contrary, it confirms and affirms the existing methods by which the Courts have come to decisions on adult child claims. If anything, it narrows down the scope somewhat, as we will see, but it does not appear to have the effect of overruling any existing judgments. The practical effect of the decision may be seen more in the orders that are made in future under section 2 of the Act than in the question of whether or not any particular claim is valid.

2.1.8 There are six things about Hughes LJ's judgment to which we should pay particular attention. The first is that he re-affirms the importance of the **maintenance standard** [see 4.5 and onwards of this book] and in fact rejects the Court of Appeal's award to Mrs Ilott on the basis that the maintenance standard was exceeded in that award. He notes that the statutory powers under the Act are for maintenance only and "not to confer capital on the claimant" [para 15]: we will look at what this means in practice at 4.5.6]. In respect of the exercise which the Court is carrying out under the Act, he affirms that it is of necessity a **value judgment** [4.3.6 – 4.3.9] on the part of the relevant Judge, and is a **single assessment of reasonable financial provision** [4.3.10], which has important consequences for the ability of either side to appeal.

2.1.9 Connected with this, in a number of places in his judgment he rejects what the Court sees as an **unduly technical approach** to the balancing exercise. A judge is not necessarily required, for example, to go through the relevant factors twice, once at each stage; there is no need to set out some "hypothetical standard of reasonable provision" and then add to it or subtract from it; and in the specific context of the *Ilott* case itself he makes significant points about the value of the **testator's wishes** [6.7.4] and **estrangement** [6.7.17]. The judgment also deals with the **relevance of state benefits** [6.3.4] when making an assessment of reasonable provision under the Act.

2.1.10 Although it is still early days, the evidence from cases decided since *Ilott* SC suggests that all of Hughes LJ's principles are being taken into account in new cases. The adult child case of *Nahajec v Fowle* [2017] EW Misc 11 (CC) refers in detail to, and closely adopts, Hughes LJ's approach. In *Ball & Ors v Ball & Ors* [2017] EWHC 1750 (Ch), heard on 18–19 July 2017, *Ilott* SC was not referred to during the trial, but the trial Judge invited submissions on it prior to judgment. The claimants laid stress on four aspects of Hughes LJ's judgment: the "reasonableness" factor, the fact that a "moral" claim is not essential, the importance of the testator's expressed wishes, and the relative weight of a long estrangement: the judge considered these factors and endorsed

Hughes LJ's approach. In Nahajec the claimant obtained a modest lump sum; in Ball the claimants received nothing. However, in both cases, there appears to be a distinct shift towards a wider approach to the value judgment and weighing exercises. Nahajec and Ball are considered later in this book.

2.2 History

2.2.1 From the most recent development, let's look back to the most distant. Between 1837 and 1938, there was in essence nearly total testamentary freedom: a man (and for most of this period, only a man) was entitled to leave his property in his Will exactly as he chose, without recognising any obligations of any kind to his next of kin or dependents. Inevitably, this had caused hardship and in some cases actual destitution. From the mid-1920s onwards, the National Union of Societies for Equal Citizenship (NUSEC), had campaigned for a change in the law. It took the dogged persistence of the President, Eleanor Rathbone, and the Parliamentary Secretary, Eva Hubback, against very considerable parliamentary and professional opposition, to finally achieve the Inheritance (Family Provision) Act 1938.

2.2.2 The 1938 Act however made very limited provision for adult children. As far as sons were concerned, only disabled adult sons were eligible; for daughters, the applicant had to be disabled or unmarried. No person who had been treated as a child of the family but who was not in fact the biological child of the deceased could make any claim at all, leading to some quite substantial unfairness. The 1938 Act did however establish that the relevant standard of provision was maintenance, the lodestar feature which was to remain fixed in the 1975 Act and which as we will see is still causing problems to this day.

2.2.3 The 1938 Act was replaced in 1975 by the Inheritance (Provision for Family and Dependants) Act. The 1975 Act considerably widened the scope of potential applicants, but it did not specifically provide that adult children were among them: it specified only that any child of the deceased, or a person treated as a child, could apply. Importantly, however, it also extended the definition of "child" to include any person who had been treated as a "child of the family" at section 1(1)(d). In fact it was not until *Re Callaghan* in 1984 (reported at [1985] Fam 1) that there was an unequivocal finding by a Court that the word "child" in section 1(1)(c) and 1(1)(d) included an adult child, although by that time the application of another adult child in *Re Coventry (Deceased)* [1980] Ch 461 had already been decided.

2.2.4 How the machinery of the Act works has been clear from its beginnings in 1975, but it has proved difficult to square the operation of the Act with wider concepts about property, inheritance and entitlement. From 1938 onwards, there have been three conceptual problems with family provision on death legislation that the Courts have struggled with: the belief in testamentary freedom, the question of whether or not it is relevant that an applicant under the Act is "deserving", and the question of what, in every case, the Court should decide is reasonable provision. *Ilott SC* specifically raises these questions again in the judgment of Hale B and expressly warns that the Act does not provide the tools to resolve the difficulties. For better or worse, whether you are acting for a potential applicant or for the estate, these are issues that you are going to have to grapple with.

CHAPTER THREE
BEFORE YOU START

3.1 *Preliminary*
3.2 *Disputes About Parentage*
3.3 *Domicile*
3.4 *Limitation*
3.5 *Costs*
3.6 *The Settlement Imperative*
3.7 *Proportionality*

3.1 Preliminary

3.1.1 Before you start considering the merits or quantum of your client's case, there are three important preliminary matters to think about. The first is whether your client is a "child of the deceased" within the meaning of section 1(1)(c) or 1(1)(d) of the Act, the second is whether your client is still in time to make an application, and the third is whether DP died domiciled within the jurisdiction. Any of these matters can mean that your client is not eligible to make a claim. This section deals with those three matters, and it then goes on the deal with some other points that you should consider at the earliest possible stage: the need to consider settlement from the outset, costs considerations, and the proportionality principle.

3.1.2 First, however, a word about adulthood.

I do not agree that the words in section 1(1)(d) require such a narrow construction. "Child," for the purposes of section 1, clearly includes an adult child. [*Re Callaghan* [1985] Fam 1]

3.1.3 *S*ection 1 (1)(c) of the 1975 Act makes no mention of adulthood: it simply provides that any "child of the deceased" is eligible to make an application. In this book, I have taken my definition of adulthood from section 1 of the Family Law Reform Act 1969, which provides that a person attains full age when she reaches the age of 18. An adult child, for the purposes of this book, is therefore anyone between the ages of 18 and, say, 98. Although the likelihood of a 98-year old having a surviving parent is pretty remote, it is not at all unusual in these days of longer life expectancy for a potential claimant to be in her sixties: in *Re Hancock (Deceased)* [1998] 2 FLR 346, the claimant was 69 years of age by the date of the trial.

3.1.4 However the claims of infant children -- whether as applicants under the Inheritance Act 1975 or as beneficiaries under the estate -- will inevitably take a high priority, because DP had a strong legal obligation to provide financial support for them. In distinct contrast, in adult child claims the estate will often argue that there was no obligation at all on the part of DP to provide for AC.

3.1.5 A claim made by an 18-year old is inevitably going to differ quite markedly from one made by a 68-year old, not least because they are usually in very distinct financial circumstances. There is an informal "sliding scale" of financial dependency between the 18-year old in full-time further education who was still being supported by DP at the time of death, to an independent married woman, such as Mrs Ilott, who had not had financial support from DP for many years. The scale begins to slide upwards again where AC has reached her sixties, when health and mobility problems may mean that she requires increased financial support. Otherwise, however, the Court approaches the claim of any child -- whether infant or adult -- using exactly the same method and the same set of criteria.

3.1.6 The Relevance of Dependency and section 1(1)(e)

Section 1 (1)(e) of the Act allows those who have been maintained by the Deceased to make a claim. Most adult child claimants will choose to concentrate on their eligibility under section 1(1) (c) or (d), because the extent to which DP did in fact maintain and assume responsibility for maintaining her (and they are not the same things, as we will see) are matters that the Court specifically has to address at section 3(3). There is therefore not usually a great deal of point in adding a claim as a dependent under section 1 (1) (e).

3.1.7 However, there may be doubt in some cases whether a claimant has been treated as a "child of the family" within section 1 (1) (d), and claimants with that doubt in mind may choose to make an application as dependents under section 1 (1) (e) instead. This was the course adopted by the claimant in *Baynes v Hedger* [2009] EWCA Civ 374. At that time, an application under section 1(1)(d) could be brought only if the deceased had treated AC as a child of her marriage: for the current position, see 4.2.10 below. The deceased had been married, but the relevant relationship had been with AC's mother, with whom the deceased had been in a relationship (but not a civil partnership) for many years. An AC in the position of Hetty Baynes could now bring a claim under section 1(1)(d), and *Baynes v Hedger* is considered several times in the course of this book for that reason.

3.2 Disputes About Parentage

3.2.1 Obviously, if your client is a recognised legitimate child of the deceased, with the deceased's name as a parent on their birth certificate, she will have no difficulty in persuading the Court that she comes within section 1(1)(c) of the Act as a "child of the deceased". But what about a potential claimant who believes that she is the child of DP, but has no documentary evidence to prove it?

3.2.2 Claims are often disputed from the outset on the basis that the claimant is not a biological child of the deceased, and in these cases there may be a preliminary issue on that point on which some scientific evidence -- usually, these days, DNA evidence -- may be needed. Before considering scientific evidence, however, consider whether any of the legal presumptions about parenthood may help your client.

3.2 3 Common Law Presumption of Legitimacy

First, there is the common law presumption of legitimacy. Legitimacy itself is no longer an issue in Inheritance Act proceedings because s.25(1) of the Act defines "child" as including illegitimate children, but of course a presumption of legitimacy includes a presumption of parentage: if the presumption is that AC is the legitimate child of DP, it is also a presumption that DP is the natural parent of AC. The presumption is, in essence, that a child born to a married woman during the subsistence of her marriage is also the child of her husband. It can be rebutted by evidence proving the contrary, including evidence that the mother and DP did not have "access" to each other during the relevant time, or that DP was impotent. The presumption does not apply -- in fact, it is reversed -- if the parties were separated under an order of the court, but if they were separated by agreement, the presumption is that there was a legitimate child.

> Mariana makes a claim against the estate of her deceased father, Orsino. The executors of Orsino's estate dispute her claim on the basis that, although Mariana was born while Orsino was married to her mother, he did not have access to her at the material time because he was serving a lengthy prison sentence. The Executors will have to produce solid and reliable evidence of the fact of that imprisonment and possibly also evidence that there were no opportunities whatever for conjugal visits.

3.2 4 Birth registration presumption of legitimacy

Because an entry in a register of births and deaths is *prima facie* evidence of all the facts required by statute to be entered in it, it is at least a starting point for an AC in order to make a claim on the basis that the persons entered in the Register are her parents.

3.2 5 Findings in other proceedings

This presumption is likely to be of considerable assistance to many AC claimants. The fact that a person has been found to be the father of a child in any relevant proceedings before any court in England, Wales or Northern Ireland is admissible in evidence for the purpose of proving that he was the father of that child: Civil Evidence Act 1968 s. 12(1)(b). If such a finding is made then DP must be taken to have been the father of that child unless the contrary is proved, and the contents of any document which was before the court in the other proceedings are admissible in evidence if the question arises again in any other civil proceedings. As "civil proceedings" includes proceedings in any of the ordinary courts of law (s. 18(1) CEA 1968), this includes any application made under the Inheritance Act in the County Court and in both the Chancery and Family Divisions. "Relevant proceedings" include pre-Children Act 1989 proceedings: CEA s. 12(5). For this reason, if your client anticipates that there will be a dispute about paternity or if there is an element of doubt, you should specifically check whether or not there were child maintenance, affiliation or divorce proceedings in which there may have been evidence about your client's position.

3.2 6 If you are acting for AC and you are able to put forward any of these presumptions, you will discover very quickly whether the other parties intend to lead rebuttal evidence. If DP's paternity of AC is not accepted, that matter will have to be dealt with as a preliminary issue. It should not, however, be a reason to delay issue of the Inheritance Act claim.

3.2.7 Scientific Tests of Paternity

The rapid expansion of DNA technology has meant that this evidence of paternity has eclipsed pretty well all others, partly because of its conclusivity: it can establish the probability of parenthood to an extremely high degree of accuracy. The rules are now governed by the Family Law Reform Act 1969 as amended. The Act provides that the Court may in any civil proceedings in which the parentage of any person falls to be determined give a direction for the use of scientific tests which show that a person is or is not the father or mother of that person; and for the taking of "bodily samples" from the relevant parties: FLRA 1969 s. 20(1).

3.2.8 However, there is no power under the FLRA to direct post-mortem scientific testing: *Spencer v Anderson* [2016] EWHC 851 (Fam), so taking samples from the deceased after death is not a possibility. What the Court was able to do in that case was to order under the High Court's inherent jurisdiction that a stored DNA sample of the deceased could be tested, but if there is no extant DNA available it is likely that another means will have to be found of proving parentage. If you are representing AC, it may therefore be worth enquiring whether there are some relevant samples in the possession of third parties, such as blood or tissue samples taken for other purposes by the police, a hospital, or medical professional.

3.2.9 There may items which would yield DNA among DP's effects -- a hairbrush, for example -- but it may be impossible in practical terms for AC to establish that the objects exist. Note that only the High Court has inherent jurisdiction, and this remedy will not be available to your client if the matter was issued in the County Court unless she makes a free-standing application in the High Court for the purpose.

3.2.10 One other possibility might be to trace paternal DNA via a child of DP's that he acknowledged as his, but bear in mind that bodily samples can only be taken with the consent of the relevant person, even if the Court has ordered the test. The Court can draw inferences if a person refuses to comply with an order for testing, such inferences being those that appear proper in the circumstances: s. 23(1) FLRA 1969. In a case where a putative father refused to take a DNA test, it was said that the obvious inference to be drawn is that he is, in fact, the father, and that inference has indeed been drawn on several reported occasions: see, eg. *Re G (Parentage: Blood Sample)* [1997] 1 FLR 360. The same inferences could presumably be drawn if a putative sibling refused to take a DNA test, particularly if that sibling was a beneficiary of DP's estate. In *Re A (A Minor: Paternity: Refusal of blood test)* [1994] 2 FLR 463 Waite LJ said that to avoid an adverse inference being drawn the putative father (or, in our case, his heirs) would have to advance very clear reasons which would make it just and reasonable to allow him to maintain a refusal to undergo tests [@ 473].

3.2.11 Note that the costs of the taking and the testing of bodily samples are to be paid by the person seeking the direction of the Court that the test should be carried out, but the amount paid will be treated as part of her costs of the proceedings (s. 20(6) FLRA 1969) and should therefore be recoverable on the usual grounds.

3.2.12 The Court has a discretion as to whether it will or will not order a DNA test to be made, although in the case of an adult child with a reasonable claim against the estate, it is likely to exercise that discretion in her favour, not least because a DNA test may establish conclusively that she is not DP's child and therefore close off her claim under section 1(1)(c). It may not however close off her entire claim, because she is often able to assert that she was treated by DP as a child of the family within the meaning of section 1(1)(d). Section 3(3) of the Act specifically directs the Court to consider in section 1(1)(c) and 1(1)(d) applications whether DP knew that the applicant was not his own child.

3.2.13 The question of when and whether to pursue DNA testing can be a fraught one, particularly where DP did not acknowledge AC as his child during his lifetime, and even more so when the existence of AC comes as an unwelcome surprise to DP's other family. The immediate reaction of other beneficiaries and family members can be to dispute AC's claims of blood ties, sometimes aggressively, and in particular to resist any move towards DNA testing. Approach the matter with sensitivity, but do not be surprised if the initial answer is a brusque refusal.

3.2.14 "Treated as a Child of the Family": section 1(1)(d)

A dispute that your client was treated as a child of the family will not normally be dealt with as a preliminary issue unless the facts on either side are very stark. It is therefore unlikely to be an issue which can be resolved at a preliminary stage, so it is considered at [4.2.10] below, where we will also look at further issues relating to eligibility including those facing stepchildren and adopted children.

3.3 Domicile

3.3.1 In order for the English Courts to have jurisdiction over the claim, DP must have died "domiciled in England and Wales" [s. 1]. Domicile is a complex issue, most recently dealt with in *Kebbeh v Farmer* [2015] EWHC 3827 (Ch), where the Court decided as a preliminary issue that the deceased had died domiciled in The Gambia. Domicile issues are complex and you should look at specialist textbooks and take further advice if it appears that this is going to be a factor. You should note, however, that the fact that DP owned property abroad does not in and of itself mean that DP was domiciled abroad. Foreign property owned by DP is discussed at [6.2.19].

3.4 Limitation

3.4.1 Limitation of Action: Check the date of the Grant or Administration FIRST

Before 1 October 2014, AC could not bring a claim before the grant of probate or letters of administration had been made, but there is now a new s.4 as amended by the Inheritance and Trustees' Powers Act 2014 (Sch 2, para 6). The result is that if DP died after on or after 1 October 2014, AC does not need to wait until the grant is made if she wishes to issue proceedings. There have been cases where beneficiaries and/or executors have deliberately postponed applying for a grant in order to put off or wear down an applicant, or to attempt to make distributions or transfers. This provision should assist the applicant in such cases. In every case, however, write a letter before action first and follow the ACTAPS protocol: see 3.6.

3.4.2 Once probate or letters of administration have been granted, however, the initial claim cannot be issued more than six months after the date of grant without the permission of the Court (s.4). Step number one therefore when considering a claim is to make sure that you are still in time to issue, or if it turns out that you are already out of time, to take immediate and efficient steps to try to remedy the matter. If there has been a false start, for example when probate has been granted under a Will but has later been revoked and there has then been a new grant of probate related to a previous Will, then time starts running from the later date: see *Re Freeman Deceased* [1984] 1 WLR 1419.

3.4.3 If the time limit has already expired

AC can now only make an application with the permission of the Court: s.4 of the Act. Potential claimants have an uncanny knack of seeking advice just as the primary limitation period is coming to an end, leaving the legal adviser with the unenviable choice of either issuing immediately to protect the position, with possible costs consequences, or approaching the other side to try to negotiate a short-term solution. It is generally possible, where time is short, to obtain the Estate's agreement that it will not object to the issue of proceedings after the end of the time limit, thus partly protecting your client's position while you carry on negotiations. Such an agreement does not, however, absolve AC from the necessity of applying to the Court for permission to issue, and the Court can still refuse to grant permission even where the other side take no objection. Where time is very short -- that is, where the deadline is within a few days -- the better course is to issue protective proceedings and then approach the Estate seeking a stay while negotiations are attempted and explaining why you have had to issue.

3.4.4 Section 4 itself gives no guidance as to when the Court's permission will be granted or refused, but the basic guidelines were set out in *Re Salmon Deceased* [1981] Ch 167 and *Re Dennis* [1981] 2 All ER 140 and were recently helpfully restated in the judgment in *Berger v Berger* [2013] EWCA Civ 1305. Generally, the Court's discretion to grant permission is unfettered, but must be exercised in accordance with what is right and proper. The onus is on the claimant to show sufficient grounds for the granting of permission to apply out of time. The Court must consider whether she has acted promptly, and the circumstances in which she applied for an extension of time after the expiry of the time limit: one important factor is whether negotiations were begun within the time limit. A further point of great importance is whether or not the estate has been distributed; it is only in very exceptional circumstances that a claim out of time will be allowed when that has happened because of the difficulty of rewinding the clock. There are two further factors: one is whether AC has an arguable case under the 1975 Act, and the other is whether she has any other remedies if her 1975 Act claim is dismissed.

3.4.5 Reasons for delay

Your client may not have known that she had an Inheritance Act claim, or she may have known that she had a claim but have been understandably reluctant to pursue it because it involves taking legal proceedings against other members of her family; or the full effect of the Will, intestacy or the combination of both may not have been immediately clear to her: as to that, see [4.4.11]. The Court will be sympathetic to such factors, but not boundlessly sympathetic. One distinction that has been made is between the potential claimant who knows that she has a case, but delays for a significant period of time because she does not want to cause family upset, and a potential claimant who was unaware until long after the deadline had passed that she had any Inheritance Act case at all: compare *Escritt v Escritt* (1982) 3 FLR 747 and *Berger v Berger [supra].*

3.4.6 If your client has delayed until after the estate has been distributed, she will probably find it extremely difficult to persuade the Court to give her permission to make an application. If an estate has already been distributed, it is almost impossible for the Court to put the clock back in order to deal with her claim. Furthermore, even if there has not been full distribution, beneficiaries and executors may have taken decisions on the basis that there would be no Inheritance Act claim, decisions which may now be very much to their disadvantage if AC is allowed to make her application. A beneficiary may have entered into new financial commitments in the expectation that she was going to receive a substantial sum under the intestacy provisions, for example, and it may now be unfair to her to unravel those arrangements, particularly where AC has known for some time that she had a claim but has done nothing to advance it.

3.4.7 The fact of negotiations progressing in the background may help. In *Beckett v McMillan* [2015] NI Ch 8, the claimant widow had issued her claim in time but had then not pursued it for a period of over ten years while the parties, including her adult son, attempted to compromise with the beneficiary. The beneficiary did not pay anything under the resulting consent order (to which the claimant was not a party) and the claimant then successfully sought to revive her claim. Deeny J remarked that the context, including the fact that negotiations had taken place throughout, meant that she got "just about to the excusable level although it is a very finely balanced judgment". The case does however provide some support for an applicant who has been strung along by other beneficiaries and the estate until her claim has become stale.

3.4.8 Another Northern Irish case, *McNulty v McNulty* [2002] EWHC 123 (Ch), approved in B*erger*, noted that the time limit was not a disciplinary provision to be enforced for its own sake, but is designed to give a measure of protection for executors and a measure of certainty for beneficiaries by enabling the estate to be distributed once a six-month period has elapsed. If you have to make an application to issue out of time, focus on these two factors.

3.4.9 New information

The fact that new information about the estate or about AC's own situation has come to light may be a powerfully persuasive factor in granting permission, but generally the claimant must have sought advice and then taken steps to issue very speedily. In *Stock v Brown* [1994] 1 FLR 840, the provision for the widow under the Will appeared to be sufficient just after death, but there was then a dramatic fall in interest rates and the costs of her care increased. She was allowed to apply 5 ½ years out of time. In *McNulty*, the widow discovered only three years after the event that the deceased's sons had significantly undervalued the deceased's business in order to reduce the income they were obliged to pay her under the settlement. Note that Mrs McNulty's delay of about ten months between discovering the truth and issuing her application was described as "inexcusable tardiness" by the Judge. She did succeed in obtaining permission to apply out of time, but the general message is clearly not to delay once relevant new information has been discovered.

3.4.10 Joint tenancies

There is one absolutely inflexible deadline, although its significance is likely to fade over the next few years. It relates to property owned by the DP under a joint tenancy if DP died before 1 October 2014. If your client wishes to make an application to sever a joint tenancy under section 9 of the Act in these circumstances (as to which, see section [6.2.24] below), that application **must** be made within six months of the grant of probate or of letters of administration or it will be completely lost: s.9(1).

3.4.11 For this reason, you need to make careful enquiries when you take instructions: for the appropriate point, see 5.3.6. The most common case is joint beneficial ownership of DP's home, which may pass to DP's surviving spouse under the joint tenancy rules, but there may also be substantial amounts in joint bank accounts which may not pass into the net estate. You need to establish as soon as possible whether or not there are any significant jointly owned assets, because if

DP died before 1 October 2014 and AC does not issue within six months, her right to DP's share of those assets is lost forever.

3.4.12 For deaths from 1 October 2014 onwards, the position is simpler. Section 9(1) now provides that the DP's share under any joint tenancy is included in the net estate if DP died after that date.

3.4.13 Using caveats

At the risk of stating the obvious, if the executor or administrator has not yet been granted probate or administration, the time limit has not started to run. For this reason, potential claimants have sometimes attempted to fend off the grant of probate by entering a caveat at the probate registry to prevent the grant from being made. The Courts have made it clear that caveats should not be issued to protect a potential Inheritance Act claim: see, for example, *Parnall v Hurst* [2003] WTLR 997. The only reason for entering a caveat is because there is a concern about the formal validity of the Will. There are certainly many Inheritance Act cases where your client will also have an alternative claim in probate, and we look at these in Chapter 9. Where your client has a case that the Will was not properly executed, for example, or that DP did not have the mental capacity to understand what she was doing by making the Will, you must enter a caveat. However, it is good practice not to do so if your client cannot challenge the probate process.

3.5 Costs

> *"While it may be that a 'no holds barred' approach to certain types of litigation is entirely appropriate, it is not in my judgment at all appropriate in the context of claims under the Inheritance Act, where, even in a big money case, the costs are likely to form an ever-increasing part of the subject matter of the dispute until, as appears largely to have occurred in the present case, it is the costs burden alone which prevents settlement."*

Briggs LJ in *Lilleyman v Lilleyman (Costs)* [2012] EWHC 1056 (Ch)

3.5.1 Costs should be at the forefront of every legal advisor's mind, whether you are acting for the estate or AC, from the very first moment that you are instructed in an Inheritance Act claim. Like most claims involving probate, Inheritance Act claims are expensive to mount and contest, and legal costs can exhaust even a substantial estate. For that reason, litigation should be a last resort.

3.5.2 It is vital, particularly for those who are advising applicants, to make a **realistic** assessment of whether your client has a claim for reasonable provision, and if so, to consider very carefully how the Court should exercise its discretion in order to provide it. To do this, you need to carry out the exercise set out in section 3 of the Act, set out in this book in chapters 8 and 9. To protect your client's position, you then need to make **reasonable** settlement offers as early as possible: see section 3.6 below.

3.5.3 Bear in mind that the normal costs rules apply in Inheritance Act claims. Costs are at the discretion of the Court, but will generally follow the event, and the Part 36 regime is in full force. The popular belief that all or any party will have its costs automatically paid by the estate in probate actions is without foundation. Personal representatives will usually be able to have their costs of acting as a personal representative out of the estate, but not necessarily their costs as beneficiaries if they also benefit from the estate.

3.5.4 In *Palmer v Lawrence* [2011] EWHC 3961 (Ch), the applicant widow had already spent £50,000 on getting the claim to trial and included this expenditure in her statement of her financial resources and needs. The beneficiaries argued that the issue of her spending on legal costs should be ignored because "*otherwise every family provision claim in the case of someone of modest means would be self-justifying because the means of the claimant would always be reduced by legal costs*" [29]. Judge Purle QC doubted that there was a simple answer to the dilemma applicable in all cases, but remarked also that "*where the court concludes, leaving aside the impact of costs, that the will does make reasonable financial provision for a claimant, it is difficult to see how a self-induced costs burden can make the reasonable unreasonable*" [30].

3.5.5 The claimant in *Palmer v Lawrence* had intimated to the Court that if she was successful, she would seek an order that her costs should be paid out of the estate, thus leading to a "swings and roundabouts" effect in which the net estate would be depleted. The judge took the view that he should deal first of all with the question of whether the Will had made reasonable provision and disregard the costs issues, bringing them back if the claimant passed stage 1 (which, in *Palmer*, she did not).

3.5.6 When acting for any party in Inheritance Act proceedings, but perhaps particularly when acting for AC, you must bear in mind from a very early stage that an adverse costs order can sometimes destroy the effect of any award that your client receives, and at worst can be a financial disaster for her.

3.5.7 You should note particularly that the deciding factor for the trial Judge in *Palmer* in dismissing AC's claim was a value judgment he made about AC's conduct. The risks that any AC runs in the post-*Ilott* climate are obvious. Do not embark on litigation without a clear strategy, and make sure that you advise your client at all stages about the costs risks she is running.

3.6 The Settlement Imperative

> *"Legal representatives **in all cases** should consider with their clients and the other parties concerned the possibility of attempting to resolve the dispute or particular issues by ADR and **they should ensure that their clients are fully informed about the most cost-effective means of resolving the dispute**." Chancery Guide 2016 para 18.1. (Emphasis added)*

> *"Parties and their legal representatives are encouraged to enter into discussions and/or negotiations prior to starting proceedings. The parties should bear in mind that the courts increasingly take the view that litigation should be a last resort, and that claims should not be issued prematurely when a settlement is in reasonable prospect."*

> ACTAPS Code paragraph 2.9

3.6.1 The Practice Guidance Note of the association of Contentious Trust and Probate Specialists (ACTAPS) is seen as the benchmark of good practice in contentious trust and probate proceedings, including Inheritance Act claims, and you need to be aware of it and follow it. It is available online at http://www.actaps.com/draft.cfm. The two aims of the Code are "to encourage the resolution of disputes without hostile litigation; and even where litigation may be necessary to ensure that it is simplified as far as possible by maximising the scope for the exchange of relevant information *before the litigation process has commenced.*" [My italics.] Substantially the same point is made by the Chancery Guide.

3.6.2 Note the ACTAPS stress on early disclosure of evidence. One of the advantages of the Form E-based method that I set out in this book is that it focuses your attention on getting in the evidence supporting your client's case from the time of your first instructions. We are going to look at the tactical and strategic importance of early disclosure at [10.3], but one extremely beneficial aspect of disclosing supporting evidence early is that it cuts down on issues and therefore also on costs. If for example your client has significant health problems and you are able to produce medical evidence about her conditions at an early stage, you are likely to cut down dispute about that aspect of the case considerably.

3.6.3 It is vital to have potential settlement solutions in mind from a very early stage, not least because of the costs protection they offer.

3.7 Proportionality

3.7.1 CPR Rule 1.1 provides that the purpose of the Civil Procedure Rules is to enable the Court to deal with matters justly and (since April 2013) at proportionate cost, including at 1.1(2)(c) dealing with the case in ways which are proportionate to the amount of money involved; the importance of the case; the complexity of the issues; and the financial position of each party. It is the Court's duty to manage the case so that the overriding objective is complied with (CPR 1.4), but it is the parties' duty to help the Court to further the overriding objective (CPR 1.3).

3.7.2 While all of the individual elements within the overriding objective are important, it is particularly important in Inheritance Act cases to keep at the forefront of your mind that everything you do in the case will need to be **proportionate** to the issues and the amount at stake. As we will see in some of the cases that I discuss in this book, costs in Inheritance Act matters can quickly begin to run out of control if the parties, as well as the Court, do not take a sensible view of the issues and how they are to be resolved.

3.7.3 Clients in Inheritance Act cases will often give instructions to the effect that they would rather that the entire estate was spent on legal costs than on going to the beneficiary or family member who is the object of their ire, as for example the executor did in *Wright v Waters* [2014] EWHC 3614 (Ch). You must therefore explain the proportionality principle at the earliest possible moment, and ensure that your client understands that the Court may well punish this "down to the last penny" approach with punitive costs orders, or may simply not allow your client to conduct the case in the way she would wish to.

3.7.4 One common example is the use of expert evidence. This issue is frequently encountered in adult child Inheritance Act cases where AC is claiming that she cannot work due to ill-health. We will look at the specific questions which arise at 6.3.28, but where the estate is modest and AC's claim is proportionate, the Court will be very reluctant to allow costly expert medical evidence unless there is no other realistic option. Your executor client may well believe that AC is exaggerating her symptoms, but if she has been diagnosed with a serious illness by a reputable medical professional, there would seem to be little point in obtaining expert medical evidence to refute that diagnosis, particularly where the estate is small.

3.7.5 Beware also of putting forward a case with a plethora of issues, most of which cannot really form the basis of a dispute, and try to agree what the material issues are with the other side at the earliest possible opportunity. If you quantify your client's claim at a maximum of £50,000 whether it is paid as a lump sum or satisfied in some other way, it is unlikely to be proportionate to have five or six separate points of dispute. You may well have your initial claim drastically pruned at the directions stage either by applications from the other side or by the Court of its own motion on the grounds that the sheer number is disproportionate.

CHAPTER FOUR
THE MACHINERY OF THE ACT

4.1 What the Act Does, and What It Doesn't
4.2 Eligibility: The Portal
4.3 The Threshold: Stage 1
4.4 Making Provision: Stage 2
4.5 The Maintenance Standard
4.6 Starting the Balancing Exercise Under S.3

4.1 What the Act does, and what it doesn't

> *"My second observation is that at times the argument came near to saying that what the Court had to consider was how the available assets should be fairly divided. That, of course, is not the position under the Act, and is not what the Court has to decide."*

Goff LJ in *Re Coventry* @ 486F

4.1.1 Having investigated whether there are any issues that you need to deal with in order to establish that your client has a claim, we can turn to the way that the Act works. Under the machinery of the Act, the Court's only job is to decide whether the disposition of DP's estate, whether it is being effected by a Will or by intestacy, or a combination of the two, does not make reasonable provision for AC.

4.1.2 "Reasonable provision" means reasonable provision for A's maintenance: section 1(2)(b). We have already seen, and will see again at 4.5, that *Ilott SC* has reinforced the authorities on the existing definition of "reasonable provision". In making that decision, the Court must have regard to the factors that are set out in section 3 of the Act.

4.1.3 The Court certainly does not commence its considerations on the assumption that an adult child should get something from the estate. On the contrary, it has to start off making no assumptions whatever. It is instead taking a 360-degree survey around the factors in section 3 of the Act and then deciding, having taken that survey and noted the salient features of the landscape, whether the provision that has been made for AC is reasonable.

4.1.4 The issue was helpfully addressed in *Re Coventry*, where the Judge had found that AC's circumstances were close to subsistence level (possibly even below that level), and it was then submitted that on that basis the Court should have found that the provision left for him (which was nothing) was not reasonable. But for Goff LJ, that did not follow. The question was not whether it might have been reasonable for D to assist his son; the question is whether in all the circumstances it was unreasonable that the disposition of the estate did not do so. [*Coventry* @ 488F.] This is a much more open question, and it crucially depends on looking at the other section 3 factors as opposed simply to the needs and resources of AC.

4.1.5 It is vital to good client relations and communications that you give the client an accurate picture of what the Act can and cannot do for her at an early stage, and then remind her of it throughout your association as necessary. In my experience, it is very difficult for a distressed and anxious client to keep in mind the fundamental "reasonable provision" concept of the Inheritance Act. It is probably not the factor in the situation which is uppermost in her mind. If you follow the route set out in this book, there is a good opportunity to give this Advice when you are discussing her financial information with her at paragraph 4.4 of Form E: see [5.5] below.

4.1.6 We are going to look in detail at each aspect of how the Court decides whether reasonable provision has been made for AC. But before we go on to look at that, it is helpful to start off by removing a few preconceptions about how the Act does **not** operate.

4.1.7 What the Act *Doesn't* Do

In summary, the Act does ***not***:

- Decide whether DP acted unreasonably in leaving her estate as she did;
- Correct any provision made (or not made) out of malice or spite simply because of that malice or spite;
- Consider whether the distribution of the estate is fair;
- Consider whether AC is "deserving" of a legacy on any moral basis;
- Make reparations for past parental behaviour;
- Rewrite the Will to correct any of these perceived problems.

4.1.8 If your client's case depends on these points alone, then she is highly likely to fail in proving that the disposition of the estate did not make reasonable provision for her. This can be extremely difficult for an adult child to understand, and advice should be given sensitively, and bearing in mind the enormous emotional significance of disinheritance in most cases. But in every case you need to take full instructions from the client, because although AC may be approaching the case in a way that is not helpful, she may still have a claim that the disposition of the estate did not make reasonable provision for her.

4.1.9 DP acted unreasonably

This is a common mistake in formulating Inheritance Act cases. DP can act as unreasonably as she likes, provided the Court is satisfied that the result was to make reasonable provision for AC in all the circumstances. The test is whether or not the disposition of the estate has made reasonable provision for AC, which is an entirely different matter.

> Fernanda leaves her substantial fortune to seven strangers that she picks out of the telephone directory. If her reason for doing so is that she disapproves of her children being left large sums of money and wishes in principle not to make them financially secure, then her gift is not on first examination unreasonable. If her adult children are not only capable of earning their own livings but are comfortably off, then there is very unlikely to be a viable Inheritance Act claim by any of them.

4.1.10 Hughes LJ noted in *Ilott SC* [@17] that the reasonableness of DP's decisions are undoubtedly capable of being a factor under section 3(1)(g) of the Act, which is the "sweeper" section directing the Court to put into the scales any other matter which it considers relevant, and sometimes also section 3(1)(d), which directs it to consider any obligations or responsibilities which DP might have had towards AC. He noted that it can sometimes be difficult in practice to keep considerations that the Will did not make reasonable provision apart from considerations that DP acted unreasonably in failing to make that provision and commented that for this reason "*it is very easy to slip into the error of applying the wrong test*".

4.1.11 He then returned to the dictum of Oliver J in Re Coventry that "*it must be shown, not that the deceased acted unreasonably, but that looked at objectively, his disposition or lack of disposition produces an unreasonable result*". If Mrs Ilott had been able to afford all of the necessities of her lifestyle without any need for extra funds, Mrs Jackson's decision to leave her estate to charities with which she had no connection would still have been unreasonable, but it would not have produced an unreasonable result.

4.1.12 Some DPs may well take a principled view that they oppose inherited wealth and for that reason will not leave the bulk of their estates to their children: Sting has previously expressed this view about his own fortune, and so have Bill and Melinda Gates about theirs. That may seem unreasonable to an adult child who could find a use for the money, but it is not an unreasonable disposition unless it leaves AC struggling in difficult or uncomfortable financial circumstances with no means of self-help. Standard of living will still be relevant, however. We will look at this in more detail when we examine the concept of maintenance more closely.

4.1.13 We will see, when we consider some of the potential factors under section 3(1)(g), that DP's motives for leaving the estate as she did may sometimes be a relevant factor. Although the Courts try hard not to bring a moral compass to the actions of DP, there are times when the Court's decision reflects a clear finding that DP's conduct has been harsh as well as unreasonable. DJ Million in *Ilott* at first instance formed the view that Mrs Jackson had been harsh to Mrs Ilott, and indeed that some of the matters that she had set out in her letter of reasons appeared not to have been "founded on fact". That unreasonableness was a factor which he took into account when he made his award, as we shall see. The case of *Ball & Ors v Ball & Ors* [2017] EWHC 1750 (Ch) demonstrates the difficulties than can arise where reasonableness becomes an issue under section 3(1)(g). In that case, the three AC claimants had been disinherited by their mother after they had made allegations that their father had sexually abused them. The allegations in fact led to the father's criminal conviction. The trial Judge found that DP had accepted (probably with some considerable reluctance) that her husband had sexually abused the claimants, although she considered that the claimants had exaggerated their accounts. This did not make her decision to disinherit the three claimants unreasonable.

4.1.14 Irrationality

If you or your client have real grounds for belief that the Will is so unreasonable that it is actually irrational, and that in layman's terms DP was not in her right mind when she made it, there may be a claim that DP lacked testamentary capacity, but not one for provision under the Inheritance Act. In fact, challenges to the validity of the Will are often combined with an Inheritance Act claim, but you need to make a clear distinction between the two. I have set out the claims which are most frequently made in conjunction with an Inheritance Act claim at Chapter 9 below.

4.1.15 The role of spite

One of the most difficult aspects of the law for lay clients to understand is that the fact that DP has possibly disinherited AC out of spite may not be relevant. *Ilott* was an example where there had been a long estrangement between mother and daughter, and DP had deliberately left her entire estate to charities with which she had had no real connection in life so that -- as she had indeed foretold -- Mrs Ilott would not get any of the money; but this was by no means the decisive factor. If the beneficiaries have no need of the legacies, that will be a factor to be considered under section 3 and weighed up with the other factors; but there is no rule that spite or malice will make a Will less reasonable (in Inheritance Act terms) in its provisions. Testamentary freedom is a freedom to be spiteful, or indeed unreasonable, as well as kind.

4.1.16 "It's Not Fair"

A decision about "reasonable provision" is *not* a decision about whether the disposition of D's estate is fair or unfair to AC on the basis that "X got £Y, so it is only fair that I should get £Z". In *Zarrinkhat v Kamal* [2013] W.T.L.R. 1477, the Judge commented on AC's claim, "*She had misconstrued the correct approach; her main thrust was that she had received substantially less than [her siblings]. That was not the relevant test. T's will made reasonable provision for Z when all the s.3 factors were taken into account.*"

4.1.17 DP may have had perfectly adequate reasons for leaving more to one child than another, even to the extent of excluding one or more of their children completely. In *Re Garland* [2007] EWHC 2 (Ch), DP left his residuary estate to one of his two daughters, M, and some small specific bequests to his grandchildren. He left nothing to his other daughter, G. He had had a close relationship with M and her family for the last fifteen years of his life, and during the same period he and G had been estranged; they met very rarely and there was little contact. The Court found that his decision to leave the majority of his estate to M, and nothing at all to G, made reasonable provision for G, who was financially independent of him and who had in fact received financial benefits from him during his lifetime.

4.1.18 Disappointed adult children often complain that a beneficiary of the Will has had a "windfall" in the sense of obtaining an unexpected and substantial legacy and that this is unfair to AC because that person was, for example, not a blood relative or had not done as much for DP as AC had. The classic example is a legacy to a carer or to a neighbour who helped DP in their final days: one good example (where AC was unsuccessful in overturning the provisions of the Will) is *Carapeto v Good* [2002] EWHC 640 (Ch). Indeed, it is human nature for an elderly DP who has been cared for during a long period by friends, neighbours or even professional carers who have gone the extra mile, to wish to thank those carers by leaving them something or more than something. Such an expression of gratitude is not necessarily evidence of some sinister mind control on the part of the beneficiary, particularly where AC has (for whatever reason) not been around to care for DP in her declining years. Again, provided that the Court is satisfied that the estate makes reasonable provision for AC, other beneficiaries can take very substantial legacies, up to the entire estate.

4.1.19 Reward the deserving

Hughes LJ in *Ilott SC* remarked [47] that "*care must be taken to avoid making awards under the 1975 Act primarily rewards for good behaviour on the part of the claimant or penalties for bad on the part of the deceased*". In Coventry itself, Oliver J noted that the purpose of the Act was not to "reward meritorious conduct"; this is not a contest about who "deserves" a share of the estate on any moral basis. Notions of "deserving" applicants are not relevant to the exercise the Court has to carry out. This is often a particularly bitter pill for an adult child to swallow. It is worth noting, however, that if an adult child has made significant sacrifices for a parent -- giving up a well-paid job and a career path to look after them in their old age, for example -- that may be a "special circumstance" under section 3(1)(g), and it may lead to a finding that DP had a moral obligation to AC under section 3(1)(d).

4.1.20 Rewrite the Will, either to reflect "what DP would have wanted" or otherwise

The Act furthermore does not give the Court any general power to rewrite the Will in the terms that the Court thinks that D would, if s/he had put her mind to it, have specified. The Court can only interfere with DP's absolute right to leave her property as she wishes to the extent of making reasonable financial provision for AC (*Re Bunning* [1984] Ch. 480), and no further.

4.1.21 Nor is it about "what D would have wanted". Goff LJ noted in *Re Coventry* @ 488H: "*Any view expressed by a deceased person that he wishes a particular person to benefit will generally be of little significance, because the question is not subjective but objective. An express reason for rejecting the applicant is a different matter and may be very relevant to the problem.*" However, D's wishes can be a relevant factor under section 3(1)(g): see 6.7.

4.2 Eligibility: The Portal

4.2.1 So far, we have flagged up some jurisdictional issues that you need to look at straight away before you take detailed instructions, and we have cleared away some misconceptions about the purpose and the function of the Act. Now, we need to examine more closely whether or not your client is eligible to make a claim under section 1.

4.2.2 In order to make a claim at all, an applicant has to fit within one of the categories set out at section 1 of the Act. I have called this the "Portal". For an adult child the relevant section is 1(1)(c) or 1(1)(d): that is, the applicant has to be a child of DP, or to have been treated as a child of the family if not DP's natural or adopted child.

4.2.3 Section 1(1)(c): a Child of the Deceased

Natural/Biological Children

They are entitled to apply whether or not they are legitimate: s. 25(1) of the Act, which also provides that the phrase "child" includes children in the womb *(en ventre de sa mere)* at the time of DP's death, although that clearly is not going to affect adult child claimants.

4.2.4 A person who has been recognised as acquiring a different gender by means of a gender recognition certificate under the Gender Recognition Act 2004 does not lose their status as the child's father or mother: that is, if DP was born a woman but was later recognised as male, she will continue to be a parent of AC.

4.2.5 Disputes about Parentage

We have looked at these at section 3.2. It is worth remembering though that if AC can prove that in any case she was always treated as a child of the family under section 1(1)(d), the importance of a biological link between AC and DP may not be so crucial. The more problematic cases are those where DP has had some sort of relationship with AC but it has not amounted to recognition of AC as his child, and DP has supported her to some extent but not to the extent that she was clearly treated as a child "of the family". In these cases, the biological link is going to assume a greater importance.

4.2.6 Adopted Children

Adoption at law is a legal process by which the court extinguishes for all time the ties between the child and her natural parents and creates analogous ties between the child and her adoptive parents. In the UK, the historical and primary focus has been the desire to nurture a child within a new family unit, and not specifically to give the child property or citizenship rights -- although the child may acquire these having become the child of her new parents. The position is now governed by the Adoption and Children Act 2002, which came into force in 2004.

4.2.7 Adoption in the UK is certainly not an entirely legal concept; it is underpinned by a belief that the fact of adoption gives a child (and also the parents) "*an extra and psychologically and emotionally important sense of "belonging"*. Since the coming in to force in 1950 of the Adoption of Children Act 1949, an adopted child has gained the right to inherit on the intestacy of her adoptive parents, but lost the right in respect of her birth parents. That principle was confirmed by the Adoption Act 1976 and re-confirmed in the Adoption and Children Act 2002, and that principle remains good for intestacy.

4.2.8 Re Collins Deceased [1990] Fam 56 confirmed that the adoption rules under section 39(2) have conclusive effect as far as Inheritance Act applications are concerned. The applicant there was still an infant. He was born in 1979, his mother had died in 1980, and he had been adopted in 1987. It was accepted on his behalf that s.39(2) meant that he had no standing to apply as a child under Inheritance Act 1(1)(c), but argued that because his mother had died before he had been adopted, s. 42(4) of the Adoption Act 1976 applied. S. 42(4) provides that "section 39(2) does not prejudice any interest vested in possession in the adopted child before the adoption, or any interest expectant (whether immediately or not) upon an interest so vested". The Court found (1) that s.42 applied only to instruments and not to rights under a statute, and even if that were incorrect, (2) that as a right to apply for Inheritance Act relief is not an "interest", it could not be preserved by s. 42.

4.2.9 Free-Standing Application under Family Law Act 1986

The Family Law Act 1986 s. 55A(1) provides that any person may make an application to the High Court or the Family Court for a declaration that the person named in the application is the applicant's parent. It is unlikely that many Inheritance Act applicants will wish to avail themselves of this possibility given that the matter can be dealt with in the course of the proceedings.

4.2.10 Treated as a child of the family: s. 1(1)(d)

In its updated form this subsection grants eligibility to

> *"any person (not being a child of the deceased) who in relation to any marriage or civil partnership to which the deceased was at any time a party, or otherwise in relation to any family in which the deceased at any time stood in the role of a parent, was treated by the deceased as a child of the family".*

The subsection as amended by the Inheritance and Trustees Powers Act 2014 now relates to any family in which DP at any time "stood in the role of parent", including cohabitee relationships and single-parent households, so there is no longer any bar to looking at DP's treatment of AC if DP was looking after AC together with DP's long-term partner, or was the sole parent of AC. This had become a fairly artificial requirement given the wider recognition of non-traditional families elsewhere on the statute book, and the amendment is a welcome advance.

4.2.11 Section 1(1)(d) Special Factors

Section 3(3) of the Act specifically directs the Court, where AC is applying under section 1(1)(d), to consider:

"(a) ... whether the deceased had assumed any responsibility for the applicant's maintenance and if so, the extent to which and the basis upon which the deceased assumed that responsibility and the length of time for which the deceased discharged that responsibility;

(b) ... whether in assuming and discharging that responsibility the deceased did so knowing that the applicant was not his own child;

(c) ... the liability of any other person to maintain the applicant."

4.2.12 Section 3(3), which I consider in more detail at 6.8 , is of obvious assistance if your client was brought up by DP from infancy, but is of limited help if AC and DP only became related after AC had attained her majority. However, the leading cases of *Re Callaghan* [1985] Fam 1 and *Re Leach* [1986] Ch. 226; [1985] 3 W.L.R. 413 demonstrate that AC can be a person treated as a child of DP's family even if DP did not in fact assume any responsibility for AC's maintenance at all, because AC was an adult at the time that they became associated. In *Re Leach,* AC had been 32 when her father remarried, and she had a very close relationship with her stepmother. When AC's father died, he left all of his estate to the stepmother; but the stepmother then died intestate, so that all of her estate went to her legal next of kin. AC successfully claimed that she had been treated as a child of DP's family.

4.2.13 Apart from these cases, however, there is surprisingly little direct guidance in the authorities about what being "treated as a child of the family" actually means in Inheritance Act cases. There are quite a few reports where it is clear that an applicant may well have been treated as a child of the family as well as having been maintained by DP, but there is often no clear line drawn between the two. Treatment as a child of the family is something that most Courts seem to see as fairly obvious, though there can certainly be occasions where it is not *that* obvious.

4.2.14 Cases in the Family jurisdiction can be of significant help. In *Re A (Child of the Family)* [1998] 1 FLR 347, the Court considered the concept, looking back to a line of cases decided by Ormrod LJ in the 1980s, and expressly approved the test as being whether the child in question was not treated just as a *member* of the family, but as a *child* of the family. *Re A* was a case where grandparents had stepped in to look after the child when her natural mother was not able to do so. The case turned, incidentally, on the question of whether the grandparents had assumed responsibility for A's maintenance under s. 25(4) of the Matrimonial Causes Act, the wording of which is broadly mirrored by s. 3(3) of the Inheritance Act.

4.2.15 Grandparents often step in to help out when natural parents are unable, for whatever reason, to look after a child, but the question for the Court in *Re A* was whether they were simply stepping in for a temporary period and that everyone's intention was that the child would return to the parental home, or whether this was a more permanent arrangement. Judge LJ in *Re A* said that in his view, the fact that the mother had asked to take her daughter back and the grandparents had refused was "*strong evidence of the degree to which they assumed long-term responsibility for A and treated her as a child of the family*".

4.2.16 The principle of "not just a member, but a child" obviously does not apply only to grandparents, but to the extended family generally, including blended families, so it applies to stepchildren, whether by marriage or in a cohabitee setting. In every relevant case, you will want to consider whether the arrangement was considered by DP to be permanent, and, if AC was an infant, whether DP was asked (and refused) to return AC to her parents at any stage.

4.2.17 Special Guardianship

A brief word about special guardianship, which was introduced in 2007 as an amendment to the Children Act 1989. A special guardianship order grants parental responsibility, and everything that goes with it, to the person named in the order. It is the midway point between a residence order and an adoption order, giving the guardian control over the child's life without breaking the natural parental bonds. Once appointed, a special guardian can exercise that parental responsibility to the exclusion of the child's natural parents. The detailed rules on applying for and obtaining a special guardianship order are outside the scope of this book, but these orders are likely to begin to have some impact on Inheritance Act claims in the near future. Grandparents, aunts and uncles of the child are frequent applicants for special guardianship, but applications do not need to come from the child's close or even extended family. The existence of a special guardianship order in favour of DP is likely to be a powerful factor in influencing the Court towards a conclusion that AC was treated as a child of DP's family.

4.2.18 Mistaken Belief that AC is DP's Biological Child

This difficult and by no means unusual problem has to be approached through the case law on maintenance. The case may already have commenced on the basis that AC was DP's biological child; it may be that DP genuinely believed during his lifetime that AC was his biological child and treated AC accordingly; AC held the same belief, and no doubts ever arose until after DP died. The Estate, on the instructions of DP's family, now put forward a case that AC is not in fact DP's child at all. AC's siblings may well have known or suspected for some time that there was a cuckoo in the nest and have given instructions that will make matters worse, not better.

4.2.19 As with many aspects of acting for clients in Inheritance Act cases -- whether you are acting for AC or for DP's estate -- bear in mind that this will probably be distressing, and possibly even devastating, news for AC. It is unfortunately very common for those representing the estate or the beneficiaries in these circumstances to come across as brusque and unsympathetic, which will certainly not make the problem go away; quite the opposite. It may assist to short-circuit the disputes which can arise by pointing out that the case law indicates that where such a mistaken belief exists, it will not impact on any maintenance provision provided the child was treated as a child of the family: see *W(RJ) v W(SJ)* [1972] Fam 152.

4.2.20 *Quasi-adoption*

It is of course possible that AC may have become so established within a family other than DP's that DP's estate will attempt to use her position in that second family as a defence to a claim, particularly where there has been long estrangement between DP and AC. In *Re Debenham* [1986] 1 F.L.R. 404, DP had rejected AC for all of AC's life and had left her to be cared for by DP's mother/AC's grandmother. When AC made a claim on DP's estate, the executors claimed that AC had in fact been quasi-adopted by her grandparents and that as a result DP owed her no, or minimal, obligations. DP's rejection of AC in *Re Debenham* was drastic but not total, and the Court rejected the argument that she had no obligations to AC, but it is possible that such an argument might be more successful in similar circumstances where the estrangement was in fact total, and DP and AC had had no contact whatever during DP's lifetime. For estrangement generally, see [**6.2.17**] and following.

4.2.21 Children born as a result of IVF/Human Assisted Reproduction

The Inheritance Act machinery has not yet caught up with the very rapid advance of human cell technology, but it is only a matter of time before a child born in these circumstances makes a case against a biological or natural parent. I suggest that the Court will be strongly guided by the principles of legal parenthood set out in the Human Fertility and Embryology Act (HFEA) 2008. The rules are complex, and reference to a specialist textbook is going to be required.

4.3 The Threshold: Stage 1

4.3.1 The Threshold: Establishing that the Provision was Unreasonable

Once AC has got within the portal, the next step is to cross the threshold. She does this by demonstrating (1) that the effect of the Will, or the intestacy, or both combined -- we are going to call this "the disposition of the estate" -- is not to make reasonable provision for her. Once she has demonstrated that, the Court will then consider whether or not it should exercise its powers in order to make reasonable provision for her. These have been called fairly consistently throughout the case law "Stage 1" and "Stage 2".

4.3.2 Both Stage 1 and Stage 2 depend entirely on an assessment of **all** of the factors set out at section 3 of the Act. The Court is mandated to look at all of the factors set out at sections 3(1)(a) to (f) of the Act, so you must too. Section 3(1)(g) is a "sweeper" section, allowing the Court to consider any other matter which in the circumstances the Court may consider relevant, including the conduct of any of the parties. The effect of section 3(1)(g) is that if the Court considers that another matter is relevant, it must consider it, although one would hope it would consider a relevant fact in any case. "Conduct", where it is relevant at all, falls within the parameters of section 3(1)(g), and we will look at the specific mention of "conduct" when we consider section 3(1)(g) in detail below.

4.3.3 This book is organised to examine Stage 1 first, (so when I refer to "the Threshold", I am also referring to Stage 1) and then to examine Stage 2. Because the Court considers the same section 3 factors under Stage 2, there is inevitably quite a bit of duplication in practice between the two stages, and in many cases, a reported judgment does not distinguish section 3 factors which were more important at Stage 2 than Stage 1, or vice versa. In *Ilott SC* Hughes LJ commented that separating out the two stages can be an artificial exercise. Where there is a serious issue as to whether DP should have made any provision for AC at all, it may be convenient to separate the s.3 considerations into two distinct stages, but there will also be many cases in which exactly the same conclusions will both answer the question whether reasonable financial provision has been made and what that reasonable financial provision should be.

4.3.4 Ironically, given the new guidance given in the *Ilott* judgment about the maintenance standard, it is possible that there may be more doubts about reasonable financial provision than there have previously been, leading to more separation between the two stages, but we will deal with that when we come to look at the maintenance standard. Hughes LJ expressly approves of the practice of the Judge "*simply setting out the facts as he finds them and then addressing both questions under the Act without repeating them*" [para 24].

4.3.5 It is obvious however that the size and nature of the net estate, and the resources and needs of beneficiaries or other claimants, may well have a very significant impact on Stage 2 and what the Court is able to do by way of reasonable provision.

4.3.6 Discouragement of Appeals in Ilott: *Get the Evidence Right First Time*

One point which should be apparent by now is that -- in spite of the impression that the multiple appeals in *Ilott* may have left -- it is not at all simple to challenge a first-instance Inheritance Act decision, because to do so the appellant must establish that the trial judge was "plainly wrong", as Aldous LJ said in *Espinosa v Bourke* [1999] 1 F.L.R. 747. It is vital that your case is well-prepared and that you have all of the relevant **and updated** information before the Court.

4.3.7 In *Ilott SC* Hughes LJ emphasised that the first instance judgment should only be challenged **only** if there is an error in principle or at law and referred to Hoffman LJ's comment in *Piglowska v Piglowski* [1999] 1 WLR 1360 @ 1373 - 4 that allowing parties to bring marginal appeals on "*what are essentially individual value judgments*" is to "*kill them with kindness*". You may not agree, for example, with the Judge's assessment that your client could have done more to increase her earning power, but unless the Judge ignored evidence to the contrary or gave it plainly insufficient weight, your client's prospects on appeal are fairly limited.

4.3.8 This part of *Ilott SC* is likely to cast a long shadow. It means that it is more vital than ever to get your case right first time. You may not get another chance. Wall P expressly noted in an earlier *Ilott* appeal that if DJ Million had decided at the first trial that Mrs Ilott had been reasonably provided for and that therefore her claim should be dismissed, there was considerable doubt whether that decision could have been successfully appealed. Hale LJ specifically referred to this passage from the earlier judgment in her judgment in *Ilott SC* @ 65. She considered that a "respectable case" could have been made for this option as well as the two (very different) others.

4.3.9 The Role of Value Judgment

We saw at the beginning of this book that one of the most important aspects of the Supreme Court judgment in *Ilott* was that it re-affirmed that the Court is making a **value judgment** when it decides whether or not the disposition of the estate has made reasonable provision for AC. Before you continue onwards to carry out the balancing exercise for your client, you need to consider this point carefully, because it carries some dangers.

4.3.10 As we have already seen, Hughes LJ's judgment in *Ilott SC* emphasised that the Judge is usually making a single assessment of reasonable provision [@34] and that the Judge does not generally need to separate out the two stages of the exercise and apply the section 3 factors individually to each (although she might need to do so on some occasions). The Judge can adopt a "broad-brush" approach and simply set out the facts (which will be the relevant facts under section 3) and then address both of the questions without repeating the facts. Paragraph 24 of the judgment goes on to consider the dictum of Goff LJ in *Re Coventry* [1980] Ch 461 that stage 1 was a question of value judgment and stage 2 was one of discretion, and concludes that it is preferable to consider *both* stages as questions of value judgment.

4.3.11 In *Piglowska v Piglowski* [1999] 1 WLR 1360, Hoffman LJ gave a contemporary definition of value judgments as matters *"on which reasonable people may differ. Since judges are also people, this means that some degree of diversity in their application of values is inevitable and, within limits, an acceptable price to pay ... The appellate court must be willing to permit a degree of pluralism in these matters. "*

4.3.12 There are some value judgments which would probably be unacceptable: for example, if DP had left a clear expression of wishes that nothing should be left to AC simply on the basis that she was illegitimate, or indeed that she was a woman, those wishes are probably not a factor that the Court would make decisive. For the most part, however, the spectrum will be within a general standard of how today's families in the UK operate, which obviously is itself a concept susceptible to value judgments (and, as Hale LJ's judgment in *Ilott SC* set out, not terribly clear in any event). Is there a general belief in the UK that you have a moral obligation to an adult child who is very poorly or financially almost destitute, even if you have adamantly said that you do not accept any such obligation? Inheritance Act cases would suggest that the Court recognises that there is such an obligation no matter how vehemently DP denies that it exists in her particular circumstances. This is a value judgment, describe it how we will.

4.3.13 The Court has however an extremely wide field over which to train its binoculars when making its value judgments. The only guidance it has are the section 3 factors. As the *Ilott* judgment says, "both stages of the process are highly individual in every case", and the order made by the Judge should be upset only if she "has erred *in principle or in law*" (my italics). In passing, I will note that it is the width of the field, and the fact that there are no fixed criteria by which to judge what are its most salient features, which troubled Hale J in *Ilott SC.*

4.3.14 This heightens the risks of litigation in Inheritance Act disputes, because it is extremely difficult to be strongly confident about the outcome except in the clearest of clear cases. Heightened risk means an extra impetus towards settlement at the earliest possible opportunity.

4.3.15 Value judgments vs discretion

When is a decision a "value judgement" and not an "exercise of discretion"? *Ilott SC* does not give detailed guidance about this, but one way of looking at the difference between the two is that one can make a value judgment -- "Mrs Jackson's behaviour to Mrs Ilott was unreasonable", for example -- without exercising a discretion in the sense of using a court power to remedy the situation. I suggest that this is the sense in which Goff LJ was saying in *Re Coventry* that Stage 1 was a value judgment but Stage 2 was a discretion.

4.3.16 It is of course possible to argue that a judge exercises discretion about which evidence to consider and on the weight that she gives to particular items of evidence, and that a "value judgment" is therefore simply another type of discretion, but a "value judgment" appears to involve more than simply weighing up evidence; the judge must bring some external factors to bear on her decision. This the way the terms seem to be used in *Ilott SC.*

4.3.17 One luxury therefore that you and I have that Judges in Inheritance Act cases do not is that we are able to make a value judgment without having to exercise any discretion. In contrast, if a trial Judge finds that reasonable provision has not been made in an Inheritance Act case, she *must* go on to decide whether she can exercise her discretion and use one or more of the powers available to her.

4.3.18 Ilott SC states that the Stage 2 exercise is also a value judgment. It may well be that in most Inheritance Act cases, there will be no real difference in the positions of the parties whether the exercise is called one thing or the other, save that a "value judgment" is intended to be less open to challenge on appeal, as we have seen from Hughes LJ's comments at paragraph 24.

4.3.19 This conception of the exercise as a "value judgment" therefore extends both widely and deeply through the evidence in the case and the orders that are made. To exercise her value judgment about whether or not the estate has made reasonable provision for AC, the judge will first have had to make value judgments about, for example, what the appropriate standard of living for AC should be (see 4.5) and to what extent DP had any obligations towards AC (see 6.4). The overall decision about reasonable provision is therefore a value judgment based on a number of other value judgments, some of which may be very contentious but may not necessarily form a sound basis of any challenge or appeal.

4.3.20 This inevitably means that when you and the other side consider the evidence for the first time, you are all going to have to make a value judgment about, among other things, what AC's standard of living was; whether AC could have done more to help herself financially, including increasing her income; whether the conduct of either AC or DP has a bearing on the case; and how far the needs of other beneficiaries or other claimants should impact on the claim. It will not surprise you to read that it is very likely that you and the other side are going to differ in your value judgments. A trial judge might agree with one or other side in respect of value judgments, or may introduce a different value judgment of her own.

4.3.21 There are two main consequences of this. The first is that it is extremely difficult except in the clearest cases to accurately predict the detailed outcome of a trial. This increases the litigation risks exponentially. The second is that when you approach the other side to discuss settlement, as you must, you have to allow for the fact that there is a broad degree of what engineers call "tolerance" in respect of value judgments and you have, in most cases, to be flexible. If necessary, this is also a matter about which you need to remind your opponent and your client.

4.3.22 In *Nahajec v Fowle* [2017] EW Misc 11, the trial judge expressly considered the question of value judgments when deciding how far the AC claimant had been responsible for the estrangement between herself and DP, and also the accuracy of DP's letter of wishes accompanying his Will, which among other things noted that his children, including AC, was of sufficiently independent means to support herself and had no interest in his welfare. On the evidence before him, the Judge found that both of these representations were not accurate and that AC had tried to maintain a relationship with DP but DP had consistently rejected her.

4.3.23 The post-Ilott case of *Ball & Ors v Ball & Ors* [2017] EWHC 1750 [Ch] also demonstrated how difficult the value judgment exercise can be, although most of the weighing of evidence was carried out in connection with the ACs' claims in contentious probate. There, the ACs had made a complaint to the police about their father which had resulted in his conviction for sexual offences against them. Their mother had very shortly thereafter made a will disinheriting them, which she did not alter thereafter, though she lived for a further twenty years. The Judge found that the mother in *Ball* had been obliged to accept that the father had committed offences against the children, albeit her acceptance was somewhat reluctant, but that she considered their allegations exaggerated and had in any event never forgiven them. The question was whether her decision could be considered under section 3(1)(g) in particular as being unreasonable. Clearly, it could be said that the ACs had right on their side: their evidence had been believed to a criminal standard of proof and some might say that it was therefore objectively unreasonable that their mother had chosen to disinherit them nonetheless. However, the Court found that her decision to disinherit them was reasonable in the circumstances.

4.4 Making Provision: Stage 2

4.4.1 As Hughes LJ noted in *Ilott SC*, by the time you have finished balancing the statutory considerations to decide whether or not the disposition of the estate has made reasonable provision for your client, you will often be more than halfway to deciding what that reasonable provision should be -- either in cash terms or equivalent -- and how the Court should use its powers to make that provision. It can indeed sometimes be slightly artificial to try and separate out the two stages, though you should always try to do so. In this book, we are going to carry out the information-gathering exercise with Stage 1 uppermost in our minds, but where we come across points which could be relevant to Stage 2, we will note them so that we can return to them later.

4.4.2 What we need to bear in mind for the moment is that the Court has a wide range of powers that it can use to make reasonable provision if it finds that such provision has not been made, so try not to develop a fixed idea at the moment about how your client's needs should be met. We will look at that in more detail when we get to Chapter 8, but we have our fact-finding exercise to get through first.

4.4.3 Will or intestacy

The first question is whether DP died intestate or left a Will. She can, indeed, have done both, where there has been a partial intestacy. The same considerations apply to AC's application whether DP left a Will or died intestate, and for the purposes of this book the phrase "the disposition of the estate" refers to the way the property is to be distributed whether by Will or under the Intestacy Rules.

4.4.4 Will

If you are acting for AC, she will probably have a good idea of its contents, though there are occasions where AC is simply told by the executors "DP left you nothing" and is given no further information. If this is the case, then you should write an ACTAPS-compliant letter to the representatives of the estate asking for information about the provisions of the Will, the identity of the beneficiaries, the value of the estate for probate and the types of property in the estate: see 3.6.1. Any estate representative who does not provide that information at an early stage will be at risk of costs. It is obviously essential that any person contemplating an Inheritance Act claim should have full information about the disposition of the estate at the earliest possible moment. Any responsible executor will supply a copy of the Will on request.

4.4.5 It is essential in my view to have the Will, if there is one, in front of you when you meet your client to take instructions: there should be no difficulty with obtaining a copy, but if you find that the executors are reluctant, remind them of the ACTAPS code [3.6]. There is usually little problem with this, particularly if DP set out reasons either in the Will itself or in the letter of wishes as to why AC was going to be left little or nothing.

4.4.6 However, there may be parts of the Will which are ambiguous or unclear, and on which you need to get the view of the executors, or specialist probate practitioners, before you take the leap into issuing. Most Wills these days are professionally drafted, but home-made Wills can crop up in the most unexpected of cases: *Wooldridge v Wooldridge* [2016] Fam. Law 451, one of the largest reported 1975 Act disputes in terms of the size of the net estate, actually featured a home-made Will drawn up by the Deceased without any legal advice at all. If there is a letter of wishes, ask for a copy. You may not get it at this stage (indeed you may not see it until litigation has commenced), but usually the executors are keen to disclose it if it sets out reasons why AC was left nothing, or left much less than she expected.

4.4.7 Challenging the Validity of the Will: All or Nothing?

An Inheritance Act claim is not necessarily a claim that the Will is invalid: it is a claim that the estate does not make reasonable provision for AC, whether the Will is valid or not. There is nothing in theory to prevent AC from making a claim under the Inheritance Act and then making another claim that the Will is invalid: *Pinnock v Rochester* [2011] EWHC 4049 (Ch). *Pinnock* was a case in which AC had actually settled his Inheritance Act claim for a lump sum, then brought an action that the Will was invalid due to lack of testamentary capacity. The Estate claimed that his second claim should be struck out because he had already impliedly accepted the validity of the Will in the earlier proceedings, but that argument was rejected.

4.4.8 AC conceded in *Pinnock v Rochester* that the payment made to him under the Inheritance Act claim had to be brought into account if the Will was set aside. The judge commented that there may be occasions where the facts of the Inheritance Act claim were so closely bound up with the facts of any potential probate claim that issue of the probate proceedings may be vexatious or oppressive, but in that case they were not.

4.4.9 Since *Pinnock v Rochester*, anyone acting for the estate or the beneficiaries would be well advised to make it a condition of any settlement that AC accepts that she will not bring any further actions arising out of the disposition of the estate.

4.4.10 We look in Chapter 9 at other claims that adult children can make against the estate of DP, in addition to or instead of an Inheritance Act claim.

4.4.11 Intestacy

Partial intestacy

Your client's interest under a Will may have been adversely affected by a partial intestacy. These occur where DP has made an effective disposition of part of her estate by Will, but for some reason has failed to dispose of the other part or some other parts. One frequent example is a Will creating a life interest in an asset which does not set out what is to happen to the remainder.

> Isabella leaves her home to her surviving spouse, Jago, for life, remainder to Hermia, her daughter from her first marriage. The Will fails to set out any provisions as to her residuary estate, including significant sums held in her bank accounts. At the time Isabella makes the Will, Hermia has no immediate need of maintenance. However, by the time Isabella dies, Hermia is in poor health and unable to support herself. The partial intestacy in respect of the residuary estate may now mean that Isabella's Will does not make reasonable provision for Hermia, even though the remainder interest might have seemed to be reasonable provision at the time the Will was drafted.

4.4.12 Another fairly common example of a partial intestacy is a Will which provides for specific beneficiaries who do not exist, either because they are dead or because they were never born. The executors will have considered in these cases how the distribution rules under the

Administration of Estates Act 1925 s. 49(1) will operate in the particular circumstances of this Will and should be able to tell you without any significant delay what their proposed distribution will be.

4.4.13 Total Intestacy

There is a tendency to think about intestacy as something that happens by accident: unexpected or sudden death, for example. or because DP could not bring herself to make a Will, or because there are problems with the formalities of execution of a home-made Will. In fact, it is reasonably common for the deceased to have deliberately decided not to make a Will and to allow the provisions of intestacy to apply, either because she considers that these are broadly fair to everyone involved, or because she simply cannot bring herself to make a choice which will favour some beneficiaries over others. This can be the case particularly where DP has children who are claiming that they should receive more than their siblings under the Will, because the statutory trusts on intestacy provide that DP's children will inherit in equal shares.

4.4.14 The difficulty for your client may be that a share equal to her sisters and brothers does not constitute "reasonable provision" in her particular circumstances. However, as we have noted, it is not going to be enough to claim that the distribution is not "fair". Your client would certainly have to demonstrate that her assets and needs made a greater share necessary and that in the circumstances DP had some obligation to assist her; she would also have to take into account the needs and responsibilities that the DP had to others.

4.4.15 Distribution on intestacy

The rules as to distributions on intestacy changed for deaths after 1 October 2014. If a person died intestate before that date leaving a spouse or civil partner whose fixed net sum (often called the "statutory legacy") under the intestacy does not exhaust the residuary estate, then one-half of the residue is held on trust for that surviving spouse and the absolute interest on the other half on statutory trusts for the deceased's "issue", namely children, grandchildren or remoter descendants. In very broad terms, "issue" will include adopted and illegitimate children, but there can be some problems with both of these categories. The current value of the spouse's statutory legacy for deaths after 1 February 2009 is £250,000.

4.4.16 The change effected for deaths after 1 October 2014 was that the spouse/civil partner's share in the residue became an absolute interest. If there is no surviving spouse/civil partner then the whole of the estate is held for the issue on statutory trusts.

4.4.17 The statutory trusts themselves are set out at Administration of Estates Act s. 47(1)(i). Children of the deceased who are living at the death of the deceased are beneficially entitled in equal shares. If any of the deceased's children predecease her but leave children of their own (ie the deceased's grandchildren), then those children take their parent's share *per stirpes* in equal shares. Grandchildren cannot take an interest under the statutory trusts unless their parent, the deceased's child, is no longer living. These provisions can have a drastic effect on AC, as the following example shows.

> Clarinda has cared for her granddaughter, Amanda, since Fenella, Clarinda's daughter and Amanda's mother, abandoned her to move to the USA. Clarinda and Fenella have not communicated with each other since. Amanda is now 19 and studying at art school. There is no dispute that Clarinda treated Amanda as a child of the family and she has supported Amanda financially with her studies. Clarinda has been killed in a car crash and has not left a Will. Under the intestacy rules, her estate will be divided between her three children, Arthur, Thomas, and Fenella. Amanda will receive nothing unless she makes an Inheritance Act claim.

4.4.18 What provision has actually been made for AC?

Generally this is fairly easy to establish because in the nature of things, DP has generally left AC either a small fixed legacy or nothing at all. There are however some cases in which it is not immediately clear how much AC has been left. The fact that AC's entitlement cannot be given even a ballpark figure means that some tough choices may have to be made about whether or not to issue within the time limit: it may turn out that the provision is better than AC had anticipated and there was in fact no need to issue at all. Given that the estate will know of the difficulties with valuing AC's legacy, it should be possible to obtain agreement from the defendants to issue and serve and then if necessary agree a stay until a better estimate of the value can be made. Unreasonable refusals on this point can be pursued via costs orders.

4.4.19 Provision which looks reasonable but actually isn't – "poisoned chalices"

4.4.20 Life interest in a house: trustee and beneficiary at war

The provisions of the Will need to be considered carefully. In some cases, they can leave AC worse off than she was before the death. That was the case in *Iqbal v Ahmed* [2011] EWCA Civ 900. The Inheritance Act claim was made by a wife, so was to the higher maintenance standard, but the provisions of the Will could affect an adult child in very much the same way. H's Will gave his widow the right to occupy the matrimonial home rent-free, but legal ownership remained with H's stepson and another trustee. W and the stepson did not get on, and the arrangement both did not give W secure housing, and left her at the mercy of her stepson. H had left all of the rest of his estate, including what cash there was in the residuary estate, to the stepson. W was dependent on benefits and had very meagre savings. The house needed £30,000 of repairs and was in danger of becoming uninhabitable if they were not carried out. There was no doubt that W passed through the Stage 1 threshold; although the higher maintenance standard clearly applied, it is likely that an AC in the same position would also have passed Stage 1, simply because the position DP left her in was unsustainable.

4.4.21 Life interest in a house: no funds for upkeep

Another poisoned chalice is the bequest of a property which is expensive to maintain, but no bequest of capital or income with which to maintain it. *Stead v Stead* [1985] FLR 16, [1985] Fam Law 154 was a claim by a widow, and therefore on the higher maintenance standard, and it was decided in 1985, when the case law on proper provision at the end of the marriage was in a less enlightened state than it now is. Bearing those points in mind, however, the case still has relevance for adult child claimants today. The Will had left Mrs Stead a life interest in a house which was much too large for her needs (she and the deceased had previously run it as a B&B) and income from an invested sum of £6,000. She was responsible for all of the upkeep and repairs on the property. Mrs Stead was 82 years old at the time of the trial and managing a house of this size was obviously beyond her physical abilities even if she could have afforded it. She was awarded an immediate lump sum of £2,500, income of £1,500 per annum, and the Court made clear that if she wished, the current property could be sold and another more modest property purchased (she seems to have been looking at sheltered housing at the time). The responsibility for managing the repairs and upkeep was shifted to the trustees. That case made an express order that a substitute property could be purchased. Note that since the Trusts of Land and Appointment of Trustees Act (TLATA) 1996, the trustees have a general power to purchase a substitute property if they think it necessary.

4.4.22 Life interest in a house: property unsuitable

The property may be unsuitable in other ways: in *Re Watson* [1999] 1 FLR 878, it was in the wrong place. The property was in Ipswich, a town with which the applicant cohabitee had no connection and she had no reason or wish to live there. Her close friends were in Dedham; she had lived in Dedham for 47 years; she could not drive. It was a "reasonable requirement" for her to live in Dedham and the judge (Neuberger J) ordered accordingly. Note that he found the existence of a garden at the Ipswich property was in the circumstances an "expensive burden" because her mobility was very severely restricted. There is no such thing as an unmixed blessing.

4.4.23 Discretionary trusts

In *Berger v Berger* [2013] EWCA Civ 1305, the deceased's widow had been left a life interest in a Surrey property so substantial that she had required the assistance of a housekeeper and a gardener. She had also been left some further capital, but the real issue was her income. The Deceased had left his residuary estate on discretionary trust, the trustees being his two sons from his first marriage, with a direction that his trustees should "use their best endeavours to provide [the Applicant] with income on a regular (preferably monthly) basis". In addition, he had written a letter to one of his sons asking that he and his brother should ensure that the Applicant received "maximum income during her lifetime". He had specifically directed that the trustees did not need to keep a balance between income and capital.

4.4.24 As it turned out, the fact that the Applicant's income was entirely at the discretion of her fellow-trustees, who were not inclined to exercise their discretion in her favour, meant that the provision was inadequate from the start. There were questions as to whether her claim was properly an Inheritance Act claim or a trusts claim, but on appeal Black LJ affirmed that she certainly had a meritorious family provision claim.

4.4.25 We have already seen [3.4] that in *Berger* the decision to take action and make an Inheritance Act claim was delayed until it was too late. If there are real prospects that the discretion will not be exercised fairly, then you will probably have to issue protectively.

4.4.26 Where there is a trusts question of any kind, you will need to make detailed enquiries of the trustees to establish just how realistic and substantial your client's interests are. Where your client is a potential beneficiary under a discretionary trust, these may include how has the discretion been exercised in the past, and whether your client's expectations of help from the trust are realistic.

4.4.27 Valuation Disputes

These fall into two classes: disputes about the value of the net estate, encompassing not just the valuation of individual assets, but the valuation of liabilities on the estate; and disputes about the value of what AC has been left. This is an area in which it is particularly important to remind your client that she cannot bring a claim on the basic premise that the distribution is not "fair".

> Johanna wishes to bring an Inheritance Act claim because her sister Marinka was left an end terrace house, which your client asserts is worth £1,000,000, while Johanna was left the mid-terrace next door, which she says is worth £100,000. Johanna may be totally correct about the values, but that will not in itself give her a case. The question is whether, if the net estate comprises this extremely

valuable asset, the provision made for her was reasonable. If, let us say, Johanna was holding down a well-paid job and had no health problems, but Marinka was in chronic ill-health and had been assessed by the DWP as unfit for work, the Court might well find that reasonable provision had been made for Johanna.

4.4.28 Do not expend costs on valuations in respect of matters which cannot be issues in the case. If there are genuine disputes on valuation issues, attempt to agree a joint valuer at the earliest possible stage, with provision for an agreed letter of instruction and follow-up questions if appropriate. Where it is possible to narrow the issues, do so: if your client's valuation is dependent on a grant of planning permission, how likely is that grant as a realistic prospect? For land values, remember that the Land Registry holds an extremely helpful data set of prices paid in each geographic locality, and commercial sites such as Zoopla can also be source of further helpful information, all of it free of charge.

4.5 The Maintenance Standard

4.5.1 The Maintenance Standard

"Reasonable provision" for adult children means reasonable provision **for their maintenance**. The best description of "maintenance" remains Browne-Wilkinson J in *Re Dennis* [1981] 2 All ER 140: "*Maintenance connotes a provision that is to be made to meet recurring expenses, being expenses of living of an income nature*". Less helpfully, the oft-quoted Canadian case of *Re Duranceau* [1952] 3 DLR 714 summarised the issue, rather archaically, as "*is the provision sufficient to enable the dependant to live neither luxuriously nor miserably, but decently and comfortably according to his or her station in life?*" The class-based origins and connections of the "station in life" concept are particularly dangerous where the Court is obliged to make value judgments: see 4.5.9 below.

4.5.2 In order to make any claim at all against the estate, therefore, your client will have to show that she has financial needs **for her maintenance** that she cannot meet. This means that your first task as far as the question of maintenance is concerned is to obtain the best and fullest information that you can about your client's financial resources, her needs, and her obligations to other people, including her creditors, hence my recommendation to carry out the Form E exercise.

4.5.3 Ilott SC specifically focusses on this limit of the claim to maintenance and notes that it is "*a [sic] deliberate legislative advice and important*" [13]. It has to mean "*provision to meet the everyday expenses of living*" and does not "*extend to any or every thing which it would be desirable for the claimant to have*" [14]. The judgment extensively quotes and approves Browne-Wilkinson J's definition of maintenance in *Re Dennis* [1981] 2 All ER 140 as

> "*[connoting] only payments which, directly or indirectly, enable the applicant in the future to discharge the cost of his daily living at whatever standard of living is appropriate to him. The provision that is to be made is to meet recurring expenses, being* ***expenses of living of an income nature***" [emphasis added].

4.5.4 To answer the question at threshold stage (1), therefore, you need to know what your client's living expenses are, and you need to decide whether these living expenses are proportionate to her financial and family background. Sometimes there will clearly be a shortfall between income and expenses, and the gap may have been bridged by DP; the effect of the disposition of the estate may be that that bridge has now disappeared. Sometimes AC may have been living an extremely frugal life within her means without any assistance from DP, as Mrs Ilott did. The question then becomes one of whether the provision was reasonable given that AC's financial circumstances are poor.

4.5.5 This part of the exercise is usually fairly straightforward. If your client is generally able not only to support her usual standard of living but has been able to make savings, then she would not appear to need anything from the estate to assist with her maintenance, and the claim is proportionately weakened. However, if she is living on a very tight budget or is having to do without in order to support her lifestyle, then it is more likely that there is a maintenance need. How far that maintenance need is going to stretch is, once again, a value judgment question. However, to make a claim at all, it is almost certainly going to be necessary to demonstrate an income shortfall of some kind.

4.5.6 Ilott SC gives some further guidance at [15]. Maintenance is not limited to subsistence; and although it is "by definition the provision of income rather than capital", it does not necessarily have to be provided by periodical payments, but can be provided by means of a capitalised lump sum. There can also be specific lump sums payable for specific needs such as a car. The provision of housing for AC can be maintenance; the fact that DP was allowing someone to live in a house she owned will generally mean that she was maintaining that person for Inheritance Act purposes. "*But it is necessary to remember that the statutory power is to provide for maintenance,* ***not to confer capital on the claimant***" [emphasis added]. The judgment goes on to mention with approval Munby J's decision in *Re Myers* [2004] EWHC 1944 where he ordered provision to be made via a life interest in a trust.

4.5.7 The Court will however pay particular attention to how much AC has done to support herself. In general, a parent is not obliged to support an adult child who is capable of working, and without any further circumstances or history that will not be an obligation on the estate. However the fact that AC is capable of work but not now working may not be fatal to her claim. She may have been self-supporting in the past but now be unable to work because of ill health; she may now be too old to work; she may have spent much of the past two decades as a full-time homemaker and mother and be unable to find anything other than minimum wage employment. None of these factors may be conclusive, but clearly they are going to be highly relevant.

4.5.8 Since *Ilott SC,* you now have to ask yourself searching questions about whether the provision your AC client is seeking is wholly maintenance-related and does not constitute a request for capital. We know from the decided cases that an application for a lump sum to pay off a mortgage was not "reasonable provision" (*Re Jennings* [1994] Ch. 286; [1994] 3 W.L.R. 67; [1994] 3 All E.R. 27) and neither was a lump sum to pay taxes due on a lifetime gift made to AC by the

DP (*Re Dennis* [1981] 2 All ER 140). One way of testing whether your lump sum claim is truly related to maintenance is to compare it to "recurring expenses ... of living of an income nature". Is your lump sum request capitalising these recurring living expenses, or is it asking for extra capital provision?

4.5.9 The Role of Value Judgment

This is plainly one of the areas in which a Judge's "value judgment" can have a big impact. Take, for example, the facts of *Negus v Bahouse* [2008] EWCA Civ 1002. This was a cohabitee case, with a long period of dependence/maintenance, but we can bear in mind that the maintenance standard is the same as in AC cases. Ms Negus claimed for expenditure on wine, on entertainment (particularly eating out), on cigarettes (she was a heavy smoker), hairdressing and holidays. She had been supported by the deceased in an extremely comfortable lifestyle. The residuary beneficiary opposed the making of an Inheritance Act award on the basis that provision under the Act was intended to be for needs and to prevent injustice, rather than upholding extravagant styles of living.

4.5.10 On this point Munby LJ observed that "in assessing in any particular case what is or is not reasonable maintenance, the court must have regard to the nature and quality of the lifestyle previously enjoyed by the applicant and the deceased". This cut both ways: the applicant who lived with the deceased in a hovel could not expect the same level of maintenance as the applicant who lived together with the deceased in a palace. "If the lifestyle was indeed lavish and extravagant then it is entirely acceptable, and a proper application of established principle, for a judge to reflect that in his evaluation of the proper answer to the first question [in other words, Stage 1] and in the exercise of his discretion in providing an answer to the second question [Stage 2]."

4.5.11 However, adult child claims which involve sustaining an expensive lifestyle have not on the whole met with great success. In *Robinson v Bird* [2003] EWHC 30 (Ch), DP had been extremely generous to AC during her lifetime. That generosity included buying a house for her, paying for a car and other expensive chattels, and making generous money gifts. There had also been a gift of just over £200,000 to AC during DP's lifetime by authority of the Court of Protection. AC had significant psychological problems and was unable to work as a result. The net estate was worth £361,500 in round terms, of which AC's share under the Will was £75,000. She was unsuccessful in her claim to increase that share by way of an Inheritance Act claim because although DP had been sufficiently generous to her to make her financially independent, "rather than invest prudently and live within her means, she had chosen to maintain a lifestyle, the cost of which far exceeded her income". It was highly relevant that the other named beneficiary of the Will was a grandchild who also had mental health problems and who was living on the breadline, but the judgment seems to make clear that AC's claim would have been considered excessive even if this had not been a factor.

4.5.12 We saw in our look at value judgments that they are judgments on which reasonable people can differ, that judges are people, and that they can have different views about what is reasonable without actually being found wrong by an appeal court. The position is perhaps a little more straightforward in cohabitee cases because by their nature, the applicant and the deceased shared a home and with it a lifestyle and the Court can look at that shared lifestyle when assessing the correct standard. Most AC claimants will not have been sharing an extravagant lifestyle with DP, although there may be some exceptions. What you can look at is how far DP knew of AC's more lavish lifestyle, how far she approved of it, and to what extent she subsidised it.

> Miranda is working as a university lecturer on a short-term contract. The job has good prospects, but the pay is low. Her mother, Samantha, has supported her financially by giving her a cash lump sum to use as a deposit to buy her own flat, and has also paid a fixed allowance into Miranda's account every month to help with monthly payments, including the mortgage. Samantha has expressly said to Miranda on numerous occasions that she does not want her to have any money worries. Miranda is used on her income to replacing her electronic equipment such as laptops and mobile phones every couple of years, buys a nearly-new car every three years, and takes two holidays a year. Samantha has now died and the most recent valid Will leaves all of her property to her ex-husband, Peter. The relevant standard of living in Miranda's case will be the standard that Samantha's financial contributions helped to support.

4.5.13 In *Wooldridge v Wooldridge* [2016] Fam. Law 451, where the claimant widow was seeking a very high lump sum, the problematic issue was not the level of maintenance, but that the widow's specified income needs came perilously close to making no sense at all unless the deceased had been involved in some kind of tax evasion, by so much did the claimed expenditure exceed the documented income. Note that a claim to a lifestyle which is founded on illegality is bound to fail on the ground that it is contrary to public policy: *Hunter v Butler* [1996] RTR 396. You must also be aware constantly of your money laundering notification obligations where you see a potential problem along these lines.

4.5.14 "Just About Managing"

The other side will often argue in Inheritance Act cases that because AC is living within her means, she has no financial needs. In *Re Watson* [1999] 1 F.L.R. 878, Neuberger J considered the argument put by the Treasury Solicitor in that case that because the applicant (who was a cohabitee, not an adult child) was managing to live within a "meagre" income, she could (as the learned Judge put it) "be penalised as a result of her own self-denial and prudence" was, although strong, "unattractive". Although the point is not expressly made either in *Watson* or in *Ilott* (where *Watson* was specifically referred to in the CAQ hearing), one common factor in both of these cases is that the applicant could not provide for many of what most of us would consider the normal needs of life -- a new fridge, a washing machine -- without significant financial worries. He continued:

> " ... *just because a person manages to live within his or her income does not mean that that income fulfils all his or her "needs" or "requirements" let alone "reasonable requirements". That may be particularly true in the case of a stoical and modest person such as [the applicant] ...* " [@ 890 in FLR].

4.5.15 What is reasonable financial provision should not depend on how stoical, modest, or indeed long-suffering the applicant is. Take particular care if your client is elderly, but many AC claimants will be most reluctant for reasons of pride or self-esteem to make a claim at all, and may minimise their financial hardships. Nor should it depend on whether the applicant has been prepared to incur debts, whether large or small, in order to subsidise a reasonable lifestyle, which is the only practical alternative to living very frugally within her means. Sometimes indeed the applicant's credit rating will mean that she could not borrow even if she wished to. In *Nahajec v Fowle* [2017] EW Misc 11, AC was working at two jobs, one of them a zero-hours contract. She had been ill during the period before the trial and had incurred debts of £6,600. She could have managed on her income of £1240 per month if she had not had to repay her debts. The defendant argued that reasonable maintenance would be a lump sum limited to the total amount of her debts, but the trial Judge rejected this, calling her lifestyle a "frugal existence with only occasional and modest expenditure on "fun" items". He awarded her a £30,000 lump sum and commented that he would have awarded more had he not felt himself restricted by the Ilott SC approach to capitalisation of maintenance only.

4.5.16 State Benefits

These are now very much the focus of attention if your client is receiving them following the detailed examination in *Ilott SC* of how the award will affect them. Because this is something that you will consider in detail when you take instructions from your client, I have dealt with this at 5.4.11. For the moment, there are two points to bear in mind: firstly, it has been settled law since 1966 (*E v E,* [1966] 1

WLR 709; [1966] 2 All ER 44) that DP cannot use the fact that AC will receive state assistance to justify leaving her nothing out of a large estate. The position may be different where the estate is small or there is simply not enough to go round all of the potential beneficiaries and claimants who have needs, but the basic principle is that DP cannot leave AC destitute or near-destitute on the sole assumption that the state will step in. Secondly, benefits themselves are not nececssarily "reasonable provision": in other words, the fact that AC is receiving state benefits and she can therefore pay all of her most basic necessities of life does not mean that she has no claim under the Act.

4.5.17 "Maintenance" may (exceptionally) not be financial

There may be very rare cases where your client is not actually in financial need, but the estate has not provided sufficiently for her maintenance nonetheless. *Lewis v Warner* [2016] EWHC 1787 (Ch), though a cohabitee rather than an adult child case, demonstrates how this might arise in practice. Mr Warner was 91. He had sufficient income for his needs, and substantial assets. He had made his home for 20 years with the deceased in a property that the deceased owned, but that she left entirely to her daughter, who wanted to sell it. Mr Warner had the assets and income to purchase another property, but he wanted to remain in the disputed property for multiple practical reasons. He made an application under the Act to have the property transferred to him in return for payment of its for full value. The estate argued that because Mr Warner did not have any financial needs, he could not make a claim under the Act, but Newey J rejected this, noting that maintenance was not necessarily confined to support with a person's cost of daily living (as in *Re Dennis* [1981] 2 All ER 140) and was "*capable of referring to other forms of assistance with the requirements of daily life*" [23]. If a person was in want of a particular thing to sustain a reasonable quality of life, provision of that thing could possibly represent "maintenance" regardless of financial means. This decision is however subject to appeal at the time of writing.

4.6 Starting the Balancing Exercise Under Section 3

4.6.1 It is impossible in practical terms to start the balancing exercise with a completely open mind. Something has brought your client to your door to ask about an Inheritance Act claim, and that something is generally either a disparity between the size of DP's estate and what was left to AC, which AC believes is unreasonable provision in her particular circumstances, or the fact that DP was generous to other family and friends but not to AC. Sometimes it is both. If some sort of unfairness had not been perceived by AC, you would not be advising her at all. This means that you are inevitably approaching the balancing exercise with at the very least this disparity or unfairness at the back of your mind, and the temptation is to put it at the front of your mind and let it stay there.

4.6.2 The main skill at this stage therefore is not to let this element dominate the balancing exercise and see everything else through the filter of this perception, but to "park" it until you have looked as objectively as you can at all of the other elements. You will need to come back at the end of the balancing exercise and ask the question: given all the elements that the Court has to take into account, should AC have been left more for her maintenance than she was in fact left?

4.6.3 The crux of your client's claim must be that the disposition of the estate did not make reasonable provision **for her maintenance**. My suggestion is that you use an adapted Form E from the Family divorce jurisdiction to gather the relevant details, and in the next chapter we will go through Form E in an Inheritance Act case and the additional matters that you should ask about or follow up. Full financial information is essential, but it is not nearly enough. You must find out everything you can about the other factors at section 3.

4.6.4 There is a particular danger in adult child Inheritance Act cases of becoming too focussed on one particular subsection of section 3. While some subsections may have no relevance at all -- for example, the beneficiaries may choose not to put in question either their resources or their needs, so section 3 (1) (c) cannot be considered -- you must take care to put all of the available relevant subsections onto the scales. Do not leave anything relevant out of account at this stage.

4.6.5 It may well be that when you have put all of the relevant s.3 factors onto the scales that you consider there is one particularly salient and important subsection which outweighs all of the others, but in order to make that point to the other side and the Court you will have to consider the other subsections and set out your stall on why they carry relatively little weight in your case. I cannot stress enough that you must carry out the balancing exercise in every case, and from the outset of your instructions.

4.6.6 Ironically, in *Espinosa v Bourke*, Butler Sloss LJ opined that "*however rich the deceased, if the applicant has sufficient financial resources and no financial needs, it would not be necessary for the Court to look further*": but by the time that *Lewis v Warner* [above] came to be decided less than twenty years later, it was apparent that an order could be made even when the applicant has sufficient financial resources and no financial needs. Not even section 3(1)(a) is dominant. You must put in everything that is relevant.

> Jocasta has left her entire estate, save for a very small legacy, to her infant children from her second marriage to Bertie. Marina, Jocasta's daughter from her first marriage, makes a claim against the estate, including a claim that she was promised by Jocasta that she would inherit property belonging to her maternal grandmother. If the estate cannot make this payment without significantly reducing the amount available to the infant children and taking their living conditions below the poverty line, it is likely that the financial resources and needs of the beneficiaries under s. 3(1)(c) and Jocasta's obligation to her infant children under s. 3(1)(d) are going to be the overwhelmingly important factors. But if you are advising Marina, you must still consider and weigh up Marina's resources and needs, any potential obligations Jocasta had to Marina whether legal or moral, the size and nature of the net estate, and any other section that applies to the circumstances of her case. Not to do so is to give your client incomplete advice and yourself an incomplete picture.

4.6.7 Timing

The Court must be satisfied **at the date of the hearing** that the disposition of the estate did or did not make reasonable provision for AC, so all parties are to some extent aiming at a moving target as the trial date draws near. Whether you are acting for AC or the Estate, but particularly if you are acting for AC, you need to make periodic checks about her financial resources and needs and ensure that you are up to date. If you have based your data on Form E, particularly the interactive version, it is easy to update your figures when necessary and re-calculate.

4.6.8 Be aware that you are required to file up to date evidence on income, assets and needs for the trial, make preparations in good time, and chase up the other side if necessary. Avoid the fate of the executors in *Thomas v Jeffery* [2012] EWCA Civ 693, who were faced at trial with new evidence that AC had £56,000 worth of debt that he had not previously disclosed. It is much easier to put forward an argument that your client should obtain a substantial costs order on non-disclosure if you have specifically checked that the other side has nothing else to disclose, and have been answered in the negative.

4.6.9 The Value of the Claim

Because the Court will consider all of the section 3 factors, it is in my view impossible for you to fix anything more than a very rough value to your claim until you have undergone the section 3 balancing exercise. It is emphatically not a question of looking at the value of the net estate and looking at your client's assets and coming up with a figure that is "fair". What your client may obtain as reasonable provision can vary widely, depending on whether there are other beneficiaries who were dependent on the deceased, for example, and the size and nature of the net estate. An AC with health problems and unable to work may have a claim against an estate of £100,000; but if all of that estate is tied up in a property which is occupied by the infant children of DP's second marriage, or DP's frail and elderly second spouse, a fit, healthy and working AC's prospects decline dramatically and are very likely to be totally extinguished.

CHAPTER FIVE
TAKING INSTRUCTIONS: THE FORM E EXERCISE

5.1 Form E General Approach
5.2 General Points on Completing the Forms
5.3 Inheritance Act Specific Form: Section 1 Completion Guidance
5.4 Form E Completion Guidance: Overview
5.5 Form E Part 4: Other Information

5.1 Form E General Approach

5.1.1 You have by now satisfied yourself that your client is either a child of DP or was treated as a child of the family; that you have dealt with any limitation problems that arise; that DP was domiciled in England and Wales; and you should have made contact with the other side, at a bare minimum to inform them that your client is contemplating a claim and to ask for relevant information about the estate and about the beneficiaries. You have basic instructions that at least on a first examination the disposition of the estate does not appear to make reasonable provision for your client. Now you are going to take detailed instructions so that you can undertake the balancing exercise under section 3.

5.1.2 This is obviously a critical part of the evaluation exercise and you need to obtain the best instructions that you can at an early stage. Many legal advisers use a *pro forma* to take instructions, either one from a textbook (Andrew Francis' is particularly good, if you have access to it) or one that they have developed themselves.

5.1.3 If you have no access to a specific Inheritance Act *pro forma*, a financial remedy Form E is a good starting point. Using a *pro forma* makes it less likely that you will omit important details, and it makes it much easier to make an assessment of what your client's maintenance needs are and put a figure on them. On a client care point, it also makes it much easier when you are taking instructions from an angry, distressed or grieving client, because the form gives your conference a structure to which you can both return if the discussions go off-track.

5.1.4 Form E is such an efficient way of gathering together information about assets and income that its use has spread far beyond the matrimonial jurisdiction for which it was first adapted. It is certainly not uncommon to find judges in the County Court requesting that financial information for trusts of land and Inheritance Act interim hearings should be provided by way of an informal exchange of Forms E, and that practice is likely to extend further given that the President of the Family Division, Munby LJ, commented recently that the Family Court is the "natural home" of Inheritance Act disputes.

5.1.5 Form E is widely available and anyone can download a copy at https://formfinder.hmctsformfinder.justice.gov.uk/form-e-eng-20160121.pdf. It is designed to be easily understandable by litigants in person, and in many cases you can ask your client to fill out as much as she can of the form herself (from section 2 onwards) and then bring it in to you for a consultation. Sadly, the best free online guidance for completing Form E, previously on the UK Government's AdviceNow website, has been withdrawn. AdviceNow currently gives the lay client the option of watching an advice video on Youtube or of paying for an "extended" PDF guide to completing the form at the cost of £17. However, the general Form E guidance notes (I have given the web address in Appendix 3) can be of some limited assistance. You can of course go through the form with your client in consultation if you prefer. Often this is the better approach, because you can give advice at the same time, but it is of course more costly for the client.

5.1.6 The first section of Form E deals with matters that are specific to a divorce or separation and not to a death. I therefore suggest that you replace this with a more appropriate section 1 which is at Appendix 2 of this book. I have called this the "Inheritance Act Section 1". As well as the version in the Appendix, a printable version is also available online at http://familyproperty.org.uk/inheritance-act-book/instructions-form-download/. *When I refer to Section 1 of the Form in this book, I am referring to the Form in Appendix 2 and online.*

5.1.7 The Form E exercise is also useful in that it prompts you and your client to provide supporting evidence of all relevant income, assets and needs that are set out within the Form. CPR 8.5 provides that when issuing your claim under Part 8 you must provide all of the written evidence on which your client intends to rely in the form of a witness statement, with exhibits as appropriate. The Part 8 procedure is intended to be for cases in which there is no substantial dispute of fact. There are cases where it is simply not possible to obtain the relevant evidence in time, but you should provide it where you have it and make enquiries about it in every case.

5.1.8 It also prompts you, at section 5, to consider what remedy your client seeks. This is often an extremely useful reminder for both you and your client. While it is certainly essential to take instructions from her about what she considers that she needs from the estate, remember that at this stage you are only noting this for future reference until you can carry out the balancing exercise.

5.1.9 You will eventually use the information that you gather at this stage of the process to carry out the section 3 exercise. For reference, the links between the forms and the statute are as follows:

Inheritance Act subsection	**Form E sections**
Section 3(1)(a): AC's financial needs and financial resources	Financial resources: 2.1–2.7. 2.11–2.14 (capital); 2.15–2.19 (income) Financial needs, income: 3.1 Financial needs, capital: 3.2 Maintenance standard: 4.2
Section 3(1)(b) and (c): Beneficiaries' and other claimants' financial needs and resources	Completion of Inheritance Act form at 1.18 for each beneficiary or claimant
Section 3(1)(d): DP's obligations and responsibilities	Completion of box 1.19 for each beneficiary or claimant For AC, completion of boxes 4.3 and/or 4.5
Section 3(1)(e): Size and nature of the net estate	Size: 1.10 and 1.11; nature: box 1.14
Section 3(1)(f) Health and disability	AC: Box 1.16
Section 3(1)(g) "Any other matter"	AC: 4.3; 4.4; 4.5
Section 3(3): Assumed maintenance	AC: Boxes 4.1, 4.3

5.1.10 Because there are published Guidance Notes for completion of the basic Form E, I will deal in detail only with completing the specific Inheritance Act section 1, and with any further points in the Form E about which you might want to obtain further instructions in an Inheritance Act matter.

5.1.11 If you are going to take all of your instructions in conference, it is obviously a good idea to have copies of the death certificate, the Will (with the letter of wishes if appropriate), and the grant of probate/letters of administration in front of you when you go through things with the client.

5.2 General Points on Completing the Forms

5.2.1 While you are going through this Form with your client, remember that the Court is specifically directed to take into account whether DP maintained AC, the time for which DP did so, and the extent of that maintenance (s. 3(3)(a); whether and if so to what extent D P **assumed** responsibility for AC's maintenance (s. 3(3)(b); my emphasis; whether or not DP did so knowing that AC was not his own child (s. 3(3)(c); and the liability of any other person to maintain AC (s. 3(3)(d)). At any point in the Form where it becomes apparent that DP was making a contribution to AC's living expenses, you need to follow through and ask about the overall context of those payments. This aspect of your case will be vital. I deal with section 3(3) in more detail at 6.8.

5.2.2 Interactive Form E

If you have access to the online Form E, the interactive version will automatically complete the financial summaries at 2.20 and 2.21, which is a useful time-saver.

5.2.3 Should I disclose my Form E?

There is no bar on doing so, and in negotiation and without prejudice discussions it might be helpful, but it is not the way to present your case to the Court when you issue proceedings. Instead, use the information obtained (and the supporting documentation) to draft the relevant sections of your client's witness statement.

5.2.4 These days, the Court will often suggest that the parties should complete Form E for an FDR, particularly if your case is proceeding in the Family Division where the judges are more used to seeing information presented in that form, although Chancery judges may also suggest it these days. If that happens, you have your evidence at hand and little extra preparation is required other than a brief review to ensure the information is up to date.

5.3 Inheritance Act Specific Form: Section 1 Completion Guidance

5.3.1 This section gives guidance on the amended Section 1 for Inheritance Act matters that is given at Appendix 2 of this book and online at http://familyproperty.org.uk/inheritance-act-book/ and not on section 1 of the official Form E. It is therefore helpful to have a copy of that form in front of you while you read through this section. Some aspects are self-explanatory, and I deal only with those matters where I believe some brief guidance may be required.

5.3.2 Cause of Death: Box 1.5

A useful reminder that there may be testamentary capacity issues if the cause of death was dementia, for example.

5.3.3 Place of Death: Box 1.6

If DP died outside of England and Wales, make initial enquiries about whether there is a domicile issue.

5.3.4 Gross and net values of the Estate: Boxes 1.10 and 1.11

These should be readily available on the grant of probate or letters of administration if from no other source.

5.3.5 AC's Interest under the Will/Intestacy: Box 1.15

This is often not a fixed sum, but for example an equal share of one of DP's properties with AC's five siblings, that is, a one-sixth share of the whole. Quantify where you can, and make a note to ask the estate for the probate valuation of the property if you have not yet obtained it. Note more distant interests, for example residuary or contingent bequests, and any interests under discretionary trusts. If there is a discretionary trust, who is/are the trustees?

5.3.6 AC's State of Health and Earning Capacity: Box 1.16

This tends to be a much more important factor in an Inheritance Act case than it would be in a matrimonial case, because in many cases it is AC's poor state of health (and her consequent poor income prospects) on which her case is founded. The best source of information about medical conditions which affect AC's standard of living, particularly her ability to earn, is her GP.

5.3.7 Health may also play a big part here. If your client is younger and in good health, the Court may assume that any unemployment is temporary unless you have medical evidence to put forward in rebuttal. This is one of the occasions when the Judge might well make a value judgment about your client which would be difficult to overturn. If your client's case is that her earning capacity is curtailed or even extinguished by her state of health, put forward reliable evidence to that effect from the earliest possible stage. I deal with issues related to health at 6.6 onwards.

5.3.8 Section 3(6) of the Act [6.9] directs the Court to take the applicant's earning *capacity* into account, not simply what AC is currently earning. This quite often proves to be a "hot-button" issue in adult child Inheritance Act claims, with the beneficiaries claiming strenuously that AC has a higher earning capacity that she is currently admitting to. The cases range from allegations that AC is able to work but simply unwilling to do so to contentions that AC's low-income lifestyle was one of which DP specifically disapproved, hence the disposition of the estate, and everything in between. However, Form E deals with the current income position, which is clearly the place to start.

5.3.9 Contents of the Estate: Box 1.14

Do not over-rely on the Will. It is not at all uncommon for DP to make bequests of items she does not in fact own and for the Will to fail to deal with many of the matters set out at [6.2]. Instead, get the best information you can from the personal representatives, preferably the estate accounts.

5.3.10 Knowing the total size of the estate is clearly crucial, not just because your client obviously cannot make a £250,000 claim against a £150,000 estate, but because of the issue of proportionality. If the estate is a modest one, you should advise your client from an early stage that the Court will be expecting her to be realistic about what she can and cannot achieve, even if her case is sound in all respects.

5.3.11 Estate accounts help particularly with the issue of the nature of the net estate, because they put a value on the individual assets and allow you to see straight away whether there is liquidity, where there could easily be liquidity -- share portfolios, for example -- and those assets which are going to cause more difficulty, such as properties left for someone to live in for life, or investment holdings which are to provide an income to someone for life. They can also alert you to items that may not have fallen into the net estate because DP held them by way of a joint tenancy, or because DP transferred them to someone else prior to death. I look at issues about the size and nature of the net estate at 6.2 below, so in order to give that section your best attention, you need to gather as much information as you can now.

5.3.12 Distribution of the Estate: Box 1.14.5

Set out here what you know, and what your client can tell you, about how the Estate is going to be disposed of if there is no intervention.

5.3.13 Beneficiaries and other Claimants: Box 1.18

In respect of each named beneficiary in the Will, or the heirs in intestacy, establish the basics. How old is the beneficiary? What is their state of health? Have they any disabilities? What was their relationship to the deceased? What if anything does your client know about their employment situation? Do they have anyone financially dependent on them, including elderly people as well as infant children? Have any of them received any payments from DP from joint funds such as bank accounts, insurance policies, or other investments? Did any of them to your client's knowledge receive any substantial gifts or support from DP before she died? Fill in one sheet for each significant beneficiary or potential claimant: there is no need to give details of minor legatees.

5.3.14 DP's Dependants: Box 1.19

My form also includes a section for completion about DP's dependants: again these include infant children, but also elderly people, spouses and partners, and disabled adult children. They also include young adults in full-time education or training. If there were people dependent on DP when she died, these people are likely to be the estate's first priority, whether they be beneficiaries or Inheritance Act claimants. DP may well have made provision for these people under her Will, in which case you will already have asked about them when completing box 1.16 above, but it is worth double-checking here to make sure that you have not missed anyone out. There may not be a Will in situations where DP died unexpectedly and relatively young, and your client may be your only guide to less obvious dependants.

5.4 Form E Completion Guidance: Overview

5.4.1 Having taken instructions on the Inheritance Act Form E, you can now move on to your instructions on your client's financial needs and resources using the standard Form E, commencing at section 2 and working your way through the remainder of the Form. Most of the questions are self-explanatory, but I have provided guidance to specific issues which may arise in Inheritance Act matters.

5.4.2 Sections 2 and 3 set out your client's complete income and assets position (section 2) and complete capital and income needs (section 3). Your client's capital resources are at boxes 2.1 - 2.7 and 2.11 to 2.14 of Form E, and income resources at boxes 2.15 - 2.19. Form E also asks for details of her capital financial needs [3.1] as well as income needs [3.2], although as we will see at 8.5 her claim will depend on what her maintenance shortfall is, so do not allow your client to believe that there is scope for awards of capital other than in respect of that. This is not a "wish list". It is often very instructive, however, to get details of what your client's capital needs are. It can tell you a great deal about what her income position is; clients who need capital to buy new carpets or furniture, as Mrs Ilott did, are clearly struggling financially. You will also get an idea of her standard of living from her answers to box 4.2.

5.4.3 For each item, Form E prompts you to obtain supporting evidence, which puts you ahead if you do have to prepare and file a witness statement in due course. As noted above, most items are self-explanatory. I have therefore only commented on sections of the form where some focussed enquiries are useful in Inheritance Act matters.

5.4.4 Form E Financial Details Box 2.5: Capital: Other Assets

A useful aide-memoire, listing as it does the other assets which should be considered but which do not fall within the categories already set out. One potential asset in this section is any interest that AC has under any trust, including a discretionary trust. It also includes any asset that your client is likely to receive in the foreseeable future, held on her behalf by a third party, and any foreign assets.

5.4.5 Ask about any trusts that are out there from which AC may have expectations, and whether or not there may be a life interest in her current home either under the Will or some other instrument or agreement. If AC herself has a life interest in a property not connected with DP -- usually a right to reside in a specific property until her death -- that interest can be valued, but the more important question for you is probably whether the property is appropriate or far too expensive for her needs. She may have been left (by, say, a deceased spouse or partner) with a property which is too large for her, and with no fund from which she can pay for repairs or upkeep.

5.4.6 A future asset which is not specifically mentioned on Form E but which has strong relevance to an Inheritance Act claim is an anticipated future payment in compensation or damages as a result of injury or death. First of all, if your client is not employed because of illness or injury, has she made a claim for damages and if so, what is the current position? Secondly, is your client likely to receive a payment personally as a result of DP's death? This includes nominated death in service benefits from pensions. Thirdly, has your client any claim (such as a Fatal Accidents Act claim) as a result of the injury or death of someone on whom she depended?

5.4.7 Form E Financial Details Box 2.6: Income (employment, self-employment, investments)

Form E asks for supporting evidence in the form of the last available P60, the last three payslips and the last Form P11D (expenses) if your client has one.

5.4.8 This is obviously a useful place to return to your client's employment status in general, and history if relevant; you will have already discussed her capacity to keep herself at box 1.15 above. It redirects your client's attention to the fact that the relevant standard is the maintenance standard. Is she working at the moment? If not, is that a temporary or permanent situation? A young adult claimant, particularly one currently in full-time education, is likely to have earning potential in the foreseeable future, but it may not be that significant. Research the starting salaries for graduates in her discipline. A junior doctor is likely to start on a basic salary below £25,000, for example, although that may be boosted by unsocial hours payments.

5.4.9 It is also a good place to pick up on poor earning potential which is not linked to health issues. Remember that if your client is over 50 (and particularly if she is a mother who has not worked for some years), it may now be extremely difficult for her to get employment at anything above the minimum wage, if that.

5.4.10 Form E Box 2.18: Income from State Benefits

The benefits question can cause particular difficulties -- indeed it did so in the *Ilott* case -- so if it is relevant, get the best information about it that you can. This section includes income from the state pension and from child benefit. One of the difficulties with state benefits is that many of them are means-tested and AC will not be eligible for payment of them if her assets are above a certain level. At the time of writing, means-tested benefits are:

- Income-based Jobseeker's Allowance
- Income-related Employment and Support Allowance
- Income Support
- Pension Credit
- Child and Working Tax Credit
- Housing Benefit
- Council Tax Support
- Sure Start Maternity Grant
- Funeral Payment
- Cold Weather Payment
- Universal Credit.

5.4.11 Go through this list with the client and specifically check in each case whether or not she receives the benefit. She will certainly have documentary evidence from the relevant government department about her benefit entitlement for the present financial year, and you should obtain copies of this.

5.4.12 Financial Requirements: Form E Section 3

Form E divides these into income and capital needs. At this stage, try not to jump ahead into considering what order would best suit your client's needs, although I accept that it can be almost impossible not to reflect on this to some extent. Remember that we are approaching the information-gathering exercise without any preconceptions as far as we can do so. Be sure of the figures first. You can then approach the second stage of the balancing exercise from a more detached position.

5.4.13 The question of what your client needs may seem obvious, but it is worth considering the context first of all. It is now almost universally recognised that all human beings need food, shelter and water as primary needs, and generally in that order. Air and sleep are also essential. These are the physiological foundations of human life. Above those foundations there is a hierarchy of other needs, which you can check if you search online for Maslow's hierarchy of needs, but none of these upper needs can be satisfactorily met if the primary needs are not. The second-tier needs include health, employment, property, family and stability. There are obviously financial factors connected with all of these needs. Above those are the more self-referential needs of love and belongingness, self-esteem, and self-actualisation. Failure to meet any of the needs at lower levels will mean that upper-level needs cannot be met.

5.4.14 For the moment, we will concentrate on the questions you should ask when completing Form E in order to establish whether your client has any relevant basic needs. We will return to the needs question generally at 6.3.15.

5.4.15 Food

If AC cannot pay for her weekly or monthly food budget without help, she obviously cannot meet her basic needs, but it is worth asking about this aspect of the matter with care and tact. Visits to food banks should of themselves prove that there is a significant maintenance problem, but many clients will be most reluctant to admit that they have done so. Benefits payments are intended to cover all food costs, but there is very little room for manoeuvre if an emergency arises and money has to be diverted elsewhere. We saw at 4.5.13 that "subsistence" will almost always fall below a reasonable maintenance standard, whether income is coming from benefits or simply low pay.

5.4.16 Shelter

For the purposes of the Inheritance Act, the question is not whether AC has any roof over her head, however temporary, but whether she has a *secure* roof over her head. There is a serious housing shortage in the UK with equally serious financial consequences. ONS figures show that private rents have been rising in England and Wales at an average of between 1.4% and 3% annually since 2012. The RICS market survey for February 2017 is forecasting rent rises of 2.7% in the next twelve months and an average growth of 4.4% per annum over the next five years. There were reports last year that the average rent of a one-bedroom property in England accounted for more than 50% of the average salary of a young adult. You must take this context into account when considering your young AC client's needs in the foreseeable future. In every case, bear in mind the proportion of AC's income that she is paying in housing costs, and note whether any of it is being paid by housing benefit.

5.4.17 Fuel

Do not overlook the need for, and the cost of, domestic fuel, which is an element of shelter. This is now a major factor in the household budgets of even the relatively well-to-do. "Fuel poverty" is currently defined as having required fuel costs that are above the UK average, which if paid would leave the household with a residual income below the poverty line. In the most recent UK government figures, over 10% of UK households were in fuel poverty by this measure and approximately 20% of households in the private rented sector. A more rough and ready guide is to use the previous official definition of fuel poverty: is your client spending more than 10% of her disposable income on fuel?

5.4.18 Details of household spending

Form E does not set out budget headings, but it is certainly worth taking specific instructions from your client about her usual monthly household expenditure. Most clients are able to give you a very accurate idea of where the money goes, particularly if things are tight. If she needs some help, there are many budget forms online which she can go through on her own or together with you. The Money Advice Service has a good online budget planner at:
https://www.moneyadviceservice.org.uk/en/tools/budget-planner

5.4.19 It is particularly important to get an accurate picture at this stage of whether AC is able to meet her immediate and her reasonably foreseeable financial needs. Don't forget to look forwards. Personal circumstances such as severe or chronic illness, or advancing old age, can mean that the foreseeable future looks much more bleak than the present.

5.4.20 Your client's financial needs are going to be totally dependent on her appropriate standard of maintenance. If your client has always lived modestly, she will not now be entitled to a lavish lifestyle from the estate, regardless of its size or nature. If you need guidance on appropriate figures, you can consult the Joseph Rowntree Foundations's *Minimum Income Standards* for the lowest acceptable point in the scale, and *At a Glance* to slide the scale upwards. On extravagant lifestyles and the likelihood that an AC's wings will be clipped, see 4.5.9 and 6.3.13.

5.4.21 Form E Boxes 3.1.2 and 3.2.2: AC's Dependants

These sections in Form E refer specifically to children, but you should widen the scope to include your client's income and capital needs in respect of anyone who is dependant on her, including elderly relatives, partners or spouses with serious health problems, and indeed anyone for whome she is a carer. As well as infant children, include disabled adult children, and young adults in full-time education or training. Section 3(6) of the Act obliges the Court to take into account when making its assessment AC's financial obligations and responsibilities. These obviously include financial obligations and responsibilities to infant children, but more generally to any other dependent such as a disabled adult child.

5.4.22 AC's responsibility to provide for and support her children (who will very often be DP's grandchildren) can be a most important factor in deciding whether reasonable provision has been made. In most cases, the Court will look at whether or not DP has helped with the costs of support in the past. If DP was a loving grandmother who has consistently paid for her granddaughter's school fees, for example, but who has died unexpectedly without making any provision in that respect, and AC is unable to afford to pay the school fees herself, this can form the basis of a claim by AC.

5.4.23 The picture may be different with other dependants. In *Palmer v Lawrence* [2011] EWHC 3961 (Ch), one point made by the claimant widow was that she was living in one of the deceased's properties with her adult daughter (not the deceased's daughter), who could not contribute to the household expenses (although the judgment does not say why not). The Judge found that the deceased "was under no moral or other obligation to house his wife's daughters" [@43] and that the fact that she was "a caring and loving mother who looks after her children" was "not in itself a reason for increasing the burden on the estate". Nonetheless, include all of your client's dependants at this stage.

5.5 Form E Part 4: Other Information

5.5.1 Significant changes in assets or income: Boxes 4.1 and 4.2

The questions cover a 24-month span, for the whole of the 12 months up to the date of the Form, and for the next 12 months thereafter. Note that the section is intended to include foreign assets and any intended disposals. However, you should take instructions for a wider time period than this where appropriate.

5.5.2 Timing: Immediate past

This can be a particularly relevant matter in Inheritance Act claims, where AC's financial position may have become significantly worse since DP's death. Form E asks for details of the current position, but also at Box 4.1.1 for significant financial changes over the past 12 months. In most cases, given the requirement to issue within six months of probate, this should suffice, but if your client instructs you that the relevant period of change stretches back over a longer period -- if, for example, there was a delay in taking out probate -- keep the longer period in mind and ask about it.

5.5.3 Timing: Foreseeable Future

Section 3(1)(a) obliges the Court to consider the financial resources and financial needs which AC "has or is likely to have in the foreseeable future", so you are not simply looking at AC's situation today, but in a specific forward period, though that period is going to differ from case to case. If, for example, your client struggling financially at the moment but will within the next 18 months receive a very substantial legacy from an uncle's estate, that will be a relevant matter for the Court to consider. If the DP also knew about it, it may also be a factor under section 3(1)(g) or 3(1)(d), but we will look at that in the appropriate place.

5.5.4 Form E has specific prompts about the future; for example, sections 3.1 and 3.2 ask about about anticipated changes in income or capital needs in the "near future" and "reasonable future". The form asks for an explanation of the anticipated change and an estimate of the future cost. It also asks about significant changes to assets or income over the next 12 months at 4.1.2. "Foreseeable future" under the Inheritance Act extends beyond 12 months from the date of completing the form, but responses to these questions should lead you to the relevant period in your client's case.

5.5.5 The concept of "foreseeability" in the Inheritance Act is wider than the Form E scope, however. It was said in *Challinor v Challinor* [2009] EWHC 180 (Ch); [2009] W.T.L.R. 931 that the Court is not restricted to considering only those needs that AC is more likely than not to have, and can take into account any needs that AC is reasonably likely to have, but should not consider possibilities which were "remote" or "speculative" as specific needs. The Court can still consider these possibilities as part of the overall picture, but it has to take into account the probability of their occurring. At this stage, make sure that you have covered all of the matters which your client considers as reasonably foreseeable.

5.5.6 Standard of living

If you are a family practitioner, you will be experienced in asking the right questions for this section, but let's examine the general things you will want to find out about. AC's home is a good place to start: whether it is rented or owned will tell you a great deal about her standard of living. So, of course, will the size of her home. You will already have completed a budget which will have shown you what AC is currently spending her income on. It will have told you about holidays, about how much AC spends on birthday and Christmas presents, about health and beauty treatments, and other leisure activities including expensive hobbies; it will also have told you something about how much AC is spending on travel or motoring costs. What are considered as "needs" in a more affluent household would be considered luxuries in less well-off households, as we have seen. Rather than wrestling with whether DP had a responsibility to maintain the standard of living, whatever it was, at this stage, simply note down the household budget and any gap between income and expenditure.

We have already seen at 4.5.9 that there is no formal cap on reasonable maintenance and that if DP subsidised a "luxury lifestyle" then AC may certainly refer to her high standard of living, but you should bear in mind that the Courts are likely to consider that DP's duty was limited to giving AC the best financial start in life rather than indefinitely supporting a child who is able to earn her own living.

5.5.7 Particular contributions: Box 4.3

This section of the form asks for particular contributions to the family property and assets or outgoings, family life or the welfare of the family. Although the standard Form E refers to contributions by "you, your partner or anyone else", in this context only contributions by AC herself are going to be relevant. Discussing this section with the client can if appropriate reveal the existence of either a proprietary estoppel claim or at the very least a promise to leave property which may fall within sections 3(1)(g) or 3(1)(d). AC may have contributed her labour, expertise and even her cash to a family business which has now been left elsewhere.

5.5.8 This section may also reveal sacrifices that have been made by AC, in particular by giving up paid employment to move back home and care for DP in her declining years. Again, this can often be linked to a promise made by DP that if AC did this, DP would leave her all of the estate or a specific part of it.

5.5.9 Conduct: Box 4.4

Your client will generally have something to say under this heading, sometimes a good deal, and this is a good point to give her general advice about what the Inheritance Act does and how it works, including explaining to her if necessary that "the DP did not leave her estate equally between me and my sisters" and "the DP was unreasonable (or even spiteful)" are not grounds on which to apply for provision under the Inheritance Act. Conduct matters will fall into section 3(1)(g) if the Court considers them to be relevant.

5.5.10 Conduct matters which are likely to be relevant are:

(1) DP made promises to AC about how the estate would be left, or allowed AC to believe that she would inherit;

(2) DP behaved cruelly and unjustly to AC, particularly if this was the cause of a long estrangement which AC tried to mend, or if it had financial consequences for AC, and/or if it resulted in AC being unable to become financially independent;

(3) AC cared for DP over a lengthy period either in serious illness or old age;

(4) If the claim is under section 1(1)(d), any conduct relating to DP's treatment of AC as a child of the family will be helpful - see 4.2.10 above;

(5) Although you may not get a complete picture from AC at this stage, how AC treated DP may well also be relevant; bad conduct on the part of an adult child can, on occasion, result in a claim being dismissed [see *Wright v Waters* [2014] EWHC 3614 (Ch)].

5.5.11 Other circumstances (specific list)

The list here is a useful memorandum of "foreseeable future" events, including the prospects of redundancy, retirement, and inheritance (from another source than DP, obviously). It also asks about earning capacity and disability. Earning capacity can increase as a result of the AC acquiring professional qualifications or simply expecting a promotion; it can decrease because ill health makes it impossible to carry on with AC's present employment. As for disability, progressive conditions like MS may dramatically affect the foreseeable financial needs of AC. We have already looked in brief at health issues, and will look at them again at 6.6.

CHAPTER SIX
SPECIALLY SIGNIFICANT SECTION 3 FACTORS IN ADULT CHILD CLAIMS

6.1 *Overview of Section 3*

6.2 *Section 3(1)(e): The Size and Nature of the Net Estate*

6.3 *Section 3(1)(a): AC's Financial Resources and Needs*

6.4 *Sections 3(1)(c) and (d) Any Obligations Which D Had Either Towards AC, or to Any Other Beneficiaries, or to Any Other Claimants*

6.5 *Sections 3(1)(b) and (c): Resources and Needs of Other Beneficiaries and Claimants*

6.6 *Section 3(1)(f): Health and Disability*

6.7 *Section 3(1)(g): 'Sweeper' Section*

6.8 *Section 3(3): Assumed Responsibility*

6.9 *Section 3(6): Earning Capacity and AC's Own Obligations*

6.1 Overview of Section 3

6.1.1. The Court must consider the section 3(1) categories in every Inheritance Act claim, but it is clear from the reported cases that some factors are particularly likely to crop up in relation to claims made by adult children. Section 3(3), which we have already come across briefly [4.2.11], relates specifically to claims made either by a child of the family or a claimant who was treated as a child of the family and is likely to have particular importance for claims by young adults.

6.1.2 Section 3(6) directs the Court in every case to consider the applicant's earning capacity when considering her financial resources, and her financial obligations and responsibilities when considering her financial needs; although the subsection therefore applies to every applicant, the question of earning capacity has been most keenly contested in applications by adult children. We will look at the section

3 factors which have been most relevant in adult child applications to date.

6.2 Section 3(1)(e): The Size and Nature of the Net Estate

6.2.1 Opinions differ as to whether it is better to start your section 3 exercise by looking at your client's financial needs and obligations under section 3(1)(a), or to clarify the size and nature of the net estate under section 3(1)(e). Obtaining the best information available under both subsections is crucial to making a good realistic assessment of your client's claim, so the best view is that you certainly need to start with one or the other, but it matters less which you deal with first. Here, we are going to start by considering what you need to look out for when considering the net estate, and then go on to look at what you need to know about your client's financial needs and obligations.

6.2.2. Size

There is obviously no point at all in making a claim against an estate that is almost or actually insolvent, or where the assets are of minimal value. If probate has been granted, the estate will already have passed information to HMRC for taxation purposes, so you will at least have the net value for probate, including the IHT400 forms which set out the substantial assets of the estate; if not, then the estate will certainly have information about the overall value of the assets which it will usually supply to you on request.

6.2.3 The disclosure of how much property is in the net estate can sometimes be an unpleasant surprise for your client. Long-held, or even recent, family assumptions about what the deceased owned may turn out either to be unfounded or to be out of date. In particular, the deceased may have made lifetime transfers of property to other family members or friends, sometimes with the intention of tax efficiency, and sometimes deliberately and specifically to attempt to prevent any Inheritance Act applications.

6.2.4 Section 8 of the Act provides that the subject matter of certain dispositions made pre-mortem by DP will, regardless of where they have gone and who holds then, be considered to be part of the net estate. The relevant dispositions are (1) a nomination by DP of any person to receive money or other property (this will obviously include nominations for life insurance payments and death in service benefits from pensions); and (2) any money or other property received by a donee as a deathbed gift (*donatio mortis causa).* The effect of this is to extend the scope of the net estate, but also to extend the reach of the Court. It applies to any disposition made for any reason, and there is no need to prove an intention on DP's part to avoid the operation of the Act.

6.2.5 Section 10 of the Act is the anti-avoidance provision, and this does require proof of an intention to avoid the Act. It is discussed at 8.5 below.

6.2.6 On the other hand, some very substantial assets may not fall into the net estate at all. Death in service and other end of life pension benefits will usually pass directly to the person nominated by the deceased during her lifetime; the same may be true of payments on life and other insurance policies. Any 1975 Act claim can only be against assets in the net estate. However, if a beneficiary or another claimant has benefited from a pension or insurance payment, that can be taken into account by the Court as part of his or her assets under sections 3(1)(b) or (c).

6.2.7 The relevant value of the assets is their value at the date of the trial: section 3(5) of the Act. In *Dingmar v Dingmar* [2006] EWCA Civ 942, the correct approach to a jointly owned asset was said to be to determine the proportion of the asset owned by the deceased at her death and then value it at the date of the trial, and that has been generally followed since.

6.2.8 There can be dramatic and unexpected fluctuations in value of the net estate between death and trial: see for example *Re Hancock* [1998] 2 FLR 34 where the estate was worth about £80,000 at death but well over £630,000 at trial. The fact that the deceased had probably made reasonable provision for the adult child applicant at death in the £80,000 context was no reason why this should now bar her from relief in the increased value context, where DP had had a good relationship with AC, and had thought at the time of making the Will that she ought to have something.

6.2.9 Estate includes "family money"

Another feature of the net estate can have particular relevance for adult children: situations where the net estate includes assets which the claimant says should have passed to her, usually because they belonged to the other parent, or in which she claims some equitable interest. The former was arguably the case in *Ilott* itself, where Mrs Jackson's estate included assets bought with Fatal Accidents Act compensation money paid over following the death of Mrs Ilott's father while Mrs Ilott was still in her infancy. The money had clearly not been paid over for the benefit of Mrs Jackson alone as his widow, but also for the benefit of his child. This formed a part of the arguments in the cases in the lower courts, but the Court of Appeal did not consider that it was a significant factor and this aspect of the case seems not to have been pursued in the Supreme Court. However, in some cases this may be a factor of some importance, and should always be considered.

6.2.10 Sometimes, for example, the first parent to die has left all of his estate to the surviving parent on an understanding that she will leave a substantial legacy to your client. If your client can show that there was indeed such an understanding, the point will fall within DP's obligations or responsibilities to AC at section 3(1)(d): see 6.4 onwards.

6.2.11 Disputes about value

Disputes about the value of assets within the estate are fairly common, and depending on the size of the gap between the parties' valuations and the importance of the issue at stake, it may be necessary to seek expert valuation evidence or, if that is not cost-effective, to agree a value for the purposes of litigation. Sometimes even expert evidence will not help, because the value is dependent on claims being made against the property by third parties, or by HMRC, and it is not realistically possible to give an accurate figure without the claim being concluded. In these circumstances, a trial judge may simply have to do the best she can with the information provided, as Kushner J did in *Musa v Holliday* [2012] EWCA Civ 1268; [2013] 1 F.L.R. 806, where there were claims pending against all of the properties comprised in the estate. Although her valuations were later appealed, the Court of Appeal expressly affirmed both her reasoning and her valuations.

6.2.12 In *Ilott* itself, DJ Million was presented with financial evidence, particularly about Mrs Ilott's needs, which he described as "*ill thought out and unhelpful*" and admitted that he had been "*left to deal with this case with a more rough and ready approach*", although it is apparent from *Ilott SC* in particular that he was doing himself less than justice. What is however clear is that the trial Judge can take a "*broad brush*" to "*very variable personal and family circumstances*" [24], including financial circumstances. If you have particular points to make about valuation and you want to restrict the operation of a trial Judge's broad brush, then ensure that you have evidence available to do so. Where the Court has refused to order expert valuation evidence, you will have to look further afield. If the disputed property is land, the Land Registry maintains house price data which can assist in giving a general picture of value. Commercial sites such as Zoopla have further information which builds on this data.

6.2.13 Where's it all gone?

There are occasions when your client may be on the receiving end of a nasty surprise, in that the estate, whether net or gross, is much less than she was expecting it to be. In *Dellal v Dellal* [2015] EWHC 907 (Fam), the deceased had while alive appeared in various rich lists as having a net worth of around £500m, but on his death the net estate was worth £15.4m. All of this had been left to his wife, from whom he was separated at the time of his death, but she then brought an Inheritance Act claim including contentions under section 10 of the Act that the deceased had, within six years of his death, transferred out most of his estate to other family members.

6.2.14 If a claimant can establish that transfers have been made out of the estate, the Court can order that the recipient should hand back that property, whatever it may be, or its equivalent value. This includes money and other property passed into the hands of trustees under section 11. Family practitioners may see a resemblance to the s.37 powers under the Matrimonial Causes Act 1973, but it is vital to note that sections 10 and 11 do not, unlike s.37, make the initial transfers invalid. Instead, the Court will make a money judgment to repay a specified sum to the estate, where it will again become available for distribution. Section 10 is dealt with in more detail at 8.5 below.

6.2.15 The issue can affect even modest estates. In *Re Beaney* [1978] 1 WLR 770, a DP with dementia had made a gift in her lifetime of the only substantial asset in the estate to one of her three children. In that case, the two disinherited children brought their case on the basis that the donor's mental capacity had rendered the gift void; if they succeeded on that point (as they did), they inherited under DP's intestacy and had no need to bring an Inheritance Act claim. However, the same or similar facts can occur in an Inheritance Act context. Your client therefore has a choice of remedy here, depending on the strength of the evidence that DP had insufficient mental capacity at the time of making the gift. Again, note that a declaration that DP did not have capacity will make the transfer invalid, whereas a s.10 or s.11 claim will result in an order to repay a specified sum to the estate.

6.2.16 Nature

The next thing to consider is how the estate's assets are held, in particular whether there is any significant liquidity in the estate. It is not enough to know that the net value, is, say, £300,000; your client needs to know whether that £300,000 is held in investments, or in property, and in particular whether other beneficiaries are reliant on that property for either a home or an income.

> Dolina has been left a small legacy by her mother Sandra, but the bulk of the value in the estate consists of a property over which Dolina's elderly stepfather, Torquil, has been bequeathed a tenancy for life. Other than this property, there are very few liquid assets in the estate, and certainly not enough to satisfy Dolina's claim. If Dolina succeeds in her claim, the property would have to be sold to pay her. The balance would not be enough to buy a replacement property for Torquil, who has no means of his own. Satisfying Dolina's claim would therefore make Torquil homeless.

6.2.17 As this example shows, the Court may be faced with extremely difficult decisions: do not make its life more difficult, and your client's case more precarious, by ignoring issues that are clearly there. You must take some account of Torquil's needs when you put together your case. The nature of the net estate makes it much more difficult to come to a straightforward solution. In fact, any case where the net estate is substantially comprised of assets which provide other parties with a home or a living -- a family business, or a farm, for example -- is going to be a complex one.

6.2.18 Totally Unique Assets

There are times when the focus of the dispute between the claimant and the defendant is an asset which cannot be replicated. The most obvious example is a property which has been a family home, sometimes for several generations. The Court's ability to award a lump sum to purchase a substitute may be poor consolation to a claimant who has lived in a property for all of her adult life. In *Lewis v Warner* [2016] EWHC 1787 (Ch), the house in dispute was not strictly speaking "unique" but it was unique to this particular cohabitee claimant. There was, in fact, no practical substitute because another property, even in the same village, would involve him in moving house at the age of 91, and in the current property he had medical help on tap, because the doctor and the doctor's wife lived next door and kept an eye on him. "*The one thing that Mr Warner's means could not buy him without the intervention of the Court was what he needed, his home as a consequence of Mrs Blackwell making no financial provision for him.*" He was able to purchase the house at a market price determined by the Court.

6.2.19 Property outside the jurisdiction

The English courts will generally be either unable or unwilling to make orders binding upon property situated outside the jurisdiction, but it will still be necessary to fix a value to that property as part of the net estate, and establish how the foreign property will pass under the laws of the relevant jurisdiction to complete the picture on resources and needs of the beneficiaries. For an example where the property was situated in North Cyprus, see *Holliday v Musa* [2015] EWCA Civ 1268.

6.2.20 Business assets

It can be difficult to separate out DP's personal assets from assets owned by DP's business, whether that was a limited company or a partnership; and indeed the same is true of her liabilities. Seek clarification from the company or partnership accountants of their position at the earliest possible opportunity; you need to know whether the company is claiming substantial assets which might otherwise fall into the residuary estate. Company directors and partners often take out life insurance policies which are guarantees for company debts or are to be paid to discharge them, as happened in *Wooldridge v Wooldridge* [2016] Fam. Law 451. In that case, the deceased had a loan secured on the family home which was paid off from the proceeds of one of his personal insurance policies. The result was that the property passed to his wife mortgage-free, but a part of her Inheritance Act claim was that the money loaned had been borrowed for the benefit of the business, and that the proceeds of the policy should not have been used to repay it. She was unsuccessful in that claim, but it gives an indication of how far the boundaries between personal and business assets can become blurred.

6.2.21 Partnership shares

A partnership at will (as opposed to a partnership by deed) is dissolved by death. At that point, the estate of the deceased partner becomes entitled to the appropriate share of the partnership assets, including goodwill. The surviving partner(s) (one or more of whom may well be the defendants - see, eg, *Ames v Jones* [2016] EW Misc B67 (CC)) can choose to carry on the business or wind it up. If the other partner(s) continue to trade, the estate is entitled to a proportionate share of the profits which are attributable to the use of that deceased partner's net assets: *Sandhu v Gill* [2006] Ch 456 at [49]. Remember, however, that the key date for valuation is the date of the hearing and not the date of death, so that if the partnership assets are worth little or nothing by the date of the hearing (as in *Ames v Jones*), there is nothing for the claim to bite on.

6.2.22 Fatal Accidents Act Claims and Payments

FAA claims payments are made to the individual claimants and do not form part of the estate; they do, however, fall to be considered as part of the resources of the relevant recipients if they are either beneficiaries or other claimants under sections 3(1)(a)(b) and (c).

6.2.23 "Deathbed" gifts / **Donatio Mortis Causa: section 8(2)**

They are called death**bed** gifts for a reason: as recently confirmed in *King v Dubrey* [2015] EWCA Civ 581, the giver has to contemplate **impending** death, and not merely that she will die at some point in even the near future. Death, or the shadow of it, has to be on the doorstep. Furthermore, the gift must only take effect on death, and the giver has to give control of the subject matter of the gift to the recipient. Most reported cases concern land, where the control is given by passing over title deeds or land certificates. It remains extremely difficult to establish that a gift has been given *donatio mortis causa,* but if the facts can be established, s.8(2) of the Act provides that such a gift (minus inheritance tax) will be treated for the purposes of the Act as part of the deceased's estate. As was the case in *King v Dubrey* itself, a deathbed gift claim will often be combined by an AC with an Inheritance Act claim in the alternative.

6.2.24 Jointly Owned Assets

There are special rules relating to assets that DP owned jointly with others: see 8.4. Check whether there are any assets which have passed to another person by way of survivorship. These may include not just land, but the proceeds of insurance policies and the contents of joint bank accounts. In *Cunliffe v Fielden* [2005] EWCA Civ 1508, for example, the applicant wife had by survivorship in respect of joint funds and policies acquired £226,000. These were of course taken into account as her assets, but they did not form part of the net estate.

6.2.25 There was no need in that case to consider whether to sever the joint tenancy because it was the applicant herself who had received the benefit, but there will be cases where the principal beneficiary of DP's Will has also received substantial assets by survivorship and it may then be in the interests of your client to apply to sever so that DP's share will remain in the net estate. We have already seen that to sever a joint tenancy in any of these assets where the death is before 1 October 2014, the claim must be brought within six months of the grant of probate, or it is lost.

6.2.26 Property treated as part of the net estate under s.8

There is one other section of the 1975 Act which you need to look at when considering the size and nature of the net estate, and that is section 8. In brief, it provides that where a person has received a sum of money or other property from DP as a donatio mortis causa (s. 8(2)) or where DP has "*in accordance with the provisions of any enactment*" nominated another person to receive a sum of money or other property after his death (s8(1)) that sum of money or other property (minus any capital transfer tax payable) will be treated as part of the net estate for the purposes of the Act.

6.2.27 The provisions prevent DPs from avoiding the effect of the Act either by making a nomination or a deathbed gift, and a recent case has looked particularly at s. 8(1).

6.2.28 In *Goenka v Goenka* [2014] EWHC 2966 (Ch), the deceased had left the family home and a lump sum to his wife, but had nominated his father to receive the death in service benefit payable under his NHS pension. Mrs Goenka successfully argued that the nomination was made "in accordance with the provisions of an enactment". The nomination itself had been made under the National Health Service Pension Scheme Regulations 1995, which in their turn had been made under the power conferred by statute in the form of the Superannuation Act 1972. As a result, the lump sum of £201,000 fell into the net estate.

6.2.29 Note that section 8(1) does not apply to pensions generally and will presumably never apply to private pensions. The key in *Goenka* was that the NHS pension scheme was itself a creature of statute, hence the nomination was in accordance with the provisions of any enactment. Nonetheless, there are many statutory pension schemes in existence, many of them with very valuable benefits, and you should check on the nomination position if DP was enrolled in such a scheme. If she was, then any nomination is likely to fall within section 8(1).

6.3 Section 3(1)(a): AC's Financial Resources and Needs

6.3.1 Your information on AC's financial resources and needs will come from the fact-finding Form E exercise. Looking through your completed form, you should now have a clear picture of whether AC's income is providing her with enough for **her** reasonable standard of living. You are able to calculate what the shortfall is, and you also know what high-price items would assist her to keep up that standard of living, and what lump sum she would need in order to purchase them.

6.3.2 AC's Resources

As well as the figures in your completed Form E, you must also direct your attention to your client's earning *capacity* as set out at section 3(6) of the Act. Although the requirement to consider earning capacity is not confined to child claims under the Inheritance Act, it is in adult child claims that the question of earning capacity is most closely contested, and the question of how far AC has earning capacity is to a large extent a value judgment, which means that you should pay particular attention to it.

6.3.3 There are some clear cases: if AC has been judged by the DWP to be unfit for any work at all, then it is probably unwise to contest that finding, because the assessment process is acknowledged to be rigorous. At the other extreme, there are claimants who have a very successful business and career history who are choosing not to work but who plainly could earn considerable sums if they chose otherwise. The problematic cases are those in the middle, where AC may be claiming that she has a limited earning capacity which she cannot increase, and the beneficiaries are claiming that she could, and should, do more to help herself, and it is these that are most susceptible to judicial value judgments. The most common limiting factor on earning capacity is physical or mental health, as to which see 6.6.

6.3.4 State Benefits

Not Reasonable Provision by Themselves

Benefits have a double relevance in Inheritance Act cases. In the first place, there is strong and consistent authority that even if AC is having her main needs met by benefits, that may not be reasonable provision for her. The point was first made in *E v E* [1966] 2 All ER 44, in which it was said that reasonable provision is not limited to keeping a dependant above the breadline. In that case the applicant was surviving on benefits. Stamp LJ stated that "*the fact that the very badly off can obtain national assistance, and will not be left to starve, would not in my judgment afford* ***any good reason of itself*** *to justify a deceased from making no provision for a claimant out of a large estate.*" [emphasis added]. A decision by DP not to leave AC anything simply on the basis that the state will look after her does not, without further investigation, appear to be reasonable provision.

6.3.5 However, claims by ACs and others depending on benefits are often still opposed on the basis that benefits are meeting all of their financial needs; this is wrong in principle. At paragraph 69 of *Ilott* CAQ in 2015, Ryder LJ noted that as a matter of public policy, the court is not constrained to treat a person's reasonable financial provision as being limited by their existing state benefits, and that remains the law. In fact a detailed examination of the Ilotts' financial circumstances established that although they were living within their means, there were present needs that they could not actually afford.

6.3.6 Lump sum awards and means-tested benefits

In the second place, the Court has to be careful if making a lump sum award to a claimant on means-tested benefits. To take an example, housing benefit (an extremely valuable resource to a low income client) is not payable if the applicant for it has more than £16,000 of capital. If, therefore, any award made under an Inheritance Act claim would take your client over the capital limit, she may lose her entitlement to housing benefit until her capital is again reduced below the limit: in other words, she would have to use the capital to pay her rent. In *Ilott CAQ,* Arden LJ equated this situation with "little or no financial provision for maintenance at all", though the Supreme Court did not agree.

6.3.7 The Supreme Court also expressly disapproved of the Court of Appeal's decision that a claimant in receipt of state benefits should be treated in the same way as a claimant who is elderly or disabled in that she has increased needs for living expenses, and that the existing benefits must be preserved by any order made. Since *Ilott SC*, there is certainly no principle that any order made by the Court must preserve existing benefits. It will generally be sensible, however, for both parties to try to preserve AC's existing benefits as far as that is possible. This change in approach means that Courts will probably be asked to use their existing powers under s.2 more inventively: see Chapter 8.

6.3.8 On the other hand, Hughes LJ said in *Ilott SC* @ 39 that an order for an award which had little or no value to AC because of the impact on benefits might in itself be a legitimate error of principle justifying an appellate order to set the award aside, and that there certainly would be an error of principle if the original award had been made in ignorance of the true position.

6.3.9 In summary, an award can result in the loss of some benefits, but if it is of little or no value to AC because of that loss, then it is wrong in principle.

6.3.10 Deprivation of capital

In the past, there has been a widespread assumption that a lump sum payment would reduce benefit entitlements overall, however it was used. If, say, your client had £16,000 in savings and she received £4,000 as a lump sum, that sum would take her outside the capital allowance for housing benefit. If she spent that £4,000 on anything other than her rent, it was assumed that she would fall foul of the rules on intentional deprivation of capital. That automatic assumption was possibly misplaced, but you still need to take great care in this area.

6.3.11 Since *Ilott SC*, the focus has now been tightened to the specific deprivation of capital rules in respect of the relevant benefit: if housing and/or council tax benefit, the Housing Benefit Regulations 2006 SI 213/2006 at 49 & 50, and for DWP means-tested benefits, the DWP's Decision Makers Guide (DMG) on Capital (Vol 5, Chapter 29, particularly paragraphs 29805 onwards).

6.3.12 The difficulty for everyone, up to and including the Court, is that decision makers in this area have a very wide discretion and there can be no clear indication at the time of trial as to when expenditure will be seen as justifiable, and when seen as intentional deprivation of capital. For the DWP Rules, the decision maker needs to be satisfied that the deprivation was made with the object of obtaining benefit as a "significant" purpose. Payments which the claimant has no choice but to make are excluded, but these are restricted to the necessities of life such as food and fuel, immediately repayable debts and legal debts capable of enforcement, or repayment of a DWP overpayment.

6.3.13 At the other extreme, spending capital "extravagantly or imprudently even if [the claimant says] they have used it to pay for the necessities of life" and payments of more than the amount due on a debt, including more than minimum payments on a credit card or repaying a mortgage, will be payments made by choice [DWP DMG 5/29 @ 29834]. Most lump sum claims by ACs on benefits will be for purposes somewhere in the middle of these two extremes, and even a cursory look at reports of deprivation of capital decisions will demonstrate that there is no guarantee that a lump sum earmarked by the Court for, say, the purchase of new kitchen white goods will not result in the loss of benefits. There are reports that spending on funeral plans has been seen by the DWP as deprivation of capital; there are reports that spending on a modest holiday has not. Proceed with extreme caution and if necessary take specialist advice from an agency dealing with deprivation of capital issues on a regular basis before committing your client to anything. If you are in the course of litigation, it is safer to assume that the DWP will apply the rules with rigour.

6.3.14 It may be of assistance if you are dealing with these issues on your client's behalf that the DWP Budgeting Loan and Budgeting Advance schemes (the replacements for the old "Social Fund" on Universal Credit) will advance money for, among other matters, the purchase of furniture or household items (for example, washing machines or other 'white goods'); clothes or footwear; rent in advance; costs linked to moving house; maintenance, improvements or security for your home; travelling costs within the UK; costs linked to getting a new job; maternity costs; funeral costs; repaying hire purchase loans, and repaying loans taken for the above items [see the DWP pages at GOV.UK for more details]. The list appears to indicate items which the DWP sees as essential or reasonably so, although there are strict caps on the amounts of the loans, so any proposed expenditure above the level of the cap may face challenges of extravagance even if there is acceptance that the purchase is justified.

6.3.15 AC's Needs
Housing

If your client owns her home (either alone or with another person), then she may have no real housing need, though her housing position may not be as stable as it first appears: for example, if she is going through a divorce/separation, is she likely to have enough capital afterwards to re-house herself to the appropriate standard?

6.3.16 Take instructions on how the mortgage is being paid and whether or not the payments are affordable for AC at the moment or in the future. DP may have bailed her out over the years: although the applicant did not succeed in *Baynes v Hedger* for other reasons, it was relevant that the deceased had helped her with her mortgage payments over the years. In fact, at one earlier stage the deceased had purchased a home for her. Although mortgage interest rates are currently at historic lows, the position may alter significantly within the next few years. Remember that the Court needs information about your client's finances "now ***and in the foreseeable future***", and if interest rates are beginning to rise and are forecast to rise further, this is something you should take into account.

6.3.17 Rented Property

There is limited security of tenure in the UK rental market; this, coupled with consistent rent rises which make properties increasingly unaffordable, means that a question mark hangs over the housing security of an AC client in privately rented property. Since *Ilott SC*, however, it is clear that the previously favoured solution of making an application for a lump sum to purchase a property in AC's name will probably find less support in future. That outcome is likely in many if not most cases to be seen as over-provision, because it results in a capital gain. The solution put forward in *Ilott* itself is for a property to be settled on AC for life, though this may not always be a practical possibility. It is probably symptomatic of a changed economic background that the Court did not at any point consider in *Nahajev v Fowle* [2017]

EW Misc 11 whether or not the AC claimant, who was living in rented property, should be provided with a life or beneficial interest in another property to give her greater security of tenure. This may have been partly practical, given that the main beneficiary of the estate had already spent all but £44,000 of his inheritance, but it would appear that the trial Judge took the view that *Ilott* SC prevented him from making a lump sum which was not capitalised maintenance. We will look at this again when we consider lump sum orders at 8.2.4.

6.3.18 House provided by DP

AC may in fact already be living in a property that has been provided or subsidised by DP and which now falls into the general estate without any specific provision having been made in the Will: for a recent example, see *Wodzicki v Wodzicki* [2017] EWCA Civ 95 . Did AC pay any rent to DP for the property? If so, she may have a legal or equitable tenancy, although it is unlikely to give her much security of tenure. Were any promises made to her by DP about her ability to live in the property long-term? If she has been provided with a roof over her head by DP but there is a prospect that the roof may now be removed, there is obviously a strong case that the Will may have failed to make reasonable provision for her. You should also consider whether there are DP obligations under s. 3(1)(d) or other factors under 3(1)(g).

6.3.19 BoMaD (Bank of Mum and Dad)

By May 2017, loans or gifts from parents to purchase a property, the so-called "Bank of Mum and Dad", amounted to a loan book of £6.5 billion nationally, about the equivalent of the Yorkshire Building Society's loan book, according to the *Financial Times.* This makes BoMaD the country's ninth biggest lender. Arrangements for repayment differ: for example, one or both parents may become co-owners of the property with AC, or DP might have taken out a charge on the property, or the money may be regarded as a "soft loan" to be repaid at a specific or not so specific date. Because this arrangement is now so widespread, a sudden and unexpected death of DP may leave your young adult client in a difficult position.

6.3.20 Things will work out well for AC if the property was held under a joint tenancy with DP, because the entire equity will pass to her, but less well if she and DP were tenants in common and DP's share has passed under the Will to another person. There is also a possibility that DP's principal beneficiary under the Will may claim either that the soft loan now needs to be repaid because circumstances have changed, or that DP's estate is a beneficial co-owner of the property under a resulting trust and that an order for sale is appropriate. The main action in all these cases is likely to be a trusts of land action, but AC might need to consider an Inheritance Act claim as well on the basis that the estate has not made reasonable provision for her. I deal at 9.4 below with trust of land claims.

6.3.21 Other basic needs: Income Need

There is a strong temptation, particularly if you are a family lawyer, to look at the income shortfall, capitalise it over a set period, and then fix on a suitable lump sum. My view is that post-*Ilott SC*, and particularly in the current investment climate, you should keep a much more open mind. What you should do however is quantify benefits in kind, whether received from DP or others, as much as you can.

6.3.22 AC clients often have sufficient income to get by and meet their basic food, shelter and housing needs, but nothing at all to spare for other recurring expenses on top of the basics. Heating and hot water is one important category, and we have already [5.4.18] looked at fuel poverty. Even modest treats like a family trip to the cinema may be a financial struggle, and it may be impossible for your client to pay for the regular upkeep or repair of her home. Again, we enter into the arena of value judgments. Most judges would accept that heating is an essential item of expenditure and that it should not be rationed; but some judges might consider that a family unable to afford to go to the cinema should not be given the means to do so from DP's estate.

6.3.23 Other basic needs: Capital Needs

Has your client got a financial safety cushion if things go wrong? The inability to keep a financial safety cushion in the form of a small savings account is in itself an indication of an income need, and it eventually results in capital needs. This was important in Mrs Ilott's case, where the family could not afford to replace basic furniture such as beds or carpets, or kitchen white goods. While this is a value judgment, these items are regarded as necessities even in the most modest of households: in fact, Hughes LJ at least implied that he considered a holiday a necessity even for cash-strapped families like the Ilotts, although another Judge on another day might consider that a family in this financial position would have to do without holidays.

6.3.24 A family car can be an important asset, particularly if it allows the main family breadwinner to get to and from work, and where there are infant children who need to be taken to school and back, for example. It can often be cheaper to purchase a reasonable replacement than to attempt to keep the current vehicle on the road, but AC may not have the capital required for that replacement. You can examine that with her in detail, looking at the options.

6.3.25 There is one obvious capital requirement to take into account, and that is the costs of taking the claim to trial. This is a good point in an initial consultation at which to pause and consider how fighting the claim will impact the estate financially, as well as the amount that AC could expect to receive. You need to give your client the crucial advice that she cannot ordinarily expect to receive her costs out of the estate at the end of the proceedings. The cost of bringing the action should be put into the scales at the earliest possible moment because it will focus the attention of the other side on attempting to achieve an early settlement.

6.3.26 We have already seen from the discussion of *Palmer v Lawrence* [2011] EWHC 3961 (Ch) at 3.5.4 that AC can put her costs of litigation into her statement of resources and needs, but the Court is unlikely to see them as a particularly weighty factor at stage 1.

6.3.27 "Safety" Needs: Health and Education

After the primary physiological needs are taken care of, the second tier of needs relates to "safety" factors: health, education, employment, property, family and social stability. Two of these in particular, education and health, have a particularly direct connection to financial provision.

6.3.28 Health

Ill health, whether mental or physical, can bring its own needs for capital expense, including adaptation of AC's current home (or in extreme cases the need to move home completely), therapeutic aids or treatments. In these days of increasingly long NHS waiting lists, if a medical condition is preventing AC from making her living as she usually would – a need for a hip replacement, for example – it may be a good use of a lump sum to obtain private medical treatment. Older ACs may need some private nursing care. Look into the foreseeable future as well as the present. Is AC's condition going to deteriorate? This is something that you will certainly want her general practitioner to give you information about, and it is possible you may need expert medical evidence in due course: see paragraph 6.6.5 below.

6.3.29 Education

Section 3(3) specifically directs the Court to look at "the manner in which the applicant was being or in which he might be expected to be educated or trained". By the nature of things, this is going to affect the claims of young adults of university or further education age much more often than it will affect applicants in their 30s or 40s, when the focus tends to be more on employability and on educational opportunities which have already been lost.

6.3.30 The obvious application of the section is to young adult children who are either already in further or higher education, or about to embark upon it, but have not been left enough under either the Will or intestacy to fund their university or college places. Accurate assessment of needs can be very difficult in such cases, and there is not a great deal of case law to give guidance, although the recent case of *Taylor v Bell* [2015] EW Misc B3 (CC)] has given us the best idea so far not just of a basic approach, but of when variation of an order can be appropriate, and the principles on which the Court should decide how much that variation should be. It is likely that courts dealing with education and training elements in young adult claims are using maintenance claims for guidance, and applying the principles in family cases to Inheritance Act cases.

6.3.31 In *Nahajec v Fowle* [2017] EW Misc 11 (CC), the 31-year old adult child claimant intended to change her career and qualify as a veterinary nurse. Saffman J considered that section 3(3) was not relevant to her claim because that section referred to the manner in which the claimant was being educated or trained or the manner in which **he might expect** to be educated or trained and noted that these words indicated that it was not a question of whether it would have been reasonable for a deceased person to contribute towards a claimant's education or training, but a question of whether the claimant expected it from the deceased person. In *Nahajec* AC had no such expectation: her father had been estranged from her for most of her life. However the judge noted that this did not make her educational plans and ambitions irrelevant; the Court (and in this case did) consider them as a relevant factor under section 3(1)(g).

6.4 Sections 3(1)(c) and (d) Any Obligations Which D Had Either Towards AC, or to Any Other Beneficiaries, or to Any Other Claimants

6.4.1 Obligations to AC

"Obligations" are not expressly defined in the statute, but as we have seen, and will see, they have had an almost magnetic attraction in the adult child Inheritance Act case law. It became clear from an early stage after the 1975 Act was passed that "obligations" would mean more than merely legal obligations; indeed, if one was being simplistic about it, one could say that if only legal obligations came within s. 3(1)(d), there would be no need for a separate statute at all because AC would have other routes to recovery. In the cases of the late 1970s to the mid-1980s, the phrase "moral obligation" was frequently used, as much in scepticism as with approval, to be replaced with the phrase "special circumstances".

> *"Oliver J. is said to have treated the existence of a moral obligation as a condition precedent to the exercise of this jurisdiction - a moral obligation resting upon the deceased to make some provision for the plaintiff. On a correct reading of the judge's judgment, I do not think that he did so. His approach was that where an applicant*

is an adult male in employment, and so capable of earning his own living, some special circumstance is required to make a failure on the part of the deceased to make some financial provision for the applicant unreasonable."

–Goff J in *Re Coventry* @ 494–5.

6.4.2 This is a crucial passage in understanding how the Court evaluates the claim by an adult child, and it is worth breaking it down to look at it more closely. First of all, there is no need for the adult child to show to the Court that the deceased had a moral obligation to leave her a reasonable provision under her Will; note that it was argued (and, in fact, would be argued again in later cases) that this was a "condition precedent", without which the claim would not get through what I have called the "portal". That argument failed, so your client does not need to show "moral obligation" to make a claim.

6.4.3 There is a "baseline" level by which a parent's obligation, to use the wording adopted in *Baynes v Hedger* @ 187, is limited to giving a child " a sound financial start in life". Under English law, a parent has no continuing duty to do any more than that for an adult child who does not suffer a physical or mental disability. There is no rule that there has to be some sort of "moral obligation" owed by DP to AC in order for the Court to make an order in AC's favour. But where the claimant is an adult in employment and/or is capable of earning her own keep, then there probably is going to have to be something more if a failure to make provision is to be considered unreasonable [Coventry @495A per Buckley LJ].

6.4.4 In *Re Coventry* AC claimed that DP had a moral obligation to leave him something because he (AC) had given up promotion in the Royal Navy and stayed at home to look after DP for a period of over twenty years. There was no evidence however that DP had asked him to do so -- in fact there was strong evidence that DP had on the contrary wanted AC and his family to move out of DP's property -- and it was clear that far from making a sacrifice, AC had in fact obtained a valuable benefit, namely twenty years' rent-free occupation of the family home.

6.4.5 In *Espinosa v Bourke* [1999] 1 F.L.R. 747 , Butler Sloss LJ confirmed that section 1(1)(d) extended beyond legal obligations and explained the use of the word "moral" as there to underline that DP's obligations and responsibilities were not to be narrowly construed but to take into account a "broad sense of obligation and responsibility"; it did not extend to the dictionary definition of "moral" as either right or wrong. She thought that any considerations of that kind were better dealt with at section 3(1)(g).

6.4.6 However, where an adult child (the reference to an adult male is now totally out of date; see *Re Jennings* [1994] Ch 286) is either in employment or is able to earn her own living, in order to show that the estate has not made reasonable provision for her, she has to show some "special circumstance". That "special circumstance" might be a moral obligation, but can be more (or, sometimes, less) than that. But it is vital to understand that the "special circumstance" or "moral obligation" cannot simply be that the deceased parent died in comfortable circumstances, that the adult child was not well-off, and that there was therefore a moral obligation on the part of the parent to leave the child well provided for. An application based on that ground alone will not succeed. In other words, your client has to have clarified what the "special circumstance" is in her case. We will look at some of these special circumstances when we consider the categories of adult child applicants in the next sections, and also when we look at the considerations under section 3(1)(g), which I have called the "sweeper" subsection.

6.4.7 If we reverse this, the logical corollary would be that an adult child who is not capable of working, for whatever reason, does not need to show "special circumstances". That view is supported by a case like *Re Jennings* [1994] Ch. 286, but it is definitely not the case that an AC who is unable to work because of health problems will automatically receive an award under the Inheritance Act. One example is *Wright v Waters* [2014] EWHC 3614 (Ch) , where AC was wheelchair bound and suffered from heart disease, angina, diabetes, osteoarthritis, depression, vertigo and cervical spondylisis. She survived mostly on benefits. She was awarded nothing from the estate because the trial judge (Behrens J) considered that her past conduct towards DP discharged any moral obligation that DP might have had towards her. This is also, incidentally, another good example of a value judgment made by the trial Judge of the kind which will become increasingly difficult to displace on appeal.

6.4.8 By now, it will be very clear that there is no basic equation to the effect that (rich deceased parent + poor adult child = Inheritance Act claim). However, there are many instances in which the Court will consider that the facts show that DP did have financial obligations and responsibilities to AC. Just as importantly, section 3(1)(d) of the Act directs to the Court to take into account the financial obligations and responsibilities that DP may have had to other beneficiaries or claimants.

6.4.9 AC disabled, suffering from chronic illness, or otherwise vulnerable

This can encompass situations where DP did not know that AC was ill, perhaps because the parties were estranged or AC was reluctant to burden DP with the full facts of her condition; where DP knew that AC was ill or vulnerable but chose to do nothing (for a striking example, see *Hanbury v Hanbury* [1999] 2 F.L.R. 255, where DP deliberately avoided hearing anything about his disabled daughter's current state of health); or where DP has been helping AC out financially and in other ways before her death. None of these are conclusive, although if DP has been helping out, AC's case starts on a firmer footing.

6.4.10 Recognition that "something should be done" for AC

One important indication of a special circumstance or moral obligation is the admission (sometimes the reluctant admission) of DP during her lifetime that she should "do something" for AC. Even in *Re Debenham* [1986] 1 F.L.R. 404; [1986] Fam. Law 101, which is a classic example of the obdurate and unrelenting parent:

> *"One can see that such a mother might say 'It is about time I did something for my daughter', but she did not appear to take that view, except that she had said to the applicant, and to Mr Graves, that she was going to look after her daughter in her will."*

6.4.11 More recently in the case of *Challinor v Challinor* [2009] EWHC 180 (Ch), AC's father had recognised that he had a moral obligation to provide for AC, who had Down's syndrome and lived in residential care, and that that moral obligation would pass to his estate and its only beneficiary, his widow (who was AC's stepmother).

6.4.12 Promises made to AC: Family Money

One important sub-category of special circumstance or moral obligation is the fairly common situation where DP's estate included some property which had been informally promised to AC during DP's life. These informal promises can come to take on a stellar importance when the Court considers the section 3 factors. In *Espinosa v Bourke* [1999] 1 F.L.R. 747 , the Court of Appeal identified two moral obligations on DP which had arisen during his lifetime. The first was an obligation to recognise the care which had been given to him in his declining years by AC. The second was a promise that he had made to AC's mother that a specific shareholding which had passed to him on the mother's death would in turn be left to AC. In the circumstances of the case, the overall view of the Court was that the care moral obligation had probably been discharged, but the promise obligation had not.

6.4.13 DP expressly rejects any obligations to AC

These are clearly difficult cases, and are at the point where the Court must judge how far testamentary freedom should be permitted to go; and that, of course, is once again a value judgment. A parent who expressly says, to AC or to anyone else, that she has no obligations towards AC may do so for a wide range of reasons. It may be that DP believes that she has given enough financial assistance and that it is now time that AC stood on her own two feet. That decision may be reasonable, or it may fly in the face of what DP knows about AC's state of health, for example.

6.4.14 In *Baynes v Hedger* [2009] EWCA Civ 374, the deceased had given her goddaughter considerable financial support in the past but had made it clear that she was unwilling to support the applicant indefinitely, or indeed into the immediate future. Although the deceased had at times communicated this unwillingness to third parties, notes that she had made effectively to herself on letters from her solicitor were also admissible as evidence of her views at the time. One of these notes was in fact found by the Court to be an express disclaimer that she was assuming responsibility for the applicant's maintenance, and express disclaimers are always going to be treated by the Court as matters of significance.

6.4.15 Or it may be that DP does not approve of AC's conduct or lifestyle, and it may also be that the Court believes DP's disapproval is justified: see *Williams v Johns* [1988] 2 FLR 475, where AC's mother recorded in a letter accompanying her will that she had no obligation to AC, whose behaviour had caused her significant distress. Looked at objectively, the reported details of conduct do not seem beyond the pale even allowing for the fact that the case is 30 years old, but the Judge was very influenced by the fact that a number of witnesses gave evidence about DP's distress and the suffering that AC had caused her.

6.4.16 The most difficult cases of all are probably those where DP does not approve of AC's conduct or lifestyle, or simply of AC full stop, and it is clear that DP is being unreasonable in her views. *Ilott* is of course one such case; another is *Re Myers* [2004] EWHC 1944 (Fam), which was in fact mentioned in *Ilott SC* and in which DP's attitude to AC certainly appears, from the facts as they are given, to have been both prejudiced and unfair.

6.4.17 This is the point at which Hughes LJ in *Ilott* notes that the question of whether DP was reasonable is encompassed within the overall question of whether the disposition of the estate made reasonable provision for AC. The Court must decide whether, regardless of what DP has said, her estate has in fact financial or other obligations towards AC; and if it decides that it does, then it must override her express wishes. For recent interesting discussions on this topic, see *Nahajec v Fowle* [2017] EW Misc 11, where DP had left a letter of wishes saying things about the AC that the trial judge found to be inaccurate, and *Ball & Ors v Ball & Ors* [2017] EWHC [Ch], where DP cut off three of her children because they had given evidence to the police which had brought about their father's conviction for sexual assault.

6.4.18 *No Retrospective Reparations*

There is one particular obligations issue which can bedevil claims by adult children. Generally speaking, an Inheritance Act 1975 claim cannot be used to make up for a failure by DP in the past to fulfil her parental responsibilities and obligations: it is what May LJ in *Re Jennings* [1994] Ch. 286 described as the "no retrospective reparations" rule. It is very common to find AC claims formulated on the basis either that DP failed to support AC during her childhood, or (a growing trend) that DP in some way abused or neglected AC, and that as a result DP's estate now has a "moral obligation" to make reasonable provision for AC. Obviously an allegation of this stripe is also going to figure as an item of conduct under section 3(1)(g): see 6.7. It is a matter about which potential AC claimants can feel very strongly. Unfortunately, in most cases, it is not a factor which will be taken into account at section 3(1)(d) or at 3(1)(g).

6.4.19 The general rule is set out in *Re Jennings.* In that case the claimant relied on DP's obviously lamentable failure to maintain him in his infancy as a ground for claiming that he had had obligations and responsibilities towards him which had not been discharged. Nourse LJ expressly disapproved this argument as a general principle and affirmed that there is no claim if the only ground is a financial failure to maintain AC during childhood.

6.4.20 DP has caused AC lasting harm

The first was in fact identified by May LJ in *Re Jennings* itself:

> *"For instance, if a father's failure to fulfil an obligation to his child whilst the former is alive* ***results in a continuing disability, perhaps physical, perhaps psychiatric, which persists to the date of the deceased's death,*** *then as a matter of construction such an obligation and the failure to comply with it would be matters to which the court should have regard on an application for an order under section 2."* [emphasis added]

6.4.21 For "father" we can read "parent", but the case is authority for the proposition that if a parent has caused physical or psychiatric injury to her child which has persisted until death, then that is a matter which the Court should take into account. "Obligations" extend, as we have seen, to moral obligations as well as financial ones.

> Wotan was convicted in 1998 of inflicting grievous bodily harm on his baby daughter, Lyanna, by shaking her and causing brain damage. Lyanna has needed specialist care ever since, including adaptations of her home and special education. She has been totally estranged from her father since he was convicted. Wotan won £2.5million on the National Lottery in 2016. He has now died. His Will leaves all of his estate to his second wife. Lyanna appears to have a viable claim against Wotan's estate, despite the total estrangement, on the basis that Wotan's failure to fulfil his obligations to protect her has resulted in continuing physical and psychiatric disability.

6.4.22 Allegations of sexual abuse and violence made against a parent after many years, and particularly when that parent is now dead, are no less problematic in Inheritance Act cases than they are elsewhere: for a recent review of the issues, see *F & S v TH* [2016] EWHC 1605 (QB), where the allegations were made against a deceased Roman Catholic priest and appear to have related primarily to events in the 1970s and early 1980s. The general civil standard of proof applies, but the Court must guard against prejudice to a possibly innocent party in dealing with allegations that have at the very least lain dormant for decades. In many cases, the personal representatives and beneficiaries will have no knowledge at all of DP's life at the time of the alleged events, putting the estate at a particular disadvantage.

6.4.23 In *B v Nugent Care Society* [2010] 1 WLR 516 Clarke MR accepted that *"considering prejudice to the defendant [in historic abuse cases] involved considering what evidence might have been available to the defendant if a trial had taken place earlier, or it had learnt of the claim earlier: it was not sufficient simply to hear the evidence of the claimant, and indeed any other evidence now available, and decide the issue of limitation on that basis without considering what evidence would or might have been available at an earlier stage"*.

6.4.24 Although it predates *B v Nugent Care Society* by some years, *M v S* [HC ChD, unreported, 16 July 2001] appears to support this approach. M claimed under the Inheritance Act on the basis that physical and sexual abuse by his mother had left him with lasting psychological and physical injury. He adduced expert medical evidence together with the evidence of some witnesses to whom he had related the alleged abuse. The trial Judge [Etherton J, as he then was] found that there was no cogent evidence of any abuse and that DP had in all the circumstances made reasonable provision for him. He also found that there was no evidence that AC's bulimia had been caused by the alleged abuse. *M v S* demonstrates the extreme difficulty that historical allegations can cause in Inheritance Act matters, and is at the very least an extremely helpful guide in other cases. Note that the Court set out that cases involving allegations of historic abuse are better brought in the Family Division and not the Chancery Division.

6.4.25 AC's Financial Responsibilities and Obligations to Other beneficiaries or Claimants

These responsibilities and obligations are often overlooked by AC claimants when they first come to give instructions. In fact, they are of vital importance. If AC's parent died after marrying again and leaving infant children, and there is barely enough in the estate to support the infant children, then any Inheritance Act claim by AC is very unlikely to succeed, no matter how unfair AC believes the distribution to be. The same is obviously true if DP was supporting a disabled spouse or civil partner or had been maintaining a cohabitee within the meaning of section 1(1)(e) of the Act.

6.5 Sections 3(1)(b) and (c): Resources and Needs of Other Beneficiaries and Claimants

6.5.1 The subsections in full (I have combined them here for ease of reference) provide that the Court must have regard to:

> *"The financial resources and financial needs which any [other applicant for an order under section 2 of this Act: s. 3(1)(b)] / [beneficiary of the estate of the deceased: s. 3(1)(c)] has or is likely to have in the foreseeable future."*

6.5.2 There is, however, no obligation on beneficiaries of the estate to disclose either their resources or their needs. They can simply defend the case on the basis that the disposition of the estate did make reasonable provision for AC, or can expand the position by making an open offer in excess of the provision from the estate and then contesting the case without reference to their own assets. Other Inheritance Act claimants, on the other hand, will be obliged to disclose their resources and needs as part of their claim.

6.5.3 On the client care level, the consideration of the resources and needs of beneficiaries and other claimants is often a flashpoint for an adult child claimant, leading her back into legally irrelevant considerations of what is fair or unfair. You will need to give tactful, sensitive but appropriate advice.

6.5.4 Some classes of beneficiary or other claimant, such as infant children or young adults, will have significant needs and negligible resources. Others, such as disabled or elderly adults, may have more resources, but will have very significant needs. If DP has left property to any beneficiary within these classes, and the beneficiary would not have independent resources to meet her needs, it is unlikely that an adult child able to earn her own living can argue that the provision made for her was unreasonable unless there is more than enough to meet the more vulnerable beneficiary's needs. Certainly, the Court is going to give significant weight to the needs and resources of such a beneficiary or claimant. If DP was maintaining the beneficiary or claimant prior to her death, that will also be a factor under section 3(1)(d) as a relevant obligation. Interestingly, both of the post-*Ilott* SC adult child cases decided so far (*Nahajec v Fowle* [2017] EW Misc 11 and *Ball & Ors v Ball & Ors* [2017] EWHC 1750 [Ch]) have judgments in which particular attention is devoted to the circumstances of the other beneficiaries and DP's obligations towards them. This may reflect a renewed concentration on the fact that the balancing exercise must take in all relevant factors.

Classes of Beneficiaries/Other Claimants

6.5.5 Infants and young adults

If DP left behind dependant children below the age of majority, the Court will consider that as a magnetically important factor unless the total estate is more than enough to meet their reasonable needs, up to and including education, at the standard of living that they had when DP was alive. Young adults, particularly those just starting out in the world of work or still in full-time education at college or university, will also be the focus of the Court's particular attention, even if your AC client has health problems or other issues. The issue of whether it is "fair" that DP's estate should pass to the other parent of her infant children is going to be a minor issue at best, regardless of where DP's estate has been sourced.

> Simone has died leaving a net estate worth £750,000, including a property worth £525,000, to her adult daughter, Tracey, stating that she has done so because most of her estate came from Tracey's father, who predeceased them both. Tracey is an artist earning a subsistence income, but in reasonable health. However at the time of Simone's death she had two infant children, Arthur and Angus, by a second relationship with her new partner Ewan. Ewan was formerly a high earner in the City but has now been diagnosed with a chronic illness and now her only income is means-tested benefits. While the Court will certainly take into account the fact that Simone's estate came primarily from Tracey's father, its priority will be to ensure that the infant children's needs are satisfactorily met.

6.5.6 Disabled and elderly adults

A disabled or elderly beneficiary will generally have specific care or medical needs, and further specific needs for practical items to help with day to day living. They may have been living with DP, in which case DP has also been maintaining them, so that section 3(1) (d) will also be relevant. A case like *Ames v Jones* BAILII [2016] EW Misc B67 (CC) is a good illustration of how this exercise works in practice. There, the impending old age of the beneficiary widow and her needs during that period of her life clearly outweighed the claim of DP's adult daughter.

6.5.7 Charities and other institutional beneficiaries

Where the beneficiaries are charities or, exceptionally, the Crown, it is easy to slip into an assumption that they have huge resources and no needs and that therefore AC's claim is proportionately stronger. In *Ilott CAQ*, the Court of Appeal had stated that Mrs Ilott's lack of expectation from the estate was a matter of little weight because the charitable beneficiaries had had no expectations from the estate either and had chosen not to plead any needs. Hughes LJ said that these observations should be treated with caution, because the charities were the chosen beneficiaries of DP and her "very clear wishes" were to benefit them. He added:

> *"The observation ... that because the charities had no needs to plead, they were not prejudiced by an increased award to Mrs Ilott is, with great respect, erroneous; their benefit was reduced by any such award. That may be the right outcome in a particular case, but it cannot be ignored that an award under the Act is at the expense of those whom the testator intended to benefit." [46]*

6.5.8 Charities and religious bodies

In *Ilott* itself, and in many other reported cases, the charities have chosen not to defend the claim on the basis of their own assets and needs, but on the basis that the other s.3 factors meant that the disposition of the estate had made reasonable provision for AC. They are perfectly entitled to do so, as we have seen.

6.5.9 Nonetheless, this very much depends on the charity. It may be difficult for very large charities such as the RSPCA or Blue Cross to make out any sensible case on needs, but the situation may be quite different if the charity is small and short of money; and, I would suggest, if the connection between DP and the charity is demonstrably close. If the charity was a local one in which DP was a volunteer, and the gift in DP's Will was the difference between the charity surviving or being wound up, then the charity would have both an assets and a needs position that could be brought into the balancing exercise.

6.5.10 Furthermore, as Hughes LJ noted in *Ilott SC*, there is a public interest in testamentary gifts to charities. All charities -- even the very large ones -- have financial needs in the sense that if they were not given donations such as the one under examination they would not be able to function at all. The real question is whether those needs should take precedence over the needs of AC for reasonable provision.

6.5.11 The Charity Commission has published a guide for charity trustees where the charity is defending litigation. A charity defending its right to property left to it by Will is specifically mentioned. It can be found at https://www.gov.uk/government/publications/charities-and-litigation-a-guide-for-trustees-cc38/charities-and-litigation-a-guide-for-trustees. The Guidance reflects the general legal position, but note the requirement that trustees must have explored other ways of resolving the dispute before entering into ligitation.

6.5.12 The Crown

Where a person has died intestate but there are no heirs within the intestacy rules, her estate will pass to the Crown on the principle of *bona vacantia*. Clearly this will not apply where there are any living relatives of DP within the rules, including adult children, but on the rare occasions that AC is applying as a person treated by the deceased as a child of the family and DP died intestate, the Crown may be a defendant: see for example *Cameron v Treasury Solicitor* [1996] 2 F.L.R. 716, which was a claim brought by a widow. The Crown can, and does, defend Inheritance Act claims on the basis that the disposition of the estate made reasonable provision for AC, and in that respect will be treated in the same way as any other beneficiary. In *Cameron,* for example, the Crown succeeded in its defence.

6.6 Section 3(1)(f): Health and Disability

6.6.1 The category includes mental health problems and disabilities as well as physical ones. As far as your client is concerned, you will have asked about any health problems that became apparent when you were going through the Form E exercise, including any disabilities for which benefits are paid. There may well be follow-up questions that you need to ask, and if the condition is serious, you will need to put forward some evidence about it even at an early stage.

6.6.2 It is essential to obtain some basic evidence about AC's state of health by way of a letter from her general practitioner which can be disclosed to the other side and exhibited to her witness statement. GPs will generally do no more than set out a quick review of AC's medical notes in the letter, but at least you have confirmation from a medical professional that AC's evidence about her health is correct. You will need to know more, however, including whether the condition is progressive, and if it is, the pace of progress; and if appropriate you will need to know about life expectancy.

6.6.3 If your client is receiving benefits which relate to a medical condition, such as ESA or the Personal Independence Payment (PIP), obtain confirmation from the relevant government agency.

6.6.4 Questions about AC's health are often a hot-button issue in Inheritance Act claims, particularly where AC is of working age. The beneficiaries often claim either that AC is not as ill as she claims, or that she is capable of earning her living at least in part, or that her illness is to a greater or lesser extent self-inflicted, for example via alcoholism or drug addiction. The first two of these issues require detailed medical evidence and often some further evidence from mental health or occupational therapy professionals.

6.6.5 This is one of the areas where proportionality can quickly become a major issue. The value of the average net estate in the UK is around £150,000 and we have already seen the substantial inroads that can be made into that estate by legal costs alone. Judges hearing first appointments in cases involving modest estates will often be extremely reluctant to order expert medical evidence as part of the directions, particularly when it seems plain that the beneficiaries will have to accept that AC has a life-affecting health condition; or, conversely, that AC will have to accept that one of the beneficiaries has one. Prepare to meet stiff judicial resistance if you want an order for a £2,000 medical report in a case involving an estate with a net value of £100,000 or less. If you believe that the other side are obliging you to source that evidence because they are refusing to accept the obvious, then say so, and ask the Court to case manage.

6.6.6 There have been, and there will continue to be, costs penalties in taking points on the medical evidence which oblige the other side to commission medical experts and which will obviously have to be abandoned at trial. If your client's elderly stepmother has Parkinson's with serious mobility problems and needs to remain living in her specially adapted bungalow, and she has produced GP evidence to that effect, it is likely to be unwise to contend inflexibly that she has no mobility problems at all and oblige her to confirm her case via a Parkinson's specialist consultant.

6.6.7 Of course, these matters can often be questions of degree, and there can be a particular tension where AC is claiming that her health prevents her from working at all, but be aware that the Courts will expect both parties to take sensible positions where the overall estate has a modest value. Questions of degree can sometimes be resolved by asking the relevant person's GP to comment on the extent to which her medical condition affects her day-to-day functioning, though the other side is likely to object that AC's GP is not going to give unbiased evidence. At the very least, approach the issue with the other side in a co-operative spirit and attempt, whatever the attitude of your opponent, to establish as much common ground as possible.

6.6.8 If your client's medical condition is disputed and you are not permitted to obtain expert evidence for reasons of proportionality, remember that the trial Judge is making a value judgment about all of the matters at section 3 and provide her with the best information that you can in order to make that judgment. A well-organised witness statement by your client setting out what her health problems are and the practical ways that they affect her earning capacity and her day to day living will be of considerable assistance. One particularly important piece of evidence which may be readily available to your client is a DWP assessment that she is not fit for work, or that she is fit only for say light clerical work.

6.6.9 This is an area where case law is of limited help, because the general principle is clear and the s.3 considerations are fairly fact specific. One case that is of particular interest however is *Challinor v Challinor* [2009] EWHC 180 (Ch), where AC had Down's syndrome and had lived for some time in a residential home. Her father had set aside a fund of £10,000 for her in his lifetime, which had increased to £15,000 by the date of his death, but had left all of his £55,000 estate to his second wife, AC's stepmother. In addition, he had jointly owned a property with his second wife which had passed to her by survivorship; his share alone had been worth £265,000.

6.6.10 AC submitted evidence that her health had deteriorated in recent years and that she now needed physiotherapy and extra assistance with bathing and dressing. She also submitted that her needs would only increase in the future, a contention that was disputed: see the section on "Foreseeability" at 5.2.2. The Court found that although most of C's living expenses were met by way of state funding and a local authority top-up, she did not have the funds to buy clothing, holidays, additional personal care and physiotherapy. This is the kind of care that a supportive family would usually provide without it becoming a factor in litigation, and it is telling that the Court found that in the light of the evidence it did not appear that the stepmother would voluntarily give effect to the father's expectation that AC's needs would be met from his estate after death.

6.6.11 Note particularly that the Court took the view that although AC's basic needs were catered for via state and local authority funding, she was entitled to some provision above that basic level not just for her physiotherapy and personal care, but for clothes and holidays. Quality of life is important. If a case for reasonable provision is made out and the estate can bear the cost of the claim, the award will do more than provide the basic necessities of life.

6.6.11 "Self-inflicted" health issues

The main culprits here will be the health effects of alcohol and drug addiction or abuse, which can often be severely disabling. The addiction itself may have resulted in estrangement between AC and DP, because DP entirely disapproves of AC's manner of living; that will be a relevant factor, particularly if DP has expressly refused to support AC any further.

6.6.12 One case in which DP did not do so is *Stephanides v Cohen* [2002] EWHC 1869 (Fam); [2002] W.T.L.R. 1373 , an extremely sad story in which AC was in fact the defendant beneficiary in a claim made by DP's widow. AC was a heroin addict with non-Hodgkin's lymphoma, which was in remission at the time of the trial but had already recurred once, and had suffered a deep vein thrombosis as a result of drug misuse. He was addicted to LSD as well as opiates, was clearly incapable of supporting himself, and was 37 at the time of the trial. The trial judge said, sadly but probably fairly, that AC had "*so far made a total mess of his life and has squandered all of the opportunities that have been offered to him and a great deal of money*". DP had however continued to support him both emotionally and financially.

6.6.13 The case was a straightforward question of balancing the interests of widow and adult child, and the trial judge was clear that the widow's claims had priority: DP's obligation to AC was "*the moral obligation borne of his parental love for his son, and especially when that son is unable to support himself ... even though the condition causing that deficiency is self-inflicted*". He added: "*It is urged on me that it is precisely because of the wreck that he has made of himself and his life through his addiction that he needs the greater part of the estate in priority to the needs of the claimant. In my view, it is the other way about.*" After making what we can clearly see is a value judgment, he then proceeded to award DP's widow enough to satisfy her needs on the higher maintenance standard, which left AC with approximately 40% of the estate.

6.7 Section 3(1)(g): 'Sweeper' Section

6.7.1 Section 3(1)(g) directs the Court to consider any other matter which it considers to be relevant. From this wide category, a number of specific issues tend to arise, some of them of considerable weight where they appear.

6.7.2 Expectations

There are cases where, to borrow the conventional phrase, AC expects nothing from DP's Will and is not disappointed. Mrs Jackson had told Mrs Ilott she was going to leave her nothing, and Mrs Ilott therefore had no expectations from the Will at all. The fact that an AC has no expectations of receiving anything is unlikely to weigh particularly heavily when considering reasonable provision. The main underlying argument for its relevance in the cases seems to be that AC has adjusted to living in very restricted financial circumstances and so there is no reason now to give her significant assistance. How reasonable that is depends on the circumstances of the case, but particularly of course the other relevant s.3 factors.

6.7.3 The other side of the expectations coin is that AC has been led to expect provision from the Will and either gets nothing, or not enough. These situations are better considered under "Promises" below.

6.7.4 DP's Expressed Wishes

The clearest indication of D's wishes about what is to happen to her estate are usually set out in her Will. She may have added some explanation either in the Will or in a letter of wishes setting out her reasons for what she has done, and she is often advised to do so these days in an attempt to discourage an Inheritance Act claim, although she does not need to do so. As we have seen, it is not the Court's task to rewrite the Will and it will not interfere with DP's rights to dispose of her estate as she wishes except to the extent necessary to make reasonable provision for AC: see, eg, Vinelott J in *Re Bunning* [1984] Ch. 480; [1984] 3 W.L.R. 265.

6.7.5 D's expressed wishes that AC (or anyone else) should benefit

In the adult child case of *Challinor* [2009] EWHC 180 (Ch), AC had Down's syndrome and had lived for some years away from her father in a residential home. Her father had accepted that he had a moral obligation to provide for her out of his general assets during his lifetime and after his death from his estate, which he left entirely to his widow, AC's stepmother. The Court was satisfied that DP had a moral obligation to provide for his daughter, but not satisfied that the stepmother would recognise that obligation. Although therefore the issue did not arise in that case, the Court noted that recognition by the beneficiaries of an estate of the passing of a continuing moral obligation onto them and the ability and willingness to satisfy such an obligation were relevant matters under section 3(1)(g).

6.7.6 The occasions on which this may be a section 3(1)(g) factor may be relatively rare, as presumably if the beneficiaries recognise the passing of a moral obligation and are able and willing to meet it there would appear to be no need for litigation; however, there could be cases where the beneficiaries may have genuine doubt about how far they should go to meet that obligation, particularly where they need to balance the needs of other dependants.

6.7.7 D's expressed reasons why AC (or anyone else) should not benefit

This category will include letters explaining why the Will has been made as it has, or express reference within the Will itself. In *Wright v Waters* [2014] EWHC 3614 (Ch) the testatrix expressly referred in a letter accompanying the Will to the reasons why she had left nothing to her daughter. The Court will generally look at them but they may not carry great weight. Note that Mrs Jackson's letter of wishes in *Ilott v Mitson* was taken into account but did not displace the other section 3(1) considerations, partly one suspects because DJ Million, the first instance judge, found that "*[59] The letter and other evidence showed in my judgment that [Mrs Jackson] was capricious and unfair in many of the reasons she gave for excluding her daughter (and grandchildren) from the estate*", and that she was "*inflexible and unforgiving*", although he accepted that Mrs Ilott and her husband had also contributed to the difficulties of effecting a sustained reconciliation.

6.7.8 DP's Wishes that the Estate should be used in a specific way

In *Baynes v Hedger* [2009] EWCA Civ 374 , most of the Estate was made up of a property, Dunshay Manor, which had been purchased by the Deceased's father, a distinguished artist. D's father had spent the rest of his working life there, and had passed the property to D, who was herself an artist of distinction. She initially left the property to the Artists' Benevolent Trust, but later transferred the bequest to the Landmark Trust because it was her ultimate aim to preserve the property and its associated land "as a memorial to eighty years of artistic endeavour", and that determination "never wavered". A successful application would have necessarily involved setting aside the Landmark Trust bequest. Although the applicant failed on other grounds, the Court put significant weight on the deceased's long-term and fixed intention to keep the property intact and to be preserved for specific charitable purposes. If DP had a strong connection to a particular social cause or religious faith and has left a sizeable legacy to a charity or church associated with that cause, the Court is likely to bear the strong connection in mind, but not to the extent of leaving AC without reasonable provision.

6.7.9 DP was unreasonable

In *Ilott SC*, Hughes LJ said that "*the reasonableness of the deceased's decisions are undoubtedly capable of being a factor for consideration within section 3(1)(g) and sometimes section 3(1)(d)" [17]*. Sometimes, as he noted, if the Will does not make reasonable financial provision for AC, it is because DP acted unreasonably in not making it. However he also points out at paragraph [17], which is well worth careful reading in full, that there can be times that DP has acted completely reasonably and that reasonable financial provision has still not been made, and other occasions where DP has been totally unreasonable but the financial provision has itself been reasonable.

6.7.10 We have to be extremely careful to remind ourselves at every turn that the primary question is not whether DP was unreasonable, but whether the estate made reasonable provision for AC. You cannot simply say "DP was unreasonable and therefore there is no reasonable financial provision". But bearing that in mind, there may still be occasions where DP's unreasonableness can be a factor under section 3(1)(g) or (d).

6.7.11 DP was violent or abusive

Unless this has affected AC's health or earning capacity, these considerations are unlikely to form a material part of the Court's considerations: see the section on "No Retrospective Reparations" at 6.4.18 above. They will certainly attract questions as to why the allegations were not raised at an earlier time. If, however, there have been findings of fact in another court or tribunal that DP was violent or abusive, or express admissions of any kind, these certainly will be relevant.

6.7.12 Conduct

A wide and deep category, encompassing everything from truly selfless sacrifices by AC for DP (or indeed vice versa), to situations where AC's appalling behaviour caused misery to DP: see *Bye v Colvin-Scott* [2010] WTLR 1. It also encompasses DP's conduct, which can be so manifestly unreasonable that it is extremely difficult to disregard it. Inevitably, these matters are going to be value judgments: one person might see DP's conduct towards AC in *Re Myers* [2004] EWHC 1944 (Fam); [2005] W.T.L.R. 851, for example, as extremely insensitive and dismissive, while another might see it as excusable within the character of a brusque and perhaps somewhat bitter man.

6.7.13 Always be aware that conduct can tip the scales decisively. In *Wright v Waters* [2014] EWHC 3614 (Ch), AC wrote a letter to DP before DP's death, disowning DP as her mother, stating that she did not wish to communicate with her and that she wished she was dead. AC and DP did not communicate again before DP died apart from one brief telephone call. DP later wrote, in letter appended to Will, that "my daughter has been a constant source of trouble to me and my husband for many years" [66]. The trial judge carefully considered the section 3 factors and acknowledged that AC was the daughter of the deceased, that she had helped with the family business, that she was not well, in necessitous circumstances and there were no relevant needs of other claimants or beneficiaries. All of this was outweighed in this particular case by her conduct, which had discharged any obligation there might otherwise have been.

6.7.14 In *Baynes v Hedger*[2009] EWCA Civ 374 , where the adult applicant had put such considerable pressure on the deceased in the last few months of her life that the judge thought that some witnesses' use of the word "bullied" was not too strong, conduct of the applicant was also a factor. The first instance judge (Lewison J) said that "this is not conduct which, in my judgment, should be rewarded". The Applicant challenged that finding on appeal but it was not overturned.

6.7.15 Timing and General Administration of DP's Estate

If it has not been considered elsewhere under section 3(1), the fact that the Estate may have been administered or managed for some time, even for a number of years, without any anticipation of an Inheritance Act claim may be a relevant factor, as it was in *Berger v Berger* [2013] EWCA Civ 1305. If beneficiaries would be obliged to give up property they have already received under a distribution, this is likely to be a powerful factor under section 3(1)(g) if it has not been enough to stop a claim out of time under section 4.

6.7.16 Sabotaging AC's earning capacity

Musa v Holliday [2012] EWCA Civ 1268; [2013] 1 F.L.R. 806 was a dependent's claim under section 1(e), but it presented some typical features of a family fall-out where there is a family business. During the deceased's lifetime, the applicant had worked for his business and had drawn a salary from it. After D died, it would appear that life was made difficult for A while she remained working at the business and she was eventually dismissed by the other members of the family, who operated the business, for gross misconduct. The applicant was a woman in her 50s without any specialist training or indeed much in the way of education and this dismissal put her prospects of earning any significant salary to an end. The Judge took this conduct into account when calculating the amount that she would need for her income for the rest of her life, and her judgment was upheld on appeal.

6.7.17 Estrangement

The fact of estrangement is likely to be a powerful factor because, as Hughes LJ points out in *Ilott SC*, what would be "reasonable provision" for an AC who lacks the income to support her basic needs may be very different where there was an exceptional closeness between AC and DP, as opposed to the situation where AC and DP had not spoken to each other for 20 years. The fact that AC has lived completely independently of DP, regardless of whose fault it was in the first place that they have not spoken, is probably indicative of the fact that her need for reasonable provision may be limited.

6.7.18 At the furthest extreme are the cases like *Re Debenham* [1986] 1 F.L.R. 404; [1986] Fam. Law 101 where the estrangement is based on a lifelong rejection of AC by DP. In that case, the Court found that DP had made a very minimal acknowledgement of a moral obligation to help AC, and therefore an award could be made, but it was clearly a very fine balance for the judge.

6.7.19 Ilott SC however makes clear what you should **not** do:

> " ... ***first to assess reasonable financial provision on the basis of some supposed norm of filial relationship, neither particularly close nor particularly distant, and then to lift the provision by an identified amount to recognise the special closeness between the two ladies.*** *But without going through any such exercise, and yet adhering to the concept of maintenance, a judge ought in such circumstances to attach importance to the closeness of the relationship in arriving at his assessment of what reasonable financial provision requires."*

6.7.20 In other words, do not start off with some idea of what a "normal" adult child and a "normal" parent would do and then work up or down from there, but do consider how close DP and AC were in your client's particular case and whether, looking at that degree of emotional affinity, the provision was reasonable.

6.7.21 Estrangement can of course also be a rejection of DP by AC. There are some striking examples, accompanied by letters from AC to DP, in *Wright v Waters* [2014] EWHC 3614 (Ch) and *M v S* [unreported, but available on Westlaw].

6.7.22 In *Nahajec v Fowle* [2017] EW Misc 11 (CC), DP had broken off contact with AC when she was 11 years old. There had been a brief resumption of contact again when she was in her early 20s, which DP had brought to an abrupt end because DP disapproved of AC's boyfriend. The Court heard, and accepted, that from that point onwards DP had consistently rebuffed AC's attempts to rekindle their relationship and that not only the estrangement but the reasons for it were significant factors under section 3(1)(g).

6.8 Section 3(3): Assumed Responsibility

6.8.1 Education, training, and assumed responsibility

Section 3(3) of the Act sets out the special factors which the Court must consider when deciding on the claims of any child or person treated as a child of the family. *Re Callaghan* [1985] Fam 1 confirmed that the section applied to adult as well as infant children. The section reads:

(3) Without prejudice to the generality of paragraph (g) of subsection (1) above [ie the "sweeper" section that we have just considered at 6.7], where an application for an order under section 2 of this Act is made by virtue of section 1(1)(c)or 1(1)(d) of this Act, the court shall, in addition to the matters specifically mentioned in paragraphs (a) to (f) of that subsection, have regard to the manner in which the applicant was being or in which he might expect to be educated or trained, and where the application is made by virtue of section 1(1)(d) the court shall also have regard--

> *"(a) to whether the deceased maintained the applicant and, if so, to the length of time for which and basis on which the deceased did so, and to the extent of the contribution made by way of maintenance;*
> *(aa) to whether and, if so, to what extent the deceased assumed responsibility for the maintenance of the applicant;*
>
> *(b) to whether in maintaining or assuming responsibility for maintaining the applicant] the deceased did so knowing that the applicant was not his own child;*
>
> *(c) to the liability of any other person to maintain the applicant."*

6.8.2 The Court must therefore look, in the case of all adult children, at the applicant's actual or planned education or training.

6.8.3 If AC is not a natural child of DP but was treated as a child of the family, [4.2.10], then the Court must go on (s. 3(3)) and consider whether or not DP actually took responsibility for AC's maintenance, to what extent she did so, whether or not she (or more realistically, he) did so knowing that AC was not her own child, and the liability of any other person to maintain AC.

6.8.4 The factual question of maintenance, and the issue of whether or not DP assumed responsibility for AC's maintenance, have been considered at length in the case law. *Jelley v Iliffe* [1981] Fam 128 was a case based on section 1(e), that is on dependency rather than on parenthood, but the relevant provisions at section 3(4) mirror the wording of 3(3), particularly "the length of time for which and the basis on which [DP maintained the applicant] and ... the extent of the contribution made by way of maintenance", and "whether and to what extent the deceased assumed responsibility for the maintenance of the applicant". *Jelley v Iliffe* confirmed that the fact that DP was in fact maintaining AC at the time of death does not automatically mean that DP had "assumed responsibility" for maintaining AC.

6.8.5 What the Court tends to look for is a continuing *commitment* rather than to payments made as and when needed. The regular payment of an allowance from DP to AC is much more likely to be an assumption of responsibility than a history of DP stepping in when AC is financially stretched.

6.8.6 In *Baynes v Hedger* [2009] EWCA Civ 374 , the applicant had been treated by the deceased very much as a close relative, even an adopted daughter, would have been: her mother and the deceased had been lifelong friends and at one stage had been in a physical relationship. She could not make an application under section 1(1)(d) at the time, because the statute then restricted 1(1)(d) claims to persons treated as a child of DP in reference to DP's marriage, but a person in the same situation as Hetty Baynes could now bring a claim under s.1(1)(d): see 4.2.10.

6.8.7 Ms Baynes had to bring her claim as a dependant under section 1(1)(e) and as a consequence, the Court was restricted to looking at the maintenance position "immediately before" death, rather than at the long-term position under sections 1(1)(c) and 1(1)(d). It also meant that the question of whether the deceased had "assumed responsibility" for the applicant's maintenance was similarly restricted in scope, and perforce left out of consideration the fact that the deceased had in this case financially supported the applicant knowing that she was not her own child [s3(3)(b)] and that the applicant had apparently not received any significant financial support from her birth mother [s3(3)(c)]; indeed, the applicant's entire family, including her birth mother, were to some extent supported by the deceased. This restriction of the timeline made the applicant's case much more difficult – in fact, as it turned out, it made it more or less impossible because of the events within the last three years of the deceased's life.

6.8.8 "DP" had been notably generous to the applicant over the years, including buying a London flat for her as a gift, and making soft loans of cash to her from time to time to tide her over short-term problems. In the three years before the deceased's death, the applicant had asked for (and on some occasions received) substantial further soft loans from the deceased. By the last two or three years of the deceased's life, she was becoming reluctant to provide continuing financial support to the applicant; among other matters, providing continuing support was beginning to threaten her cherished objective of leaving her manor house and its cottages intact and with a charitable purpose as a memorial to her father. She had expressed her reluctance to come to the rescue any more on several occasions, both publicly and privately.

6.8.9 Baynes v Hedger is also authority for the principle that unimplemented promises to make payments to the applicant cannot be an assumption of responsibility for maintenance, and that the payment of past debts are not within the broad concept of maintenance unless the payment of those debts enables the claimant to derive a future income which he or she could not do if the debts were unpaid, or the debts represent living expenses incurred since the date of the deceased [para 45].

6.9 Section 3(6): Earning Capacity and AC's Own Obligations

6.9.1 I have already noted the tendency of categories in 1975 Act proceedings to overlap. Your client has to demonstrate either that she is not capable of earning her own living, or if she is in fact capable of earning her own living, that she has good reasons for not doing so. Her health will usually play a central part in these considerations. In *Robinson v Bird* [2003] EWHC 30 (Ch), for example, AC's anorexia had very significantly impaired her education and she was now, in her thirties, unable to undertake anything other than very low-paid work.

6.9.2 Sometimes AC's obligations to others may also have an impact: if she has taken on full-time care for a relative, for example. However, if she is caring for someone in respect of whom DP had no financial or moral obligations, the impact of this may be limited. There is likely to be a significant difference in value judgments where AC cannot work because she is looking after DP's disabled grandchild, and where she is looking after her elderly mother-in-law: the Court will probably judge that DP had an obligation to assist in the former case, but none in the latter.

6.9.2 Standard of living is not an exclusory factor. Even in very big money cases such as *Wooldridge v Wooldridge* [2016] Fam. Law 451, where the total estate was valued at over £8m and the relevant maintenance standard was the higher matrimonial one, the claimant's ability to earn a very high salary was relevant enough to be considered. Where your client is unable to prove to the Court that she has good reasons for not working, her unemployment may be considered a "lifestyle choice" and given comparatively little weight: *Ames v Jones* BAILII [2016] EW Misc B67 (CC) is a clear example of this.

CHAPTER SEVEN
COMPLETING THE BALANCING EXERCISE FOR STAGE 1

7.1 Value Judgment
7.2 Balancing
7.3 Espinosa v Bourke: A Classic Example From Practice

7.1 Value Judgment

7.1.1 Before you balance up the considerations operative in your client's case, it is worth reminding yourself that you, like everyone else approaching these facts, are going to have to make a value judgment about them. That means that the other side and the trial Judge may differ from you substantially -- and even completely -- without being wrong. What to one Judge is intolerably bad conduct, obliterating a claim altogether, may only be the darker side of ingratitude to another. Other factors very susceptible to value judgments include the fact of estrangement and the reasons why the estrangement happened in the first place, and whether the continuation AC's current lifestyle is justified or indeed possible, but all of the section 3 factors are clearly open to value judgments that neither you nor your client may agree with.

7.1.2 Ilott SC has made it clear that a Court's assessment of the "reasonable provision" issue now has a very broad bandwidth. Both Hughes LJ and Hale B expressly noted that a judge could acceptably have found that Mrs Jackson's estate *did* make reasonable provision for Mrs Ilott.

> *"Some judges might* ***legitimately*** *have concluded that the very long and deep estrangement had meant that the deceased had no remaining obligation to make any provision for her independent adult daughter -- as indeed Eleanor King J did when it appeared that she had scope to remake the decision"* [Hughes LJ @ 35; my italics.]

7.1.3 The Court of Appeal allowed the appeal [from Eleanor King J] on the basis that the District Judge had not erred in law and the exercise of his discretion had not been plainly wrong, so Eleanor King J should not have interfered. But Sir Nicholas Wall P commented that ... had the District Judge dismissed the claim "I doubt very much whether the applicant would have secured reversal of that dismissal on appeal"" [Hale B @ 65(1)]. (She goes on to say that "some might think" that the best choice was between this option or the Court of Appeal's large capital payment option.)

7.2 Balancing

7.2.1 Negative Factors

Look first for the factors that weigh heavily against your client in any balancing exercise. There is always a preference to look at your client's case first, build it up to its maximum weight, and then to consider the counterweights afterwards. The temptation then is not to assess the counterweights accurately. By considering them first, you begin to see how the Court will weigh up your client's case. The most important of these include:

- The estate is small, cannot satisfy the needs of everyone, or is tied up in illiquid assets;
- One or more of the other beneficiaries is an infant child or young adult;
- One or more of the other beneficiaries is elderly, particularly if that person has been financially dependent on DP;
- One or more of the other beneficiaries has health problems.

7.2.2 It is essential to give these items their proper weight at this stage. The claims of an infant child or of a young adult in full-time education or training are going to take precedence over your AC's claim unless the facts are truly exceptional. Even if your client's health is poor, the Court is going to consider that the first priority is to maintain infant children before assisting her. Do not be tempted into denying these considerations their appropriate importance and weight.

7.2.3 You may not have enough information to assess the value of these claims, but this part of the exercise will certainly direct you to the next questions you need to ask of the other side. How much is needed for the maintenance of the other beneficiaries? You will need to consider whether these needs have been properly assessed, but assuming they are realistic, is there anything at all left upon which your client can make a claim? If there is not, then clearly your client is very unlikely to be successful whatever you do.

7.2.4 Neutral Factors

There are then some factors which can, if we continue the balancing metaphor, be put on either side of the scales, and these are often the ones which are most susceptible to value judgments. The most important of these include:

- Conduct: either your client's or DP's;
- Estrangement: why, for how long, how did it affect expectations;
- Obligations: of DP to your client, of your client to her own dependants;
- Assumed responsibility.

7.2.5 By now, you should be able to separate out the relevant conduct factors from the ones that will not get you anywhere in an Inheritance Act claim. Remember that with conduct and estrangement, for example, there are always two sides to every story. Mrs Ilott thought that her mother was harsh and cruel to her; Mrs Jackson thought that her daughter had gone against Mrs Jackson's sensible advice and married a totally unsuitable man. Each thought the other's conduct was reprehensible and it was those views which had led to the long estrangement. It turned out that the Courts tended to accept Mrs Ilott's version of the history, but there will be many times when that will not be the case. It is likely that there will be things to be said in your client's favour on these issues, and possibly also things that are not so helpful. You need to put both categories into the scales at the weights you think they bear.

*7.2.6 **Positive Factors***

Now, and only now, go back and look at your client's case. Pay particular attention to the following as far as they impact your case:

- Your client's standard of living now that you have established it;
- What her particular needs are -- in specific and not in general terms;
- Her earning capacity and whether she is using it as best she can;
- Her income, particularly any state benefit income;
- Her health, particularly whether she is suffering from any disability;
- Any promises that were made to her by DP;
- Whether DP had given her financial support in adulthood and if so what that was;
- Did DP at any stage recognise an obligation to support AC as an adult.

7.2.7 You now have three sets of considerations: the ones that weigh against your client's case for reasonable provision; the ones that may go into either pan of the scales; and the ones that weigh heavily in your client's favour. Obviously, in your client's particular case there may be other considerations not mentioned here which outweigh all others, but most considerations that you come across will fall under one or other of these broad headings.

7.2.8 Balance up all of these considerations as objectively as you can. Refer back to previous sections in this book if you are in doubt, and read further in the specialist textbooks at Appendix 3. As you will have seen, every situation is different, and there are few objectively wrong answers. Inevitably, what you will be doing is saying that in your view one or two specific considerations have heavier weight than the rest, and it is on this basis that the disposition of the estate did not make reasonable provision for AC.

7.3 Espinosa v Bourke: A Classic Example From Practice

7.3.1 There is no better way to look at how to conduct the balancing exercise than by looking at a particularly good practical demonstration of it being carried out. If you look at the report of the Court of Appeal judgment in *Espinosa v Bourke* [1999] 1 FLR 747, you will see an outstanding example in the judgment of Butler-Sloss LJ at pp 757 onwards. If you want to follow this in detail, it will be helpful to have this part of her judgement in front of you as you read through this next section.

7.3.2 Butler-Sloss LJ has already found by p. 757 of the report that the trial judge gave too much weight to the question of conduct at the original hearing. It has now been agreed that the Court of Appeal will hear the matter afresh. She therefore goes through section 3(1) methodically, setting out what for her are the relevant and weightier matters. You will see that:

- She refers specifically at section 3(1)(a) to the facts relevant to AC's assets and needs, including the fact that she had lost her income at DP's death, which she clearly considers important;
- She reminds herself that the relevant date is the date of the hearing (s.3(5)) and sets out in detail AC's financial position at that date;
- She then considers the position of the only other relevant person, AC's son, who was the sole beneficiary of the Will (s. 3(1)(c);
- DP had an obligation to AC in respect of her mother's estate having promised to leave it to her (s.3(1)(d)), and Butler-Sloss LJ notes that for her, too little weight was given to this factor in the original judgment;
- She finds that the care given by AC to DP was a significant factor as conduct under section 3(1)(g);
- In passing, she notes that section 3(1)(f) (health) does not apply;

- She then deals with the heavy weight placed upon AC's other conduct and the wishes of the testator by the original trial judge and sets out her reasons why in her view these do not "discharge the weighty obligation arising from the promise".

7.3.3 She then concludes:

> *"Doing the balancing exercise and weighing in the scales, on the one hand, the straitened financial circumstances of the appellant and lack of prospects, the obligations and responsibilities which the deceased had towards the appellant, the lack of competing needs shown by any other applicant or by the beneficiary and the substantial size of the estate, and on the other hand, the inter vivos payments, her conduct towards him, the wishes of the testator expressed in the will and all the surrounding circumstances, I am satisfied that the balance comes firmly down in favour of the conclusion that the deceased failed to make reasonable financial provision for the appellant out of his estate."*

7.3.4 Whether you agree with her conclusion or not, this is a classic example by an experienced judge of the section 3 exercise. In particular it gives every applicable factor its own weight, and Butler-Sloss LJ sets out clearly why her view about relative weights differs from that of the trial judge. This is how every analysis of the balancing exercise should be carried out.

7.3.5 Butler-Sloss LJ continued after this to apply the section 3(1) criteria to the question of what provision should be made, and we will look at this again when we have considered the Court's powers.

CHAPTER EIGHT
THE COURT'S POWERS, AND COMPLETING STAGE 2

8.1 Overview of the Court's Powers
8.2 Powers Under Section 2: Property in the Estate
8.3 Property in the Hands of Third Parties: Section 2(4)(a)
8.4 Property Held in a Joint Tenancy: Section 9
8.5 Voidable Dispositions: Section 10
8.6 Completing the Balancing Exercise for Stage 2
8.7 A Real-Life Example of Stage 2: Espinosa Again
8.8 Over-Provision and Ambitious Claims

8.1 Overview of the Court's Powers

8.1.1 We are now moving to Stage 2. Clearly, you only reach this point if your section 3 balancing exercise has concluded that the Estate did not make reasonable provision for AC. You have made that value judgment; now you need to decide what would be reasonable provision for AC out of this net Estate, and how the Court should make that provision.

8.1.2 One of the most striking aspects of the case law is how often AC not only does not get as much as she claims, but gets something different in nature or effect from what she claims. Claims for lump sums become transfer of property orders; claims for periodical payments become lump sums. It may be necessary to come up with more than one possible solution to your client's provision problems, depending on the nature of the estate, the claims of the other beneficiaries, and the powers of the Court. We will have a look at the wide powers that the Court has at its disposal and then consider how you can use them best.

8.1.3 It is worth emphasising that in respect of every solution that you come up with using the section 2 powers, you must **always check your client's tax position** with a qualified tax adviser, before putting it forward as a settlement option or advancing it as a formal claim.

8.2 Powers under section 2: Property in the Estate

8.2.1 Section 2(1) sets out the Court's powers. In summary, the Court can order (a) periodical payments; (b) a lump sum; (c) transfer of property within the net estate; (d) settlement of property within the estate for the applicant's benefit; (e) acquisition of a property, using property within the net estate, and then either transfer to, or settlement upon, the applicant; (f) and (g) the variation of any ante-nuptial, post-nuptial settlement or pre-civil partnership or post-civil partnership settlement (including such a settlement made by will) made on the parties to a marriage or civil partnership to which the deceased was one of the parties, provided the settlement was made for the benefit of the surviving spouse or partner or any child of the marriage or partnership, and (h) variation of the trusts on which the deceased's estate is held. Variations of nuptial settlements at ss. 2(1)(f) and (g) can include redistribution of life insurance policy proceeds and some pensions arrangements, so these sections are not relevant only to the very wealthy.

8.2.2 The Court can use more than one of these powers in any combination, and frequently does. To take one example, in *Iqbal v Ahmed* [2011] EWCA Civ 900 the Judge granted to the applicant wife the right to occupy a property within the net estate for life, together with a right to half of the proceeds of sale and the whole of the residuary estate, and made provision for the costs of upkeep and repair to be divided equally between her and her co-owner. The order combined elements of transfer of property, settlement of property, and a lump sum, and was a particularly inventive use of the Court's powers to maximise the limited resources available.

8.2.3 It will come as little surprise that it is powers (a) and (b) (periodical payments and lump sum) which are most often used, although following the Supreme Court decision in *Ilott SC* we are likely to see an increase in applications for transfers or settlements under the remaining provisions.

8.2.4 Lump sum

A lump sum order is an attractive solution to most Inheritance Act claims if there is sufficient liquidity in the estate to permit it. It is a practical remedy to specific capital needs: if AC needs a car in order to increase her earning capacity, for instance, or if the roof on AC's house needs a full repair that she cannot afford. It can also be awarded so that AC can purchase a house to meet her need for secure housing, but as we have seen, the circumstances in which that award can be made are now quite tightly circumscribed in adult child cases by Hughes LJ's judgment in *Ilott v Mitson SC.*

8.2.5 Capitalised Maintenance

Lump sums can also be ordered where there is an income shortfall which needs to be bridged. The Family courts have now dealt for many years with the concept of a capitalised lump sum providing income for a fixed period, generally by means of the so-called *Duxbury* calculations, although other methods can be and have been used. The basic principle of the *Duxbury* calculation is to fix AC's income need, establish the relevant period -- usually but not always AC's actuarial life expectancy -- and then fix a sum which will provide AC with that income for her actuarial lifespan but then be exhausted.

8.2.6 The fixed period can be shorter: for example, in an Inheritance Act context, a period during which a young AC can complete study for a qualification which will enable her to achieve substantial earning power: for example, to take AC from her eighteenth birthday through to qualification as a doctor and the first two or three years of practice.

8.2.7 The *Duxbury* calculation has been referred to in matrimonial proceedings as the "industry standard", but there are other calculation tables and calculation methods. Of these, the most important are the so-called *Ogden* tables, which capitalise income losses in personal injury cases, but have also been used in Inheritance Act matters. In an article written for *Family Law Week* in 2009 and available online [see Appendix 3], Sidney Ross argued that there are circumstances in which the Ogden tables are of more assistance to the parties and the Court than the Duxbury tables, perhaps particularly where the applicant is old or elderly and the income shortfall is not in the tens of thousands.

8.2.8 However, matters have moved on since 2009 in a number of ways. Interest rates in the UK have been at historic lows since mid-2009 and the capital amounts required to produce specific income have increased to match. In addition, the Lord Chancellor announced in March 2017 that the effective Ogden table interest rate was to be reduced from 2.5% to 0.75%. This probably means that the Ogden rates are a more realistic reflection of the current investment climate, but it also means that there is now likely to be a significant discrepancy between Ogden and Duxbury calculations.

8.2.9 The difficulty with all lump sum capitalisations at the moment, whichever method you use, is the historically low rates of interest which invested lump sums will achieve. In many if not most cases, provision of the required lump sum to give AC the income she needs would not only empty out the estate but will be greater than the total net value. Where that is the case, it may be time to look for other solutions. The Court is going to require considerable persuasion to cut out all of the DP's intended beneficiaries in favour of your client.

8.2.10 The other main way to deal with an income shortfall is to seek a periodical payments order for a limited period, and we will look at those in the next section. I would suggest that in most cases a lump sum order is the preferable way to meet an income shortfall simply because it provides the parties with a clean break from each other; however, it may not always be possible, and where there is no particular animosity between the parties, periodical payments may be a better solution, particularly because they are capable of variation.

8.2.11 What we do now have to bear in mind when seeking a lump sum are the cautionary words of Hughes LJ in *Ilott SC:* "the statutory power is to provide for maintenance, not to confer capital on the claimant". If the lump sum is going to significantly enrich AC in terms of the capital that she holds, it is probably over-provision. .

8.2.12 We have already seen that AC's needs cannot be the measure of the award, because there may well be restrictions not just because of the needs of other beneficiaries but also because of the size of the estate. Factors working against a full award on the basis of need also include the quality of the relationship between DP and AC: see Hughes LJ @ *Ilott SC [22].* There may have been estrangement; there may have been feuding; there may be other relevant conduct factors. All of these factors need to be considered when you are evaluating whether or not to seek a lump sum order, and the value to fix on the claim. For a post-Ilott lump sum order based on capitalisation of maintenance, see *Nahajec v Fowle* [2017] EW Misc 11.

8.2.13 Factors Militating Against a Lump Sum Order

State Benefits

We have already looked, at 6.3.4, at the effect of the receipt of benefits on an Inheritance Act claim and seen that the difficulties involved were at the heart of the issues in Mrs Ilott's claim. One of the most important elements to take away from the *Ilott SC* judgment is that if you are going to put forward a lump sum claim when your client is in receipt of means-tested benefits, you must think the claim through to its logical conclusion and provide the figures for the Court. As I have stressed, it is going to be extremely difficult for your client to come back to Court on an appeal on the basis that the Judge did not deal with the figures properly: 4.3.6.

8.2.14 It is your responsibility as AC's representative to provide the Judge with the fullest possible information about the effect of any order she may make. Note that the Supreme Court rejected the criticisms about DJ Million's calculations in *Ilott*, which the learned District Judge himself described as necessarily "rough and ready" because he had not been given any information about the effect of the orders he could make. Hughes LJ expressly commented that he should have been provided with that information if the point was relevant, as it clearly was [38].

8.2.15 DJ Million's approach, which was expressly approved by Hughes LJ, was to assess what the net benefit to Mrs Ilott would be of the lump sum provision she asked for. She had argued that if she received the sum of £186,000 in round figures to purchase the house that she rented, this would relieve her of the expense of rent and ease her general household budget. The difficulty for the District Judge was that this payment was not coming out of the family's earned income, but out of benefits, specifically housing benefit, so buying the house would not actually free up much income. The District Judge put the figure at £912 per year, which was the amount of rent that the family paid from their own funds. He also noted that he had been given no information at all about the effect of another part of the claim, which was for a Duxbury lump sum to yield an income of £10,000 per year. He had assumed that this would have an adverse effect on the payment of benefits, and he was criticised for this in the Court of Appeal, but the SC judgment endorses this approach, not least because it operated in Mrs Ilott's favour [see Hughes LJ @ 38].

8.2.16 One of the morals of this is that if you do not want the trial judge speculating at large about the effects of your preferred lump sum order on your client's benefits position, give her evidence on which she can exercise her value judgment. There are benefits calculators online into which you can enter the relevant variables, including capital sums and increases in income: see, eg, www.entitledto.co.uk/benefits-calculator/startcalc.aspx, https://benefits-calculator.turn2us.org.uk/ and the UK government version at https://www.gov.uk/benefits-calculators. Calculations should be prepared for trial and if possible, parties should agree before trial which is the appropriate calculator to use if there is discussion about quantum, so that the trial judge is not being presented with rival calculations from more than one source. Do not leave this vitally important element to chance.

8.2.18 If the Lump sum is not primarily for AC's maintenance

We have seen what the Supreme Court have had to say about the appropriateness of a lump sum for the purchase of a house for your client. The aim of the Inheritance Act is to help with her maintenance and not to give her capital. If your client is seeking a lump sum in order to purchase a property for herself outright as opposed to seeking a life interest in a property, your calculations should be aimed at demonstrating that the effect of the lump sum order is not mainly to increase capital.

8.2.19 One potential way of doing this in a claim where your client is not on benefits is to factor in to your calculations the ability of your client to release funds from the property as part or all of her pension on retirement by way of equity release. What you are effectively doing is using the property as a Duxbury fund as well as a home for AC. This method is unlikely to be suitable for AC claimants who are younger than middle age, but it may be worth considering in some situations. This approach was advanced on Mrs Ilott's behalf in the Court of Appeal but rejected by the Supreme Court.

8.2.20 Size or nature of the Net Estate

The size issue is self-explanatory. If the total estate is worth £150,000, your client is clearly not going to succeed in making a claim for a lump sum Duxbury fund of £250,000, even in the unlikely event of the Court deciding that the other beneficiaries or claimants should get nothing at all.

8.2.21 Your client can certainly make a claim for a lump sum equivalent to the entire amount of the estate, but the Courts are extremely reluctant to ignore DP's wishes entirely even if DP's conduct has been questionable. DJ Million thought that Mrs Jackson was harsh and unreasonable to Mrs Ilott, but he did not question that at least half of her estate should go to the charities that she had selected, even though none of them put their needs into the balance.

8.2.22 The nature of the net estate may also make payment of a lump sum impossible in practice. The classic example is where all or almost all of the estate is comprised of a property in which DP's frail and elderly widower is residing. The Court must balance the income needs of your client against the elderly widower's needs and it is unlikely that the result of that balancing exercise is going to be an order that the property should be sold and the widower removed unless your client's needs are particularly acute. Problems may also arise where property is outside the jurisdiction, or is within the jurisdiction but under the control of third parties such as trustees. Note that the Court will not be deterred from making a lump sum order even if the beneficiary claims that she has spent all of the estate: see *Nahajec v Fowle* [2017] EW Misc 11.

8.2.23 Periodical payments

If most maintenance claims can be met by paying a capitalised lump sum, when would periodical payments be more appropriate? One answer might be that an award of a lump sum might be more than the estate would realistically have to pay under periodical payments. This appears to have been the thinking in *Re Debenham (Deceased)* [1986] 1 FLR 404, although it was not put in quite that way. The total value of the net estate was £172,000. £100,000 of that was in investments and the remainder in cash at the bank and a house. Apart from a few small legacies, including one of £200 to AC, DP left all of her money to charities. The judge specifically found that AC was living at the level of subsistence; she was dependent on benefits and in very poor health. At the time of the trial she was 58 years old.

8.2.24 The judge had "no difficulty" in deciding that reasonable provision had not been made for her, in spite of the long and almost complete estrangement. AC had wanted a lump sum as capitalised maintenance but in view of her life expectancy and her age, the Judge decided that a periodical payment was more appropriate. Interestingly, this solution was the one suggested by the charities defending the action. The judge provided that when AC was eligible for her state pension, the periodical payments should be reviewed downwards to reflect the fact that her basic income had increased.

8.2.25 The slightly chilling thrust of the *Re Debenham* award seems to have been that there were genuine uncertainties about how long AC would live, and in those circumstances a lump sum for capitalised maintenance on an actuarial life expectancy might turn out to be a considerable overpayment. Whether this was the case or not, it would appear that periodical payments may be more suitable to a case where there is real uncertainty about the period for which AC will need maintenance. Periodical payments were also suitable in *Re Debenham* because an order to this effect did not adversely affect the other beneficiaries. The order appears to be predicated on the periodical payments being made by the will trustees, although that is not absolutely clear, but in any event there were no beneficiaries who required capital or income which would prevent the order being made.

8.2.26 Periodical payments may also be more suitable when AC's circumstances are not settled and her maintenance needs may fluctuate. The classic example of this is if AC is a young adult, whether she is starting out in the world of work or still in further education. A periodical payments order made to take account of her current situation can be revised up or down by seeking variation under s. 6. In *Taylor v Bell* [2015] EW Misc B3 (CC), the applicant was in his early twenties and had been receiving periodical payments under an order made by consent in 2008. The original consent order made detailed provision (including a calendar of payments) for how the payment arrangement should operate while AC was a full-time student, but things did not go according to plan, AC had to take some time out of studying, and course requirements changed.

8.2.27 The original order had provided that there should be a ceiling on the total amount of periodical payments at a figure of £210,000, which was to be put aside in a separate bank account. Between the time of the original order and the application, some of the remaining balance in this account was distributed to other beneficiaries on the basis that the full amount was not going to be claimed, though as it turned out this basis was not correct.

8.2.28 Mr Taylor, having got his studies back on track, applied to the Court to have the order varied. The matter was heard by Behrens J, who noted that none of the authorities produced to him were decisions under the 1975 Act: as is fairly common in Inheritance Act cases, they were divorce financial remedy authorities which were being applied to Inheritance Act proceedings. They supported the contention that consent orders were binding, and that AC had to demonstrate that there had been some significant intervening event if he was to displace them. This line of reasoning was rejected by the Judge, who found that section 6 of the Inheritance Act gives the Court unfettered discretion to consider whether a periodical payments order should be varied. He proceeded to vary it to allow further periodical payments to be made, having satisfied himself that the delays were unavoidable and that AC had serious intentions of completing his studies.

8.2.29 In *Debenham,* as I have already noted, there was unlikely to be ill-feeling between the AC and the charity beneficiaries; in *Taylor v Bell*, most of the £2million estate had been transferred to a discretionary trust from which the AC was excluded as a beneficiary, and Mr Taylor's periodical payments were therefore not preventing any of the other beneficiaries from receiving capital and income under the Will. Things might be different, and periodical payments a less suitable remedy, where other trustee and beneficiary family members will see the periodical payments as a burden and an irritant.

8.2.30 The Act does not specify the date on which periodical payments must begin, which raises the prospect that they can be backdated to the date of death, or to the date when the application was made, as well as to the date of judgment. Statistically, the reports appear to favour payments from the date of death, which seems logical since any shortfall in maintenance will usually have taken effect shortly after death. *Eyre v Eyre* [1968] 1 All ER 968 is the main authority for payments commencing from the date of application, but that decision does not appear to have proceeded from any particular point of principle. In *Re Debenham* [1986] 1 F.L.R. 404, the judge considered whether the periodical payments order should be backdated to the date of death, but as he was apprehensive that this would cause benefits problems, he made a lump sum order for that period instead to make good the shortfall between death and the date of the order. *Re Debenham* is therefore support for the argument that the relevant date for the start of periodical payments should be the date of death, although there may be reasons why payments cannot be backdated and may have to be capitalised up to trial instead.

8.2.31 Transfer of property

The Court's power to transfer property will form a particular focus of any case in which the claimant and the deceased have been living under the same roof, and the claimant now wishes to have the property transferred to her. It is also reasonably common for the claimant to have been living in a property which the deceased had provided for her but had not been put into her name. In both of these cases, the claimant is likely to seek a transfer of property order so that she can have full ownership of the property.

8.2.32 Inevitably, many of the reported cases are either spousal cases, cohabitee cases, or dependency cases, rather than adult child cases. There are not many adult children these days who are provided with a home free of charge by their parents, although one exception is the adult child who has either cared for DP at home for many years or who has given up an independent life to return to the family home and care for DP in her declining years. However, the BoMaD factor (see 6.3.19) means that this may change in the near future.

8.2.33 As we have already seen, the claims of carers can intersect with the issue of promises made as a section 3(1)(g) factor, and also with concurrent proprietary estoppel claims. However, we have to bear firmly in mind when looking at transfer of property cases involving spouses rather than adult children that the maintenance standard is higher. What is suitable and appropriate for a spouse will almost certainly be at too high a standard for an adult child. Where the reports involve cohabitees or dependents, however, the maintenance standard is the same, so these are potentially more helpful at least as far as the level of provision is concerned.

8.2.34 There will be occasions when AC will actively seek transfer of property as the main part of her claim. This will happen when there is something particularly distinctive about the property, generally that it is the key to the family business or the family wealth or that it is unique, and therefore that no substitute in terms of money will suffice. Farmland is the epitome of this type of asset, and in *Williams v Seals* [2014] EWHC 3708 (Ch) DP's two adult sons sought transfer of DP's half-interest in the family farm as reasonable provision under the

1975 Act. The Court had to deal with the claim at a preliminary level, because the claimants had placed a caution on the Land Register in respect of the property to protect their claims not just under the Inheritance Act but in proprietary estoppel and in challenges to the Will. If the ACs had a viable claim to a transfer of property under s.2(1)(c), then it might be reasonable that the caution should remain in place.

8.2.35 In fact the Court found that there was no realitic possibility that the ACs would succeed on the claim that transfer was the appropriate remedy. In particular, both ACs had given clear evidence that they were short of money. They were not farmers, and their plans to develop the land would either require the consent of the co-owner, their aunt (which was clearly not going to be forthcoming), or they would have to buy her out, which they had no realistic prospect of doing. The case is a useful reminder of the reality check that the Courts may have to carry out when the main thrust of the claim is for property transfer.

8.2.36 *Settlement of property (existing or acquired)*
Making or Varying Settlements

The next powers of the Court that we are going to consider are centred on settlements, so it is worthwhile to remind ourselves before we go any further of what settlements actually are. A settlement is any transfer of property (it will usually be a gift on trust) which provides that the use of the property will be given to two or more people in succession. The key element is that the property is used by A up to a certain point, and then used by B, and then if appropriate by C.

8.2.37 The Court's powers to settle property and to vary settlements are wide-ranging and it is perhaps a little surprising that they have not been more widely used, although one can discern an increase in their use over the past 15 years, which will probably accelerate post-*Ilott*. Firstly, it can order that property in the estate shall be settled on AC: s. 2(1)(d). Secondly, it can order that property in the estate should be used to acquire property which should then be settled on AC; for example, it could order that money from the residuary estate should be used to purchase a property which should then be settled on AC for life and then to a beneficiary under the Will: section 2(1)(e).

8.2.38 If there is a pre-nuptial or post-nuptial settlement, it can order a variation of that settlement for the benefit of, among others, any child of the relevant marriage: section 2(1)(f), and it has the same power in respect of a civil partnership pre- or post-nup: s. 2(1)(g). Finally, it can order a variation in any of the trusts on which DP's property is held: for example, it could put new provisions into the Will trusts by which the trustees held the residuary estate: s. 2(1)(h).

8.2.39 Settling Property in the Net Estate

This has not been a popular method of satisfying Inheritance Act claims, and so there are relatively few reported decisions: that may change now that the Supreme Court has expressed a preference for settlements of property rather than outright transfers. The main practical problem is that it does not provide a clean break for the parties, and it is not an inexpensive solution if professional trustees are to be involved.

8.2.40 In *Harrington v Gill (Estate of Frederick Bailey Deceased)* (1983) 4 F.L.R. 265, the claimant had lived with the deceased for 8 years before his death and there was no doubt that she had been maintained by him. The deceased died intestate and his entire estate passed to his daughter, the defendant. At first instance, the trial judge had awarded the claimant a lump sum (amount not specified) and a life interest in a further sum of £5,000 from which to draw income, but had not awarded anything for her housing needs, on the basis that she was very likely to be re-housed by the local authority given that she was in her 70s.

8.2.41 The Court of Appeal confirmed the lump sum awards and also ordered that the home in which she had lived with the deceased should be vested in trustees on trust for the claimant for her life and then to the Defendant. The Court was particularly mindful of the facts that the deceased's maintenance of the claimant had included providing a roof over her head, and the judge's order had not made provision for that, but also that the claimant was advanced in years: Dunn LJ noted that the main objection to a settlement was that the defendant would be kept out of her money, but tactfully commented that given the facts and the claimant's age this was likely to be a temporary postponement. Matters may be very different where AC is in say her mid-forties. It may be much less practical or possible for the Court to order settlement of a property on her for life.

8.2.42 Variation of settlement
Variation of Pre-Nuptial and Post-Nuptial Settlements

I include under this heading settlements made in anticipation of and after a civil partnership as well as marriage, so this paragraph applies to sections 2(1)(f) and (g). When I refer to "marriage" in this paragraph, I am including civil partnership.

8.2.43 The category of pre- and post-marriage settlements is extremely wide and the reader is referred to the main textbooks on matrimonial finance for a detailed account of the law if in doubt. The basic definition remains the one set out in 1929 in *Prinsep v Prinsep (No. 2)* [1930] P 35, namely that the settlement must be "upon the husband in the character of husband or [upon] the wife in the character of wife, or upon both in the character of husband and wife....It should provide for the financial benefit of one or other or both of the spouses as spouses and with reference to their married state". It includes a bond executed by W giving H income for life from her property and an interest in the residue on her death (*Bosworthick v Bosworthick* [1927] P. 64); a life policy with a contingent interest in the proceeds for the other spouse if made after marriage (*Re Gulbenkian's Settlement Trusts (No. 1)* [1970] A.C. 508; [1968] 3 W.L.R. 1127); and a so-called "spendthrift settlement" providing for income for wife for life but with a power reserved to the settlor to revoke (*Janion v Janion [1929] P. 237*).

8.2.44 It was said in *Brooks v Brooks* [1996] A.C. 375; [1995] 3 W.L.R. 141; [1995] 3 All E.R. 257; [1995] 2 F.L.R. 13 that "the disposition must be one which makes some form of continuing provision for both or either of the parties to a marriage, with or without provision for their children. Conversely, a disposition which confers an immediate, absolute interest in an item of property does not constitute a settlement of that property." [Nicholls LJ @ 263]. The disposition must also be made in relation to the marriage, but it does not need to say so expressly in the instrument.

8.2.45 However, there are some nuptial settlements which are of particular interest in the Inheritance Act context. The proceeds of life insurance policies will very often be the subject of a nuptial settlement, if made after the marriage and with the proceeds payable to the spouse. Problems can arise where the proceeds of a policy are to be paid by the trustees to DP's widow, who is comfortably off, while AC is in financial need and has not received anything under the Will or the intestacy. This is a case in which the Court might consider variation of a nuptial settlement to make payment of part or all of the proceeds to AC.

8.2.46 A nuptial settlement has also been declared by the Courts where a private pension had been set up after marriage in which the husband, whose pension it was, made provision for a pension to be paid to his wife out of the same fund after his death: *Brooks v Brooks* [1996] A.C. 375. If DP's widow will receive a significant pension payout but AC will receive nothing at all and does not have enough for her maintenance, the Court may use s. 2(1)(f) to redistribute the pension funds. Note that unless the Court does so, it is probable that the life insurance or pension trustees would be absolutely obliged under the terms of the deed or instrument to make the payment to the surviving spouse. However, the characteristics of the *Brooks v Brooks* pension fund were unusual, and most pension funds will not be nupial settlements. If in doubt, take advice.

8.2.47 These powers are wide-ranging and effective, but they have their limits. In *Dixit v Dixit & Ors (1983)* [Unreported: 1988 WL 1608577], the trial judge had been faced with a situation in which the widow of a second marriage had been left a life interest in one-half of property A, and the infant children of the marriage the other half of that property under a post-nuptial settlement. The adult children of the first marriage had been left shares in property B, in which the claimant and the two children were also living. The Judge attempted to resolve matters by switching the widow's life interest and the children's interest from Property A to Property B, but this amounted to a resettlement of both properties and had capital gains consequences so adverse that all parties had to return to Court on appeal. Although the point was not decided, submissions were made that the Judge did not have jurisdiction under the Act to revoke the Property A trust and resettle it. That point remains open for another day, but both Sir Nicholas Browne-Wilkinson VC and Nourse LJ expressly said that they would have approved the Judge's approach had it not been for the CGT problem.

8.3 Property in the Hands of Third Parties: Section 2(4)(a)

8.3.1 The Court's powers extend to property which is being held by third parties. Section 2(4)(a) provides that the Court can

> *"order any person who holds any property which forms part of the net estate of the deceased to make such payments or transfer such property as may be specified in the order."*

8.3.2 This is an important provision because it allows the Court to retain some control over the net estate -- even after distribution, as was discussed in *Beckett v McMillan* [2015] NICh 8. I have already looked briefly at this case [3.4.7] in the context of time limits and delay. During the period in which the claimant did not pursue her case, the estate had been distributed, and the principal beneficiary had charged large parts of it to the Bank to fund unsuccessful land speculation. The Court refused to be deterred by the fact of distribution and used the Northern Ireland equivalent of s.2(4)(a) when allowing the claim to proceed after a ten-year delay.

8.3.3 There are also two further provisions which are of considerable help when property appears to have passed to third parties: these are section 9, which deals with property owned by DP on a joint tenancy, and section 10, which deals with property that DP passed to others during her lifetime.

8.4 Property Held in a Joint Tenancy: Section 9

8.4.1 We have already looked [5.3.8] at the vital importance of establishing early on in your preparation whether DP held any property jointly with another person. That property could be land, but it could also be rights under a joint lives insurance policy and/or critical or terminal illness cover. If DP died prior to October 2014, in order to bring these assets within the ambit of the Court, you ***must*** issue AC's claim within the six-month period after probate: see [3.4.10] above.

8.4.2 The relevant section of the Act is section 9, which now provides at subsection (1) that

> *"Where a deceased person was immediately before his death beneficially entitled to a joint tenancy of any property, then, if an application is made for an order under section 2 of this Act, the Court for the purpose of facilitating the making of financial provision for the applicant under this Act may order that the deceased's severable share of that property, at the value thereof immediately before his death, shall, to such extent as appears to the Court to be just in all the circumstances of the case, be treated for the purposes of this Act as part of the net estate of the deceased".*

8.4.3 The provision applies to all types of jointly held property, but land is the most common example you will encounter in practice. Note that section 9(1A) provides that the relevant value is the value that the undivided share would have had (a) at the date of the hearing of the application (b) if the share had been severed immediately before the deceased's death, although there is a provision that the Court can order that the share is to be valued at a different date.

> George and his wife Gillie jointly owned their home, "Niaroo", as beneficial joint tenants. Niaroo was purchased for £50,000 in 1985. When George died in 2015, Niaroo was worth £165,000. If severance had taken place immediately before George died, the value of his share would have been £82,500. By the date of the trial, the property is now worth £280,000. The relevant value for Inheritance Act purposes of George's share is £140,000.

8.4.4 Section 9(4) expressly declares "for the avoidance of doubt" that there may be a joint tenancy of a chose in action, which will include bank accounts, investments and the proceeds of jointly held insurance policies, among other items.

8.4.5 In relation to jointly held life insurance policies, the case of *Lim v Walia* [2014] EWCA Civ 1076 deals with the convoluted, but not uncommon, scenario where DP had a joint interest in a joint lives insurance policy, but the proceeds of that policy were paid into the account only after she died and the entire policy had passed into the hands of her co-owner. There was a further complicating factor in that DP was entitled to, but had not claimed, critical illness cover under the same policy. Ultimately the Court decided that s.9 could not be used, but the judgments are of considerable interest.

8.5 Voidable Dispositions: Section 10

8.5.1 Section 10 is an anti-avoidance provision to stop any attempts by DP to prevent her estate being engaged by the Act after death. If she has made a disposition to someone not more than 6 years before the date of her death, and she did so with the intention of defeating an application for financial provision under the Act, then (s.10(2)) the Court can order the donee to provide a sum of money or other property as is specified in the order. The Court must be satisfied that the donee did not give full valuable consideration for the disposition, and it must also be satisfied that the exercise of powers under the section will facilitate making financial provision for the applicant. Note however that AC must be able to prove that DP's intention was to defeat an Inheritance Act application: *Re Kennedy Deceased* [1980] CLY 2820.

8.5.2 The classic example of how powerful this section can be is *Hanbury v Hanbury* [1999] 2 FLR 255. AC was mentally and physically disabled, with multiple conditions requiring constant care. The effect of DP's actions prior to his death was to transfer almost all of his possessions into joint ownership with his widow (not, incidentally, AC's mother), with the result that the net estate was worth approximately £11,000 and the property passing by survivorship about £60,000. There was a trail of correspondence and notes demonstrating that DP had deliberately structured his affairs in order to avoid any claim by AC to the bulk of his property, although he had left her almost all of his £11,000 net estate. The Court made a declaration that one-half of two relevant investments be treated as part of the net estate, and then ordered the executrix to make payment of a capitalised lump sum out of the estate. The full report of *Hanbury* contains the wording of the full order, including the terms of the trust set up for AC, which is extremely useful as a precedent.

8.5.3 AC is likely to have a practical problem, however, in that it can be extremely difficult to establish that a determined DP has in fact given her money away. We have already looked [6.2.13] at the case of *Dellal v Dellal* [2015] EWHC 907 (Fam) in which a widow claimed that her husband had transferred money to his relatives to minimise her inheritance, although she had no supporting evidence and her claims were strongly denied. The estate failed to have her claim struck out, and the Court ordered specific disclosure under CPR 31.12, pending which the strike-out claim would be adjourned.

8.5.4 Section 10 may not be your client's only route to recovery. In *B v IB* [2013] EWHC 3755 (Fam), Parker J confirmed that the availability of a s.10 remedy does not prevent or exclude AC from seeking relief under s.423 of the Insolvency Act 1986. S. 423 is an extremely useful provision, available where DP has made gifts or entered into any other transactions at an undervalue. The "victim of the transaction", which can include a claimant under the Inheritance Act, can apply to the Court to have the transaction set aside. Despite its presence in the Insolvency Act, there does not need to be a present or impending insolvency, but there has to be a "victim". There are quite significant differences between the two provisions, so the confirmation that s.423 is available to AC is extremely helpful. Among other matters, an applicant under s. 423 does not have to prove that the transfers were made with the intention of defeating the provisions of the 1975 Act, and the Court is not limited to using its powers to make financial provision for AC. In any case where there is evidence that the estate has been significantly reduced, therefore, look at whether your client has a claim under s.423 as well as s.10. The remedies can be sought in tandem [para 56 of *B v IB*] so there is no need for your client to elect at an early stage.

8.6 Completing the Balancing Exercise for Stage 2

8.6.1 Here, you are balancing up at least three main considerations.

- What does your client actually need as **reasonable provision**?
- Is there any **realistic** possibility that the estate can meet that need?
- If there is, what powers should the Court exercise?

8.6.2 What does your client actually need as Reasonable provision?

It is worth repeating it one more time: your client's claim is pegged to the reasonable provision standard, and reasonable provision is based on recurring expenditure for her maintenance. It does not include large capital sums to pay off mortgages or tax liabilities unless that will help with her maintenance very materially.

8.6.3 More specifically, however, does she have a housing need? We have seen that it is more difficult since *Ilott* SC to claim that she should be given a lump sum to purchase a property outright, although in that case the main consideration was that it would not assist her general income position because of the housing benefit rules. You certainly do need to consider however whether your client should ask for the Court to pay her a lump sum for housing needs, or transfer a property within the estate to her, or vary a settlement in the Will to give her a life interest, or to create a settlement by which she obtains a life interest. In any proposal for a life interest, you must be very clear about how the property will be managed, whether or not AC will pay anything towards her occupation, and what will happen about the costs of upkeep and repairs. There will almost certainly need to be provision for a professional manager to collect any rent and deal with practical issues such as disrepair, and this will have its own costs.

8.6.3 A clean break is preferable wherever possible, so a lump sum should always be seriously considered.

8.6.4 Is there any realistic possibility that the estate can meet that need?

The keyword is "realistic".

> Nairi has a capitalised maintenance claim of £65,000. Her mother, Tia, has left an estate worth £100,000, of which £85,000 is tied up in the property she co-owned with her second husband, Wulstan. Wulstan is 82 years of age, has diabetes and poor eyesight, and cannot afford to re-house himself with his share of the property. In theory, Nairi can claim Tia's £42,500 share of the house and the further sum of £15,000. In practice, Tia's obligations to Wulstan are going to weigh so heavily that Nairi is certainly not going to get immediate payment -- though she might well be able, depending on how suitable the arrangement was, to seek an order that Tia's share should be settled on Wulstan only for his life and then pass to her.

8.6.5 Sometimes, there is no realistic possibility at all that the estate can come close to satisfying what would be reasonable provision for AC. If that is the case, face it now.

8.6.6 You must talk to your client and discuss the options. This is a crucial moment for any Inheritance Act claim, because an adult child who refuses to recognise reality at this stage and compromise their expectations may well end up not just getting nothing at all, but being out of pocket on costs. This tends to be the moment when the "it's not fair" argument becomes very important to AC, but you must explain again that "it's not fair" is not going to be the basis on which this claim is going to be decided. You will see that it helps enormously to explain this to the client if you have gone through the balancing exercise yourself and you have seen exactly where the danger points are.

8.6.7 If there is, what powers should the Court exercise?

Parties tend to reach first of all for either lump sum (as capitalised maintenance), periodical payments, or transfer of property, and often dispute matters pre-trial simply on the basis that a lump sum is or is not appropriate. If the estate and the other beneficiaries say that a lump sum is not appropriate, you need to evaluate closely whether or not there is anything of merit in what they say. The Act gives you, as you have seen, a very broad spectrum of possible solutions to your client's particular problems, so take advantage of them.

8.6.8 One reason why some of the powers in section 2 have not been widely used is perhaps because some practitioners who are used to and confident about lump sums, periodical payments and transfers of property, are often less confident about creating settlements or varying Will trusts. However, you should consider whether any of these powers might do better for your client than a simple periodical payments order, for example, and if necessary you should consult with the private client department of your firm where you can do so, or obtain specialist advice if you cannot.

8.6.9 Finally, remember in every case **to get specialist tax advice about any possible solution before you propose or agree to it** -- and well before that, unless the solution is only being hammered out under the pressure of a mediation. Make sure you know whether tax will arise on any potential order or agreement, and who will be paying it if there will be.

8.7 A Real-Life Example of Stage 2: *Espinosa* Again

8.7.1 Espinosa v Bourke is once again a particularly clear example of the Court's handling of Stage 2, particularly the judgment of Butler Sloss LJ. Having dealt with the relevant section 3 factors for Stage 1 in detail (see 7.3 above), Lady Butler-Sloss then summarises the balance in the lower half of p. 757. She concludes in that summary that the factor with the most weight is the moral obligation arising under section 3(1)(d) in connection with a promise made to AC's mother and rounds the discussion up by saying that in her view the "balance comes firmly down" in favour of the conclusion that DP did not make reasonable provision for AC.

8.7.2 She then immediately turns to "the provision by way of maintenance which this Court should order" -- in other words, to Stage 2. Immediately, she considers the beneficiary's resources and needs under s. 3(1)(b) and decides that the estate is large enough to accommodate his reasonable needs and also to make provision for AC. Although she does not expressly say that the beneficiary's needs are a matter of some weight to her, the fact that she addresses them first is clearly significant. She then notes that "the most weighty factors, in my view, are the financial problems of [AC], the obligations of the deceased towards [AC] which bind the estate and other matters under (g)." All of these matters were considered by Butler-Sloss LJ under Stage 1, but they have a different weight, and the Court gives them a different emphasis, under Stage 2, because at this stage it must make a practical decision about how much the "maintenance" should be, and how it can use its powers to best effect.

8.7.3 The judgment then deals with the amount of maintenance, expressly declining to fix the amount either at the value of the estate of AC's mother (which was a factor), or to the fact that the assets in that estate had increased in value, and re-iterates that "the question is how best to provide a reasonable sum for the future maintenance" of AC. For the learned Judge in *Espinosa*, the clear way forward is to award AC a lump sum which will allow her to clear her debts and give her a small cushion for emergencies, and she goes on to do so. The result is an elegant, clear and instructive example of how to conduct stage 2 in practice.

8.8 Over-Provision and Ambitious Claims

8.8.1 Ilott has brought the question of over-provision to the forefront of consideration again, because as we know the Supreme Court ruled that an order providing for Mrs Ilott to receive a lump sum so that she could purchase the house that she rented with her husband was more than reasonable provision. The suggestion of the Supreme Court is that if Mrs Ilott had had a housing need, the appropriate way to provide for it would be for the trust to purchase a property for her to live in, and that the property would be returned to the trust at the end of her lifetime or at least when she was no longer able to occupy it.

8.8.2 The difficulty with this solution is that it is often the worst possible result as far as the parties are concerned. To begin with, how is the property to be owned and managed? If there is an existing will trust, the trustees can of course become owners of the new property; but this puts them into a landlord and tenant relationship with AC, which is generally the last thing that either DP's estate or AC wants, given that the parties have been involved in litigation against each other. The alternative is to appoint professional trustees who may well then have to appoint a managing agent, which can add significantly to the costs burden of a modest estate. How are running repairs to be paid for, and will AC be expected to pay any rent for her occupation?

8.8.3 Even a swift *tour d'horizon* makes the potential flashpoints only too obvious. In *Musa v Holliday* [2012] EWCA Civ 1268; [2013] 1 F.L.R. 806 , the applicant (a dependent under section 1(e), but the maintenance standard is the same as for adult children) had been awarded assets out of the estate to allow her to purchase her home outright. The estate appealed on the basis that this was over-provision. The Court (Nicholas Wall LJ, who had earlier sat on an *Ilott* appeal) rejected this on the basis first of all that even on this basis the estate was not sufficiently large to meet all of the applicant's needs including her income needs and secondly that "if ever there was a case for a clean break on an application under the 1975 Act it is this one", and that it would be "a recipe for disaster to set up even the best drafted trusts, and even with the most robust and independent of trustees". [53].

8.8.4 The relations between the parties in *Musa* were clearly about as bad as they could be; there had even been a possibility that one of the respondents had approached a third party to kill the applicant, resulting in criminal charges, though these were later dropped. It was clear however from the way that the litigation had been conducted that it was very unwise, to put it no higher, to perpetuate the relationship between the two sides. While it is not every day that relations between the parties become as bad as this, it is very common indeed (and totally understandable) for both sides to want nothing more to do with each other after the end of the trial. One aspect of the *Ilott* case that made this solution possible was that the other beneficiaries were charities, who were less likely to feel personally aggrieved by the granting of a life tenancy. It is clearly not a solution that will work in every case.

CHAPTER NINE
OTHER LEGAL CLAIMS ON THE ESTATE BY ADULT CHILDREN

9.1 *Overview*
9.2 *Probate Challenges*
9.3 *Other Challenges*
9.4 *Claims Under the Trusts of Land and Appointment of Trustees Act [TLATA] 1996*

9.1 Overview

9.1.1 Do not attempt to force your client's case into the framework of the Inheritance Act if it clearly does not fit. If your client believes that DP did not have capacity to remember all of the potential beneficiaries of their estate, and to deal properly with their property, there may be a potential challenge to the Will on testamentary capacity grounds, or on the ground of want of knowledge or approval. If they believe that a Will was drafted substantially under the influence of a third party, there may be an undue influence claim.

9.1.2 It does however happen very frequently that your client may have both an Inheritance Act claim and a probate claim: in fact, there may be more than one probate claim, as for example lack of testamentary capacity and want of knowledge and approval are often put forward as alternative heads of claim. There is no bar to bringing the claims in the alternative and the issue of an Inheritance Act claim is not an admission that the Will is valid. *In Pinnock v Rochester* [2011] EWHC 4049 (Ch), the claimant successfully made an Inheritance Act claim as the son of the deceased, but later issued new proceedings claiming lack of testamentary capacity and want of knowledge and approval. An attempt to strike out the later claim failed. A recent example of a combined Inheritance Act and probate claim is *Watts v Watts* [2014] EWHC 668, in which AC claimed that DP's Will was fraudulently created and executed, with a family provision claim in the alternative. She succeeded on the probate claim by proving that the signature on the Will had been forged.

9.1.3 These are topics outside the remit of this book, but further guidance can be found in the main textbooks on non-contentious and contentious probate. Here, I have given a very basic "spotter's guide" to the qualities of each of the main probate claims. For our purposes, the key element is to differentiate between those cases where your client has a good, solid Inheritance Act claim and those where the better claim may be under non-contentious or contentious probate.

9.1.4 We have already looked [3.4.13] at the question of caveats and whether or not to challenge the probate process, and I have noted that if you have no substantial probate challenge you should not enter a caveat. But if your client does have a realistic probate challenge, then you should enter a caveat as soon as those instructions become clear. The main probate challenges are : no "due execution", want of testamentary capacity, want of knowledge and approval, undue influence and fraud.

9.2 Probate Challenges

9.2.1 Due Execution

The Wills Act 1837 s. 9 requires that a Will must normally be in writing, signed by the testator or by some other person in his presence and by his direction. It must appear that the testator intended by his signature to give effect to the will, and the signature must be made or acknowledged by the testator in the presence of two or more witnesses present at the same time. Each witness must either attest and sign the will, or acknowledge his signature, in the presence of the testator (but not necessarily in the presence of any other witness), but no form of attestation is necessary. If any of these requirements are not met, then there is a potential claim that the Will has not been duly executed. There is a legal presumption that a Will has been duly executed, but it can be displaced by cogent contrary evidence. Obviously, the attesting witnesses will normally have a critical part to play in any due execution case, but claims that a signature has been forged may also come under the due execution heading: see *Barrett v Bem* [2012] EWCA Civ 52; [2012] Ch. 573.

9.2.2 Testamentary Capacity

Longer life expectancy has meant that DP will often have been living for some time with illnesses which may have affected her mental state at the time that she made a Will. These include dementia in all its forms, but also conditions such as Parkinson's disease. Younger DPs may have been affected by brain injury, alcoholism or severe depressive illness, for example.

9.2.3 In all these cases, your AC client may come to you with significant suspicions about whether DP's mental state was sufficient to make a valid Will.

9.2.4 In order for any Will to be valid, the testator must have been of sound mind, memory and understanding at the time that it was executed. In practical terms, this means that DP has to be able to deal with and appreciate the various dispositions of property which she is going to sign: the relevant moment for the test is at the time that the Will is signed. Importantly, DP needs to understand the extent of her property and the nature of the claims of any others that she is excluding from inheriting her property.

9.2.5 In *Re Beaney* [1978] 1 WLR 770, DP had been suffering from dementia and had, in the latter stages of her life, executed a deed of gift which left her home, the only substantial asset in the estate, to one of her three children. By doing so she had in fact disinherited her other two children. Although this was obviously a case of a lifetime gift, the Court found that if the effect of the gift was to dispose of the donor's only asset of value and thus to pre-empt the devolution of her estate under a Will or intestacy, the degree of understanding required for the transaction was as high as the degree required for a Will: in particular, DP had to understand the claims of all potential donees and the extent of the property disposed of.

9.2.6 The question of whether DP had testamentary capacity is always fact-specific and issue-specific, so you must advise AC that even a medical diagnosis during life may not demonstrate that DP had no capacity. The evidence may show that DP had capacity even though she had been diagnosed with dementia, or was suffering from delusions: *Carr v Beavan* [2008] EWHC 2582 (Ch).

9.2.7 The burden of proof of showing that the testator had testamentary capacity is on the person propounding the Will, but that burden will switch and then switch back in most testamentary incapacity cases. The propounder will normally prove testamentary capacity on an initial basis by showing that the Will has been duly executed. The burden of proof then moves to the challenger to lead evidence to raise doubt that DP was not of sound mind. The burden of proof then moves back to the propounder to show that, in spite of this evidence, DP did in fact have capacity. This shifting burden has been re-affirmed relatively recently in *Key v Key* [2010] EWHC 408 (Ch), a case which also deals helpfully with the "Golden Rule" for solicitors taking instructions in cases of elderly clients with possible capacity issues, and with the question of "lucid intervals".

9.2.8 If DP is found not to have testamentary capacity, the Will is void and either an earlier Will, if there is one, or the rules of intestacy will operate instead. For a post-*Ilott* SC adult child case raising complex and fascinating issues about testamentary capacity (and undue influence) alongside an Inheritance Act claim, see *Ball & Ors v Ball & Ors* [2017] EWHC 1750 [Ch].

9.2.9 Want of knowledge and approval

In the most basic terms, can the Court be satisfied that DP knew what was in her Will at the time that she signed it, and had she made it clear that these were in fact her wishes? There is a broad spectrum of circumstances which can indicate that DP did not have the requisite knowledge and approval: they stretch all the way from actual fraud, so that DP was not aware that she was signing something that did not reflect her intentions, to physical problems such as failing eyesight, to the temporary effects of grief or alcohol, and to more long-term mental afflictions such as Alzheimer's or Parkinson's. (But note that a claim for want of knowledge and approval is a distinct claim from testamentary capacity. The key question here is whether DP was impaired for any reason from being able to perceive or understand the contents and the effects of a Will.)

9.2.10 Undue Influence or Fraud

Undue Influence

9.2.11 Again, this is a complex subject and only brief guidelines are given here. AC may have a suspicion that someone, usually a person who was close to DP in her final years, has obtained an inheritance from DP by exerting influence over her. This is not in itself a suspicious circumstance: in fact, if DP was being cared for by XY, whether XY was a member of her family or not, for a long period prior to death and saw AC only occasionally, it would be odd if XY had not had some influence over DP, and also odd if DP did not want to recognise XY's help in some way. In *Carapeto v Good* [2002] EWHC 640 (Ch), the testator had had a very close and dependent relationship with her housekeeper and her family, but she had been well advised, was highly intelligent and of full testamentary capacity. The undue influence claim by her nieces and nephews failed.

9.2.12 It has been said that what is needed for undue influence in probate is "coercion": not necessarily physical coercion or bullying, although these would usually constitute coercion, but pressure which "overpowers the volition without convincing the judgment". Total mental domination is required. In *Wingrove v. Wingrove* (1885) 1 PD 81 it was said that "even very immoral considerations either on the part of the testator, or of someone else offering them, do not amount to undue influence unless the testator is in such a condition, that if he could speak his wishes to the last, he would say, 'this is not my wish, but I must do it.'" The last phrase can be a useful cross-check: from your instructions, does it appear that these might have been DP's last words on the matter?

9.2.13 There is no equitable presumption of undue influence in testamentary cases, so the fact that, for example, DP has left all of her valuable property to her solicitor, does not give rise to any immediate presumption of undue influence which will vitiate the gift.

9.2.14 Fraud

Apart from the rare situation where a beneficiary has impersonated another person in order to obtain a benefit under a Will, the main head of claim is "fraudulent calumny", in which a person poisons the testator's mind against a potential beneficiary for his or her own gain. The person must either know that the stories being told about the beneficiary are false, or he must be reckless about whether they are true or false. Fraudulent calumny has recently undergone something of a revival as a cause of action after a long period of disuse since *Re Edwards* [2007] EWHC 119.

9.3 Other Challenges

9.3.1 Proprietary Estoppel

Proprietary estoppel claims are particularly associated with claims made against Estates by adult children, because adult child claims by their nature tend to centre on disappointed expectations, and among the reasons for disappointed expectations are promises or representations that were made by DP to AC during her lifetime to the effect that a particular item of land (or exceptionally a valuable chose in action or chattel) would be AC's upon DP's death.

9.3.2 The principal elements of a proprietary estoppel claim are (1) representations made by DP to AC (2) on which AC relied (3) to her detriment. In cases involving the disposition of estates, it is usual to find that promises or representations have been made on many occasions over a long period, even if they may not always have been clear and unequivocal. Sometimes the representations may amount to no more than DP encouraging AC to believe that she will inherit. Many of the cases involve family enterprises, whether they be businesses or farms. In *Wright v Waters* [2014] EWHC 3614 (Ch), the adult daughter claimed that she had a proprietary estoppel claim because of her work for the family business, a corner shop, many years prior to the death of her mother (she was unsuccessful on the evidence, but for our purposes the interesting point is that she was able to put forward both claims).

9.3.4 Suggitt v Suggitt [2012] EWCA Civ 1140; [2012] W.T.L.R. 1607 was another such case, this time a farming case, in which John Suggitt [DP's son, and one of his two children] made a claim that all of the farms and land had been promised to him and that in return he had worked for the farming business for little or no pay for an extended period. This claim was combined with an Inheritance Act claim made not only by John, but further individual claims by his partner Gemma and by each of their two infant children. Given that the DP had owned the house in which all of the family were living, this was presumably on the basis that Gemma and the children were being maintained by DP under section 1(e). Note that at trial, all of the evidence on both claims was heard in one session, but that the parties agreed that the proprietary estoppel claim should be dealt with first. As John Suggitt was successful on the proprietary estoppel claim, the Judge did not go on to deal with the Inheritance Act questions because they did not arise.

9.3.5 There is always a tension in proprietary estoppel cases where the promise relied on is one to leave property at DP's death between the enforceability of the promise and DP's testamentary freedom: at what point does it become unconscionable for DP to go back on her promise and make a Will leaving the property to someone else, or deliberately not make a Will in order to die intestate? The Courts have traditionally been extremely reluctant to restrain DP's absolute testamentary freedom except in very clear circumstances, but the circumstances in *Suggitt* were by no means totally clear and yet the proprietary estoppel claim was by and large successful.

9.3.6 Even if AC chooses to bring a proprietary estoppel claim as an alternative cause of action, she may also refer to promises made to her as part of her Inheritance Act claim, either as obligations or responsibilities which DP owed to her under s3(1)(d) or 3(1)(g) of the Inheritance Act. Proprietary estoppel claims remain highly technical in nature, and sections 3(1)(d) and (g) may allow the Court to take account of promises which would not reach the requisite standard of proof for proprietary estoppel.

9.3.7 Donatio Mortis causa

Very exceptionally, AC may argue that DP had already given property to her during her lifetime as a *donatio mortis causa,* or gift made in contemplation of death. Like fraudulent calumny, there had been few reported claims throughout the twentieth century, but after *Sen v Headley* [1991] Ch. 425; [1991] 2 W.L.R. 1308 had established that it was still possible to make a gift of land in contemplation of death, the doctrine underwent a revival. It is most commonly seen in the Inheritance Act context in relation to the size and nature of the net estate, because s. 8 of the Act provides that gifts made *mortis causa* are to be included as part of the estate, but it may also be that AC may want to argue as an alternative claim that some part of the estate, generally a fairly substantial part, was given to her *mortis causa*. This was the argument made by the claimant nephew in *King v Dubrey* [2015] EWCA Civ 581; [2016] Ch. 221, namely that his aunt had made a gift of her house to him by orally declaring the gift and passing the title deeds to him; if he failed on that point (and in the end he did), he claimed under section 1(e) of the Inheritance Act as a dependent of the deceased.

9.3.8 Again, establishing that a gift has been made *mortis causa* is a highly technical claim and the circumstances in which it can be made are fairly rare. Jackson LJ sets out a masterly and informative survey and history of the principles in *King v Dubrey* which is well worth reading, but in essence the gift must be made in contemplation of "impending" death, that is death in the very near future; there must have been delivery to the donee of the subject-matter of the gift (with land, will usually be title deeds); and the gift must be made in circumstances which show that the donor is to have the property returned to him if he should recover. In *King*, the Court of Appeal re-emphasised the fact that death must really be "impending" and not anticipated at some undefined point even in the near future, and that it was important to keep the doctrine "within its proper bounds" and not to allow it to extend it to an ever wider range of situations.

9.4 Claims Under the Trusts of Land and Appointment of Trustees Act [TLATA] 1996

9.4.1 Where AC claims that DP granted her an interest in land before DP's death, but that interest was not conveyed to AC by deed (for example, where DP has allowed AC to occupy a property she wholly or partly owns, or AC has been sharing DP's home with her), AC may have a claim to a beneficial interest in the property. The most common examples are where AC has given up her own house to care full-time for DP at DP's home, or where DP has a portfolio of properties and has allowed AC to live in one of them on the understanding that she will be able to live in the property for life.

9.4.2 Where the title to the Property in question is in the sole name of DP, the principles set out in the cases of *Oxley v Hiscock* [2004] EWCA Civ 546 and *Stack v Dowden* [2007] 2 AC 432 House of Lords will apply, namely that AC must first rebut the legal presumption that the intention of the parties was that beneficial ownership should follow the legal title: that is, she must show that the parties, and particularly DP, intended that she should have beneficial ownership. Conventionally, this can be proved by demonstrating that AC has paid money towards the acquisition or improvement of the Property, but clear evidence of an acknowledgement by DP that she was to have a beneficial interest will also suffice. If she is able to establish this, then the Court is able to fix her appropriate beneficial share by looking at what is described as "the whole course of dealing" of the parties.

9.4.3 In *Wodzicki v Wodzicki* [2017] EWCA Civ 95, AC made just such a claim. The house she lived in had been owned by her father (DP) and her stepmother (SM) as beneficial joint tenants. However, the clear purpose of purchasing the house had been as a home for AC and her children. DP and (SM) had paid the purchase money via a loan secured on their property in France. DP had never stayed at the house, but had visited; SM had never visited the property. DP died intestate in France; the fact of his intestacy made no difference as far as the property was concerned, as it passed entirely to SM because of the joint tenancy. SM then offered to transfer the house to AC if she relinquished all of her French inheritance rights over DP's property, which she refused to do.

9.4.4 At first instance in the County Court, the Judge found that SM held the Property on trust for herself and AC as beneficial owners, and that AC had a life interest in the Property and a right to occupy. AC appealed to the Court of Appeal for a declaration that she was the sole beneficial owner, but failed to overturn the order of the lower court. The key evidence was that DP had said at the time that the house was purchased that he was prepared to transfer the property to AC "when she was ready", but he had not done so during his lifetime. On this basis, there was clear evidence that there was no common intention at the time of acquisition, or indeed afterwards, that AC was to obtain a beneficial interest in the property.

CHAPTER TEN
PRACTICE AND PROCEDURE

10.1 Appropriate Court
10.2 Early Neutral Evaluation (ENE)
10.3 Early Disclosure
10.4 Settlement
10.5 Urgent and Interim Applications

10.1 Appropriate Court

10.1.1 Although this guide concentrates on pre-action steps, a word should be said about the appropriate forum for issuing a claim. An Inheritance Act claim can be issued in the County Court, or in either the Family Division or the Chancery Division of the High Court, but not at present in the Family Court. The anomaly was pointed out by Munby LJ in his "View from the President's Chambers" of May 2017, where he calls the Family Court the "natural home" of both Inheritance Act and Trusts of Land Act matters.

10.1.2 This is, as the President suggests, an added complication, and he notes that practitioners are being driven to the stratagem of issuing in the County Court and then asking the Judge to, as it were, swap hats and sit in the Family Court to deal with associated matters which can only be dealt with in the Family Court, such as questions of ancillary relief. He has recommended that s.25 of the Act should be amended to include the Family Court as one of the appropriate courts for Inheritance and Trusts of Land Act purposes. Outcomes for adult child applicants in modest estates would probably be significantly improved if this change was effected, but bear in mind that at the moment you cannot issue an Inheritance Act claim in the Family Court.

10.2 Early Neutral Evaluation (ENE)

Early Neutral Evaluation

10.2.1 Seals v Williams [2015] EWHC 1829 (Ch) has confirmed that this is an option under CPR 3.1(m), which authorises the Court in civil proceedings to "take any other step or make any other order for the purpose of managing the case and furthering the overriding objective". This includes Early Neutral Evaluation, by means of which a Judge will evaluate the respective cases of the parties and give her view about strength of evidence and legal issues. Norris LJ commented in *Seals* that the procedure was particularly useful "where parties have very differing views of the prospects of success and perhaps an inadequate understanding of the risks of litigation itself". The Settlement Judge can make non-binding recommendations about the best outcome of the case and to give short reasons for those recommendations which will not amount to a judgment.

10.2.2 It was the joint application and initiative of the legal representatives in *Seals v Williams* which led to the order for an ENE. If you believe that the views of the other side are simply not realistic, or not supported by evidence, it is definitely worth suggesting an ENE to the legal representatives of the other parties, and asking for their reasons for any refusal; if the other side will not agree, it may still be worth making submissions to the Judge or Master at the first appointment and asking for any observations she may wish to make. Parties unconvinced by prompting from the other side may reconsider if ENE is recommended to them by the Court.

10.3. Early Disclosure

> *"Civil litigation is now developing into a system designed to enable the parties involved to know where they stand in reality at the earliest possible stage, and at the lowest practicable cost, so that they can make informed decisions about their prospects and the sensible conduct of the case. Among other factors the judge exercising his discretion about costs should consider is whether one side or the other has, or has not, conducted litigation with those principles in mind."*

Judge LJ in *Ford v GKR Construction* [2000] 1 WLR 1397, quoted and approved in *Thomas v Jeffery* [2012] EWCA Civ 693 [see below]

10.3.1 The ACTAPS protocol [see 3.6] stresses the vital importance of communicating with the other side in your case. Inheritance Act claims are particularly vulnerable to the spending of disproportionate amounts of costs - sometimes because the parties are more interested in reviving old family grudges and quarrels, sometimes because they take an unrealistic view of what the Inheritance Act is able to achieve for them, and sometimes because insufficient thought went into issuing the claim in the first place. All three of these possibilities can have serious costs consequences -- costs consequences which may well extinguish any award that your client may otherwise obtain or retain, and may well eat up all of the estate. It is vital to start a dialogue at the earliest possible moment, to make comprehensive disclosure as you go, and to be flexible in your approach to the other side's case.

10.3.2 The procedural tangles which may emerge when these precepts are not followed are well illustrated by *Thomas v Jeffery* [2012] EWCA Civ 693. Richard Thomas made an Inheritance Act claim on his deceased father's estate. This was founded among other matters on the fact that Richard had, in his teens, helped out with the family farm. When he issued his claim, he gave brief details of his financial circumstances, including the fact that he was on a low income and that his expenditure exceeded his income, but it was not until midway through the trial, and on the initiative of the trial judge, that evidence was produced that he was over £36,000 in debt.

10.3.3 Matters were further complicated by the approach that the Estate had taken to the litigation, which turned out to cost it dear. The Court of Appeal noted that the Estate's case had been directed "not just to challenging Richard's account but also to blackening his name in a variety of ways". The Estate had not made any offers to settle at any time, or at least had made none which were disclosable to the Court.

10.3.4 The trial judge found that the Estate had not made reasonable provision for Richard -- in other words, that he got through stage 1 -- and that he should exercise his powers under section 2 to award Richard a lump sum of £36,375, which was approximately the amount of his debts. The net estate was £229,000, mostly tied up in land. The trial judge then ordered that costs should follow the event and that the Estate should pay Richard's legal costs, as well of course as paying their own. Although the total amounts of costs are not set out in the judgment, this order would presumably have made very significant inroads into the estate.

10.3.5 The Estate appealed the costs order on the basis that Richard's debts had not been disclosed until partway through the trial. The rationale was that if it had been aware of Richard's debts at an earlier stage, it would have made an offer to settle. It succeeded on first appeal, but failed in the Court of Appeal. The reasons for its failure are significant. Rimer LJ mentioned particularly the fact that it had never made any offer to settle the proceedings; that the basic stance was that Richard could not get through Stage 1, so there was no basis for any provision under Stage 2 (which is, one assumes, why no offer was made); that the Estate itself had at no stage sought disclosure from Richard about his debts; that it did not ask for any time to consider the new evidence when it was adduced (in fact it appears from the transcript to have accepted the new evidence), and it did not submit at trial that this new evidence fundamentally changed the overall complexion of the case. This is one of the occasions on which a lack of flexibility resulted in a significant costs penalty for the Estate. Note that the Court of Appeal was sceptical, given the conduct of the Estate throughout the litigation, that it would have made any offer had it known of the debt sooner.

10.3.6 The result was the re-affirmation of the order that the Estate was to pay Richard's costs as well as the award. Note that the Court of Appeal placed a responsibility on the part of the Estate to make further enquiries about Richard's financial position in a situation where his evidence was obviously inadequate. They had not done so, and they were not then able to claim that the fault of late disclosure was entirely Richard's responsibility. This aspect of the matter may seem unduly harsh to those representing beneficiaries and/or the estate, given that as I have noted it is the claimant's responsibility to provide all relevant parties with full proof of his needs as well as his resources. However, it shows that where there is an obvious gap in the evidence, the beneficiaries and the estate will be unwise simply to ignore it.

10.4 Settlement

10.4.1 It is your duty as a professional adviser in an Inheritance Act case to consider settlement from the earliest appropriate stage. We have already looked at your professional obligations in this regard [3.6] and the costs risks of embarking on Inheritance Act litigation without a clear strategy, including a realistic settlement figure. Throughout your settlement negotiations, be **realistic, reasonable** and **flexible**: **realistic** about what your client can hope to achieve, **reasonable** about sensible offers, and **flexible** about the best ways of using the estate to the best advantage of all those who are interested in it.

10.4.2 Failure to advise the client properly about the issues and the importance of entering into meaningful settlement negotiations is negligent and ACs can, and will, seek orders that they do not have to pay part or all of your costs on the basis that you should have advised them properly, as the claimant did in *Guney v Kingsley Napley* [2016] EWHC 2349 (QB).

10.4.3 That case followed *Musa v Holliday* [2012] EWCA Civ 1268; [2013] 1 F.L.R. 806, which we have already considered at 6.7.16. The result of that case had been that Mrs Holliday had succeeded and costs orders were made against Ms Guney and the other defendant to pay part of her costs of the action. Ms Guney then sued her solicitors, Kingsley Napley, on the basis that if she been properly advised, she would have settled the claim brought by Diane Holliday at a much earlier date and thereby avoided liability for the Defendants' costs after that date as well as those of Diane Holliday following a number of costs orders made against the Claimant. Although no figure is given for those costs in the case report, it will certainly be a significant sum. No final decision on the claim has yet been reported, but the overall message to take away is to do what you can not to put yourself or your firm in this position. If your client refuses to take your advice on sensible settlement, put your advice in writing and make a note of her responses.

10.4.4 You have seen that to make a settlement offer, you must have a clear idea of what "reasonable provision" would be in your client's case; and to do that, you must at an early stage weigh up all of the section 3 factors, which is the only realistic way you can gauge your client's claim, and never to lose sight of the fact that the appropriate standard is maintenance consistent with your client's usual standard of living. Claims for large capital assets will have to be carefully costed on the basis that they remain pegged to the maintenance standard. Offers of settlement which ignore or minimise the s.3 factors will be rejected by the estate without much discussion, and you will have lost an important opportunity to start a dialogue while giving the Estate the impression that you have not addressed the issues properly.

10.4.5 If, on the other hand you are acting for the Estate, beware of maintaining unreasonably that AC is not going to get over the threshold/Stage 1. This can have very serious costs consequences, as *Thomas v Jeffery* [2012] EWCA Civ 693 and *Lilleyman v Lilleyman)* [2012] EWHC 1056 (Ch) attest. In *Lilleyman*, the trial Judge was particularly unhappy about personal and irrelevant matters introduced by the Estate in its evidence, to which the Claimant responded in kind: "*this exchange reflected and unnecessarily exacerbated what I assume were already hostile relations between the parties, to no useful purpose*".

10.4.6 In fact, the Estate in *Lilleyman* had made a sensible and even generous Part 36 offer which the Claimant ultimately failed to beat; it was still refused 20% of its costs because of the way it had conducted the litigation, in particular maintaining that the estate had made reasonable provision for the claimant, and taking evidential points for which there was no corroboration. You must be reasonable in your own approach as a litigator, perhaps particularly if you are representing the Estate of the deceased, and you must advise the client realistically and be prepared for the anguish, or indeed anger, that may result. If it is obvious that the Estate does not make reasonable provision for AC, do not insist that it does.

10.4.7 Having come up with a suitable settlement figure and discussed it with your client, you should advise her to make an offer to settle before proceedings are commenced, unless you are coming up to the end of the six-month period following grant. This is often the moment where you have to advise your client that she is unlikely to obtain a substantial sum from the DP's estate, and that they must protect their costs position by making a settlement offer.

10.4.8 Note the wise (and realistic) words of Briggs LJ in Lilleyman: "*the unfortunate reality is that Mrs Lilleyman was, from [the date of the Estate's Part 36 offer], engaged in a high risk venture in which she played for high stakes and, in substance, lost*".

10.5 Urgent and Interim Applications

10.5.1 Section 5 of the Act gives the Court power, if it appears that AC is in need of immediate financial assistance, to make an order for payment of such sum or sums as the Court may consider reasonable, and if the Court considers that more than one sum is reasonable, the payments may be made at such intervals as the Court thinks reasonable. This useful power has not been much reported, but it provides for situations in which AC may need financial help urgently, for example where there is a possibility that she may be made homeless before the final hearing.

10.5.2 The powers were considered recently in *Smith v Smith & Others* [2011] EWHC 2133, where a wife sought interim payment of £25,000 and an order that she be allowed to occupy the former matrimonial home. She was in fact making a probate claim as well as her Inheritance Act claim, but her interim application was made under s.5. Mann J was sceptical that s.5 gave him the power to make any order at all respecting occupation of the house, given that it refers specifically to payments of sums rather than to the full extent of the s.2 powers, although he did not decide that point because in his view the applicant failed to make out a case for interim relief to the required standard.

10.5.3 What was essential to a s.5 application was witness and documentary evidence supporting a case for immediate financial need. The judgment referred to a passage in *Tyler's Family Provision* which provides that in order to succeed on a s.5 application a strong need should be established because the Court is effectively pre-empting the final decision; indeed, apart from the fact that the Court is specifically directed to consider the section 3 factors, it is very difficult to see how a Court would be persuaded to order substantial payments out of the estate without being convinced that the applicant had a very solid case on both Stage 1 and Stage 2.

10.5 4 Mann J did not make a finding on whether the bar was set as high as this, given the quality of the evidence in *Smith*. What the judge did expect however was a full and frank disclosure of all the applicant's financial resources as well as financial needs, as well as an explanation of why those needs were immediate and the applicant could not meet them. One point of particular interest was that the applicant had claimed at one stage that she required the lump sum payment to pay her lawyers. Although her evidence about the need for the £25,000 later changed, the Judge accepted that a need to pay lawyers could in principle be an immediate financial need within section 5 [para 42]. It is however likely that an applicant wishing to fund litigation in this way would not only have to demonstrate a very strong possibility of success at least as far as Stage 1, but also (by analogy with family cases) but also that there was no possibility of obtaining a litigation loan or other source of funding.

10.5.5 Although the claim for an occupation order failed on the strength of the evidence, there must be some doubts as to whether the Court does have the power to make such an order under s.5. If AC were the co-owner of the property with DP or could make out a beneficial interest in the property in some other way, it might be possible to claim interim relief under ss 14 and 12 of the Trusts of Land and Appointment of Trustees Act 1996, but this may not assist AC very materially if she is unable to pay for her other living expenses in the meantime.

CODA: A FINAL WORD ON CLIENT CARE

Even a brief survey of the cases in this book should have demonstrated the extremes of human emotion involved in many Inheritance Act claims. We have encountered examples where a DP has said to an AC in terms "I wash my hands of you" (and has gone on to do so), and where AC has told DP in so many words (and sometimes in these exact words), "as far as I am concerned I have no mother". We have seen occasions, reflecting the harsher social judgments of past decades which are happily much less common now, where a DP has been so deeply ashamed of being the parent of an illegitimate child or a disabled child that he or she has tried as far as possible to ignore the fact of that child's existence. We have seen adult children deeply disappointing their parents with their lifestyle choices, and we have seen parents being apparently harsh, unreasonable and unloving to what appear to be relatively blameless adult children. These aspects of Inheritance Act cases cannot be ignored. The deep emotions are often the reason that the client has sought your advice in the first place.

You are a legal advisor and not a grief counsellor, and you should not attempt to be the latter. On the other hand, it is one of your strengths as a lawyer and a human being that you can listen, understand, and assist. That applies whether or not the provision of the estate has been reasonable; it may be said that it applies particularly where there is nothing much you are able to do for your client by way of litigation.

Much is said these days of "the end of lawyers", and that the rapid advance of artificial intelligence will render the jobs of human legal advisors otiose in the future -- even the near future. It is certainly possible that an algorithm could be created which bases its analyses on decided cases and comes up with an answer to both Stage 1 and Stage 2 in an Inheritance Act claim; although my personal view is that if *Ilott SC* is to remain good law, a "value judgment" will always be first and foremost a human value judgment and not an assessment based on an algorithm.

One can see how an AI system can, after further development and at some future date, make a decision about whether AC's conduct in any particular Inheritance Act case means that no provision at all is reasonable; the problem is that because this is fundamentally an assessment based on human understanding, it is unlikely to be an assessment that any human being will trust. The inadequacy of such an approach to an Inheritance Act case can be seen if you imagine a distressed and grieving client feeding the relevant information into a user interface somewhere and simply being told that she has no case on the "computer says no" principle, particularly if the computer has decided that it is her conduct which has barred her from a claim. Effects which are already emotionally difficult can become devastating.

Don't be an algorithm. If you have assessed the situation and there is little or nothing that you can do for your client, and she appears to you to be emotionally vulnerable, at least refer her onwards to counselling organisations which may be able to help her with dealing with her grief.

If you can assist your client, always take account of the surrounding facts and ensure that he or she is not becoming overwhelmed by mediation or litigation on top of an already distressing situation; and if you are acting for the estate or for the beneficiaries, bear in mind that instructions to be inflexible or aggressive may cause very considerable costs damage to the estate.

APPENDIX I
INHERITANCE (PROVISION FOR FAMILY AND DEPENDANTS) ACT 1975

An Act to make fresh provision for empowering the court to make orders for the making out of the estate of a deceased person of provision for the spouse, former spouse, child, child of the family or dependant of that person; and for matters connected therewith.

1 Application for financial provision from deceased's estate.

(1) Where after the commencement of this Act a person dies domiciled in England and Wales and is survived by any of the following persons:-

(a) the spouse or civil partner of the deceased;

(b) a former spouse or former civil partner of the deceased, but not one who has formed a subsequent marriage or civil partnership;

(ba) any person (not being a person included in paragraph (a) or (b) above) to whom subsection (1A) or (1B) below applies;

(c) a child of the deceased;

(d) any person (not being a child of the deceased) who in relation to any marriage or civil partnership to which the deceased was at any time a party, or otherwise in relation to any family in which the deceased at any time stood in the role of a parent, was treated by the deceased as a child of the family;

(e) any person (not being a person included in the foregoing paragraphs of this subsection) who immediately before the death of the deceased was being maintained, either wholly or partly, by the deceased; that person may apply to the court for an order under section 2 of this Act on the ground that the disposition of the deceased's estate effected by his will or the law relating to intestacy, or the combination of his will and that law, is not such as to make reasonable financial provision for the applicant.

(1A) This subsection applies to a person if the deceased died on or after 1st January 1996 and, during the whole of the period of two years ending immediately before the date when the deceased died, the person was living—

(a) in the same household as the deceased, and

(b) as the husband or wife of the deceased.

(1B) This subsection applies to a person if for the whole of the period of two years ending immediately before the date when the deceased died the person was living—

(a) in the same household as the deceased, and

(b) as the civil partner of the deceased.

(2) In this Act "reasonable financial provision"—

(a) in the case of an application made by virtue of subsection (1) (a) above by the husband or wife of the deceased (except where the marriage with the deceased was the subject of a decree of judicial separation and at the date of death the decree was in force and the separation was continuing) , means such financial provision as it would be reasonable in all the circumstances of the case for a husband or wife to receive, whether or not that provision is required for his or her maintenance;

(aa) in the case of an application made by virtue of subsection (1) (a) above by the civil partner of the deceased (except where, at the date of death, a separation order under Chapter 2 of Part 2 of the Civil Partnership Act 2004 was in force in relation to the civil partnership and the separation was continuing), means such financial provision as it would be reasonable in all the circumstances of the case for a civil partner to receive, whether or not that provision is required for his or her maintenance;

(b) in the case of any other application made by virtue of subsection (1) above, means such financial provision as it would be reasonable in all the circumstances of the case for the applicant to receive for his maintenance.

(2A) The reference in subsection (1) (d) above to a family in which the deceased stood in the role of a parent includes a family of which the deceased was the only member (apart from the applicant).

(3) For the purposes of subsection (1) (e) above, a person is to be treated as being maintained by the deceased (either wholly or partly, as the case may be) only if the deceased was making a substantial contribution in money or money's worth towards the reasonable needs of that person, other than a contribution made for full valuable consideration pursuant to an arrangement of a commercial nature.

2 Powers of court to make orders.

(1) Subject to the provisions of this Act, where an application is made for an order under this section, the court may, if it is satisfied that the disposition of the deceased's estate effected by his will or the law relating to intestacy, or the combination of his will and that law, is not such as to make reasonable financial provision for the applicant, make any one or more of the following orders:—

(a) an order for the making to the applicant out of the net estate of the deceased of such periodical payments and for such term as may be specified in the order;

(b) an order for the payment to the applicant out of that estate of a lump sum of such amount as may be so specified;

(c) an order for the transfer to the applicant of such property comprised in that estate as may be so specified;

(d) an order for the settlement for the benefit of the applicant of such property comprised in that estate as may be so specified;

(e) an order for the acquisition out of property comprised in that estate of such property as may be so specified and for the transfer of the property so acquired to the applicant or for the settlement thereof for his benefit;

(f) an order varying any ante-nuptial or post-nuptial settlement (including such a settlement made by will) made on the parties to a marriage to which the deceased was one of the parties, the variation being for the benefit of the surviving party to that marriage, or any child of that marriage, or any person who was treated by the deceased as a child of the family in relation to that marriage.

(h) an order varying for the applicant's benefit the trusts on which the deceased's estate is held (whether arising under the will, or the law relating to intestacy, or both).

(g) an order varying any settlement made—

(i) during the subsistence of a civil partnership formed by the deceased, or

(ii) in anticipation of the formation of a civil partnership by the deceased, on the civil partners (including such a settlement made by will), the variation being for the benefit of the surviving civil partner, or any child of both the civil partners, or any person who was treated by the deceased as a child of the family in relation to that civil partnership.

(2) An order under subsection (1) (a) above providing for the making out of the net estate of the deceased of periodical payments may provide for—

(a) payments of such amount as may be specified in the order,

(b) payments equal to the whole of the income of the net estate or of such portion thereof as may be so specified,

(c) payments equal to the whole of the income of such part of the net estate as the court may direct to be set aside or appropriated for the making out of the income thereof of payments under this section, or may provide for the amount of the payments or any of them to be determined in any other way the court thinks fit.

(3) Where an order under subsection (1) (a) above provides for the making of payments of an amount specified in the order, the order may direct that such part of the net estate as may be so specified shall be set aside or appropriated for the making out of the income thereof of those payments; but no larger part of the net estate shall be so set aside or appropriated than is sufficient, at the date of the order, to produce by the income thereof the amount required for the making of those payments.

(3A) In assessing for the purposes of an order under this section the extent (if any) to which the net estate is reduced by any debts or liabilities (including any inheritance tax paid or payable out of the estate), the court may assume that the order has already been made.

(4) An order under this section may contain such consequential and supplemental provisions as the court thinks necessary or expedient for the purpose of giving effect to the order or for the purpose of securing that the order operates fairly as between one beneficiary of the estate of the deceased and another and may, in particular, but without prejudice to the generality of this subsection—

(a) order any person who holds any property which forms part of the net estate of the deceased to make such payment or transfer such property as may be specified in the order;

(b) vary the disposition of the deceased's estate effected by the will or the law relating to intestacy, or by both the will and the law relating to intestacy, in such manner as the court thinks fair and reasonable having regard to the provisions of the order and all the circumstances of the case;

(c) confer on the trustees of any property which is the subject of an order under this section such powers as appear to the court to be necessary or expedient.

3 Matters to which court is to have regard in exercising powers under s. 2.

(1) Where an application is made for an order under section 2 of this Act, the court shall, in determining whether the disposition of the deceased's estate effected by his will or the law relating to intestacy, or the combination of his will and that law, is such as to make reasonable financial provision for the applicant and, if the court considers that reasonable financial provision has not been made, in determining whether and in what manner it shall exercise its powers under that section, have regard to the following matters, that is to say—

(a) the financial resources and financial needs which the applicant has or is likely to have in the foreseeable future;

(b) the financial resources and financial needs which any other applicant for an order under section 2 of this Act has or is likely to have in the foreseeable future;

(c) the financial resources and financial needs which any beneficiary of the estate of the deceased has or is likely to have in the foreseeable future;

(d) any obligations and responsibilities which the deceased had towards any applicant for an order under the said section 2 or towards any beneficiary of the estate of the deceased;

(e) the size and nature of the net estate of the deceased;

(f) any physical or mental disability of any applicant for an order under the said section 2 or any beneficiary of the estate of the deceased;

(g) any other matter, including the conduct of the applicant or any other person, which in the circumstances of the case the court may consider relevant.

(2) This subsection applies, without prejudice to the generality of paragraph (g) of subsection (1) above, where an application for an order under section 2 of this Act is made by virtue of section 1(1) (a) or (b) of

this Act. The court shall, in addition to the matters specifically mentioned in paragraphs (a) to (f) of that subsection, have regard to—

(a) the age of the applicant and the duration of the marriage or civil partnership;

(b) the contribution made by the applicant to the welfare of the family of the deceased, including any contribution made by looking after the home or caring for the family…

In the case of an application by the wife or husband of the deceased, the court shall also, unless at the date of death a decree of judicial separation was in force and the separation was continuing, have regard to the provision which the applicant might reasonably have expected to receive if on the day on which the deceased died the marriage, instead of being terminated by death, had been terminated by a decree of divorce; but nothing requires the court to treat such provision as setting an upper or lower limit on the provision which may be made by an order under section 2.

In the case of an application by the civil partner of the deceased, the court shall also, unless at the date of the death a separation order under Chapter 2 of Part 2 of the Civil Partnership Act 2004 was in force and the separation was continuing, have regard to the provision which the applicant might reasonably have expected to receive if on the day on which the deceased died the civil partnership, instead of being terminated by death, had been terminated by a dissolution order; but nothing requires the court to treat such provision as setting an upper or lower limit on the provision which may be made by an order under section 2.

(2A) Without prejudice to the generality of paragraph (g) of subsection (1) above, where an application for an order under section 2 of this Act is made by virtue of section 1(1) (ba) of this Act, the court shall, in addition to the matters specifically mentioned in paragraphs (a) to (f) of that subsection, have regard to—

(a) the age of the applicant and the length of the period during which the applicant lived as the husband or wife or civil partner of the deceased and in the same household as the deceased;

(b) the contribution made by the applicant to the welfare of the family of the deceased, including any contribution made by looking after the home or caring for the family.

(3) Without prejudice to the generality of paragraph (g) of subsection (1) above, where an application for an order under section 2 of this Act is made by virtue of section 1(1) (c) or 1(1) (d) of this Act, the court shall, in addition to the matters specifically mentioned in paragraphs (a) to (f) of that subsection, have regard to the manner in which the applicant was being or in which he might expect to be educated or trained, and where the application is made by virtue of section 1(1) (d) the court shall also have regard—

(a) to whether the deceased maintained the applicant and, if so, to the length of time for which and basis on which the deceased did so, and to the extent of the contribution made by way of maintenance;

(aa) to whether and, if so, to what extent the deceased assumed responsibility for the maintenance of the applicant;

(b) to whether in maintaining or assuming responsibility for maintaining the applicant the deceased did so knowing that the applicant was not his own child;

(c) to the liability of any other person to maintain the applicant.

(4) Without prejudice to the generality of paragraph (g) of subsection (1) above, where an application for an order under section 2 of this Act is made by virtue of section 1(1) (e) of this Act, the court shall, in addition to the matters specifically mentioned in paragraphs (a) to (f) of that subsection, have regard—

(a) to the length of time for which and basis on which the deceased maintained the applicant, and to the extent of the contribution made by way of maintenance;

(b) to whether and, if so, to what extent the deceased assumed responsibility for the maintenance of the applicant.

(5) In considering the matters to which the court is required to have regard under this section, the court shall take into account the facts as known to the court at the date of the hearing.

(6) In considering the financial resources of any person for the purposes of this section the court shall take into account his earning capacity and in considering the financial needs of any person for the purposes of this section the court shall take into account his financial obligations and responsibilities.

4 Time-limit for applications.

An application for an order under section 2 of this Act shall not, except with the permission of the court, be made after the end of the period of six months from the date on which representation with respect to the estate of the deceased is first taken out (but nothing prevents the making of an application before such representation is first taken out).

5 Interim orders.

(1) Where on an application for an order under section 2 of this Act it appears to the court—

(a) that the applicant is in immediate need of financial assistance, but it is not yet possible to determine what order (if any) should be made under that section; and

(b) that property forming part of the net estate of the deceased is or can be made available to meet the need of the applicant; the court may order that, subject to such conditions or restrictions, if any, as the court may impose and to any further order of the court, there shall be paid to the applicant out of the net estate of the deceased such sum or sums and (if more than one) at such intervals as the court thinks reasonable; and the court may order that, subject to the provisions of this Act, such payments are to be made until such date as the court may specify, not being later than the date on which the court either makes an order under the said section 2 or decides not to exercise its powers under that section.

(2) Subsections (2), (3) and (4) of section 2 of this Act shall apply in relation to an order under this section as they apply in relation to an order under that section.

(3) In determining what order, if any, should be made under this section the court shall, so far as the urgency of the case admits, have regard to the same matters as those to which the court is required to have regard under section 3 of this Act.

(4) An order made under section 2 of this Act may provide that any sum paid to the applicant by virtue of this section shall be treated to such an extent and in such manner as may be provided by that order as having been paid on account of any payment provided for by that order.

6 Variation, discharge etc. of orders for periodical payments.

(1) Subject to the provisions of this Act, where the court has made an order under section 2(1) (a) of this Act (in this section referred to as "the original order") for the making of periodical payments to any person (in this section referred to as "the original recipient"), the court, on an application under this section, shall have power by order to vary or discharge the original order or to suspend any provision of it temporarily and to revive the operation of any provision so suspended.

(2) Without prejudice to the generality of subsection (1) above, an order made on an application for the variation of the original order may —

(a) provide for the making out of any relevant property of such periodical payments and for such term as may be specified in the order to any person who has applied, or would but for section 4 of this Act be entitled to apply, for an order under section 2 of this Act (whether or not, in the case of any application, an order was made in favour of the applicant;

(b) provide for the payment out of any relevant property of a lump sum of such amount as may be so specified to the original recipient or to any such person as is mentioned in paragraph (a) above;

(c) provide for the transfer of the relevant property, or such part thereof as may be so specified, to the original recipient or to any such person as is so mentioned.

(3) Where the original order provides that any periodical payments payable thereunder to the original recipient are to cease on the occurrence of an event specified in the order (other than the formation of a subsequent marriage or civil partnership by a former spouse or former civil partner) or on the expiration of a period so specified, then, if, before the end of the period of six months from the date of the occurrence of that event or of the expiration of that period, an application is made for an order under this section, the court shall have power to make any order which it would have had power to make if the application had been made before that date (whether in favour of the original recipient or any such person as is mentioned in subsection (2) (a) above and whether having effect from that date or from such later date as the court may specify).

(4) Any reference in this section to the original order shall include a reference to an order made under this section and any reference in this section to the original recipient shall include a reference to any person to whom periodical payments are required to be made by virtue of an order under this section.

(5) An application under this section may be made by any of the following persons, that is to say—

(a) any person who by virtue of section 1(1) of this Act has applied, or would but for section 4 of this Act be entitled to apply, for an order under section 2 of this Act,

(b) the personal representatives of the deceased,

(c) the trustees of any relevant property, and

(d) any beneficiary of the estate of the deceased.

(6) An order under this section may only affect—

(a) property the income of which is at the date of the order applicable wholly or in part for the making of periodical payments to any person who has applied for an order under this Act, or

(b) in the case of an application under subsection (3) above in respect of payments which have ceased to be payable on the occurrence of an event or the expiration of a period, property the income of which was so applicable immediately before the occurrence of that event or the expiration of that period, as the case may be,and any such property as is mentioned in paragraph (a) or (b) above is in subsections (2) and (5) above referred to as "relevant property".

(7) In exercising the powers conferred by this section the court shall have regard to all the circumstances of the case, including any change in any of the matters to which the court was required to have regard when making the order to which the application relates.

(8) Where the court makes an order under this section, it may give such consequential directions as it thinks necessary or expedient having regard to the provisions of the order.

(9) No such order as is mentioned in sections 2(1) (d), (e) or (f), 9, 10 or 11 of this Act shall be made on an application under this section.

(10) For the avoidance of doubt it is hereby declared that, in relation to an order which provides for the making of periodical payments which are to cease on the occurrence of an event specified in the order (other than the formation of a subsequent marriage or civil partnership by a former spouse or former civil partner) or on the expiration of a period so specified, the power to vary an order includes power to provide for the making of periodical payments after the expiration of that period or the occurrence of that event.

7 Payment of lump sums by instalments.

(1) An order under section 2(1) (b) or 6(2) (b) of this Act for the payment of a lump sum may provide for the payment of that sum by instalments of such amount as may be specified in the order.

(2) Where an order is made by virtue of subsection (1) above, the court shall have power, on an application made by the person to whom the lump sum is payable, by the personal representatives of the deceased or by the trustees of the property out of which the lump sum is payable, to vary that order by varying the number of instalments payable, the amount of any instalment and the date on which any instalment becomes payable.

Property available for financial provision

8 Property treated as part of "net estate".

(1) Where a deceased person has in accordance with the provisions of any enactment nominated any person to receive any sum of money or other property on his death and that nomination is in force at the time of his death, that sum of money, after deducting therefrom any capital transfer tax payable in respect thereof, or that other property, to the extent of the value thereof at the date of the death of the deceased after deducting therefrom any capital transfer tax so payable, shall be treated for the purposes of this Act as part of the net estate of the deceased; but this subsection shall not render any person liable for having paid that sum or transferred that other property to the person named in the nomination in accordance with the directions given in the nomination.

(2) Where any sum of money or other property is received by any person as a donatio mortis causa made by a deceased person, that sum of money, after deducting therefrom any capital transfer tax payable thereon, or that other property, to the extent of the value thereof at the date of the death of the deceased after deducting therefrom any capital transfer tax so payable, shall be treated for the purposes of this Act as part of the net estate of the deceased; but this subsection shall not

render any person liable for having paid that sum or transferred that other property in order to give effect to that donatio mortis causa.

(3) The amount of capital transfer tax to be deducted for the purposes of this section shall not exceed the amount of that tax which has been borne by the person nominated by the deceased or, as the case may be, the person who has received a sum of money or other property as a donatio mortis causa.

9 Property held on a joint tenancy.

(1) Where a deceased person was immediately before his death beneficially entitled to a joint tenancy of any property, then, if an application is made for an order under section 2 of this Act, the court for the purpose of facilitating the making of financial provision for the applicant under this Act may order that the deceased's severable share of that property shall, to such extent as appears to the court to be just in all the circumstances of the case, be treated for the purposes of this Act as part of the net estate of the deceased.

(1A) Where an order is made under subsection (1) the value of the deceased's severable share of the property concerned is taken for the purposes of this Act to be the value that the share would have had at the date of the hearing of the application for an order under section 2 had the share been severed immediately before the deceased's death, unless the court orders that the share is to be valued at a different date.

(2) In determining the extent to which any severable share is to be treated as part of the net estate of the deceased by virtue of an order under subsection (1) above, the court shall have regard to any capital transfer tax payable in respect of that severable share.

(3) Where an order is made under subsection (1) above, the provisions of this section shall not render any person liable for anything done by him before the order was made.

(4) For the avoidance of doubt it is hereby declared that for the purposes of this section there may be a joint tenancy of a chose in action.

Powers of court in relation to transactions intended to defeat applications for financial provision

10 Dispositions intended to defeat applications for financial provision.

(1) Where an application is made to the court for an order under section 2 of this Act, the applicant may, in the proceedings on that application, apply to the court for an order under subsection (2) below.

(2) Where on an application under subsection (1) above the court is satisfied—

(a) that, less than six years before the date of the death of the deceased, the deceased with the intention of defeating an application for financial provision under this Act made a disposition, and

(b) that full valuable consideration for that disposition was not given by the person to whom or for the benefit of whom the disposition was made (in this section referred to as "the donee") or by any other person, and

(c) that the exercise of the powers conferred by this section would facilitate the making of financial provision for the applicant under this Act, then, subject to the provisions of this section and of sections 12 and 13 of this Act, the court may order the donee (whether or not at the date of the order he holds any interest in the property disposed of to him or for his benefit by the deceased) to provide, for the purpose of the making of that financial provision, such sum of money or other property as may be specified in the order.

(3) Where an order is made under subsection (2) above as respects any disposition made by the deceased which consisted of the payment of money to or for the benefit of the donee, the amount of any sum of money or the value of any property ordered to be provided under that subsection shall not exceed the amount of the payment made by the deceased after deducting therefrom any capital transfer tax borne by the donee in respect of that payment.

(4) Where an order is made under subsection (2) above as respects any disposition made by the deceased which consisted of the transfer of property (other than a sum of money) to or for the benefit of the donee, the amount of any sum of money or the value of any property ordered to be provided under that subsection shall not exceed the value at the date of the death of the deceased of the property disposed of by him to or for the benefit of the donee (or if that property has been disposed of by the person to whom it was transferred by the deceased, the value at the date of that disposal thereof) after deducting therefrom any capital transfer tax borne by the donee in respect of the transfer of that property by the deceased.

(5) Where an application (in this subsection referred to as "the original application") is made for an order under subsection (2) above in relation to any disposition, then, if on an application under this subsection by the donee or by any applicant for an order under section 2 of this Act the court is satisfied—

(a) that, less than six years before the date of the death of the deceased, the deceased with the intention of defeating an application for financial provision under this Act made a disposition other than the disposition which is the subject of the original application, and

(b) that full valuable consideration for that other disposition was not given by the person to whom or for the benefit of whom that other disposition was made or by any other person, the court may exercise in relation to the person to whom or for the benefit of whom that other disposition was made the powers which the court would have had under subsection (2) above if the original application had been made in respect of that other disposition and the court had been satisfied as to the matters set out in paragraphs (a), (b) and (c) of that subsection; and where any application is made under this subsection, any reference in this section (except in subsection (2) (b)) to the donee shall include a reference to the person to whom or for the benefit of whom that other disposition was made.

(6) In determining whether and in what manner to exercise its powers under this section, the court shall have regard to the circumstances in

which any disposition was made and any valuable consideration which was given therefor, the relationship, if any, of the donee to the deceased, the conduct and financial resources of the donee and all the other circumstances of the case.

(7) In this section "disposition" does not include—

(a) any provision in a will, any such nomination as is mentioned in section 8(1) of this Act or any donatio mortis causa, or

(b) any appointment of property made, otherwise than by will, in the exercise of a special power of appointment, but, subject to these exceptions, includes any payment of money (including the payment of a premium under a policy of assurance) and any conveyance, assurance, appointment or gift of property of any description, whether made by an instrument or otherwise.

(8) The provisions of this section do not apply to any disposition made before the commencement of this Act.

11 Contracts to leave property by will.

(1) Where an application is made to a court for an order under section 2 of this Act, the applicant may, in the proceedings on that application, apply to the court for an order under this section.

(2) Where on an application under subsection (1) above the court is satisfied—

(a) that the deceased made a contract by which he agreed to leave by his will a sum of money or other property to any person or by which he agreed that a sum of money or other property would be paid or transferred to any person out of his estate, and

(b) that the deceased made that contract with the intention of defeating an application for financial provision under this Act, and

(c) that when the contract was made full valuable consideration for that contract was not given or promised by the person with whom or for the benefit of whom the contract was made (in this section referred to as "the donee") or by any other person, and

(d) that the exercise of the powers conferred by this section would facilitate the making of financial provision for the applicant under this Act, then, subject to the provisions of this section and of sections 12 and 13 of this Act, the court may make any one or more of the following orders, that is to say—

(i) if any money has been paid or any other property has been transferred to or for the benefit of the donee in accordance with the contract, an order directing the donee to provide, for the purpose of the making of that financial provision, such sum of money or other property as may be specified in the order;

(ii) if the money or all the money has not been paid or the property or all the property has not been transferred in accordance with the contract, an order directing the personal representatives not to make any payment or transfer any property, or not to make any further payment or transfer any further property, as the case may be, in accordance therewith or directing the personal representatives only to make such payment or transfer such property as may be specified in the order.

(3) Notwithstanding anything in subsection (2) above, the court may exercise its powers thereunder in relation to any contract made by the deceased only to the extent that the court considers that the amount of any sum of money paid or to be paid or the value of any property transferred or to be transferred in accordance with the contract exceeds the value of any valuable consideration given or to be given for that contract, and for this purpose the court shall have regard to the value of property at the date of the hearing.

(4) In determining whether and in what manner to exercise its powers under this section, the court shall have regard to the circumstances in which the contract was made, the relationship, if any, of the donee to

the deceased, the conduct and financial resources of the donee and all the other circumstances of the case.

(5) Where an order has been made under subsection (2) above in relation to any contract, the rights of any person to enforce that contract or to recover damages or to obtain other relief for the breach thereof shall be subject to any adjustment made by the court under section 12(3) of this Act and shall survive to such extent only as is consistent with giving effect to the terms of that order.

(6) The provisions of this section do not apply to a contract made before the commencement of this Act.

12 Provisions supplementary to ss. 10 and 11.

(1) Where the exercise of any of the powers conferred by section 10 or 11 of this Act is conditional on the court being satisfied that a disposition or contract was made by a deceased person with the intention of defeating an application for financial provision under this Act, that condition shall be fulfilled if the court is of the opinion that, on a balance of probabilities, the intention of the deceased (though not necessarily his sole intention) in making the disposition or contract was to prevent an order for financial provision being made under this Act or to reduce the amount of the provision which might otherwise be granted by an order thereunder.

(2) Where an application is made under section 11 of this Act with respect to any contract made by the deceased and no valuable consideration was given or promised by any person for that contract then, notwithstanding anything in subsection (1) above, it shall be presumed, unless the contrary is shown, that the deceased made that contract with the intention of defeating an application for financial provision under this Act.

(3) Where the court makes an order under section 10 or 11 of this Act it may give such consequential directions as it thinks fit (including directions requiring the making of any payment or the transfer of any

property) for giving effect to the order or for securing a fair adjustment of the rights of the persons affected thereby.

(4) Any power conferred on the court by the said section 10 or 11 to order the donee, in relation to any disposition or contract, to provide any sum of money or other property shall be exercisable in like manner in relation to the personal representative of the donee, and—

(a) any reference in section 10(4) to the disposal of property by the donee shall include a reference to disposal by the personal representative of the donee, and

(b) any reference in section 10(5) to an application by the donee under that subsection shall include a reference to an application by the personal representative of the donee; but the court shall not have power under the said section 10 or 11 to make an order in respect of any property forming part of the estate of the donee which has been distributed by the personal representative; and the personal representative shall not be liable for having distributed any such property before he has notice of the making of an application under the said section 10 or 11 on the ground that he ought to have taken into account the possibility that such an application would be made.

13 Provisions as to trustees in relation to ss. 10 and 11.

(1) Where an application is made for—

(a) an order under section 10 of this Act in respect of a disposition made by the deceased to any person as a trustee, or

(b) an order under section 11 of this Act in respect of any payment made or property transferred, in accordance with a contract made by the deceased, to any person as a trustee, the powers of the court under the said section 10 or 11 to order that trustee to provide a sum of money or other property shall be subject to the following limitation (in addition, in a case of an application under section 10, to any provision regarding the deduction of capital transfer tax) namely, that the amount of any sum of money or the value of any property ordered to be provided—

(i) in the case of an application in respect of a disposition which consisted of the payment of money or an application in respect of the payment of money in accordance with a contract, shall not exceed the aggregate of so much of that money as is at the date of the order in the hands of the trustee and the value at that date of any property which represents that money or is derived therefrom and is at that date in the hands of the trustee;

(ii) in the case of an application in respect of a disposition which consisted of the transfer of property (other than a sum of money) or an application in respect of the transfer of property (other than a sum of money) in accordance with a contract, shall not exceed the aggregate of the value at the date of the order of so much of that property as is at that date in the hands of the trustee and the value at that date of any property which represents the first-mentioned property or is derived therefrom and is at that date in the hands of the trustee.

(2) Where any such application is made in respect of a disposition made to any person as a trustee or in respect of any payment made or property transferred in pursuance of a contract to any person as a trustee, the trustee shall not be liable for having distributed any money or other property on the ground that he ought to have taken into account the possibility that such an application would be made.

(3) Where any such application is made in respect of a disposition made to any person as a trustee or in respect of any payment made or property transferred in accordance with a contract to any person as a trustee, any reference in the said section 10 or 11 to the donee shall be construed as including a reference to the trustee or trustees for the time being of the trust in question and any reference in subsection (1) or (2) above to a trustee shall be construed in the same way.

Special provisions relating to cases of divorce, separation etc.

14 Provision as to cases where no financial relief was granted in divorce proceedings etc.

(1) Where, within twelve months from the date on which a decree of divorce or nullity of marriage has been made absolute or a decree of judicial separation has been granted, a party to the marriage dies and—

(a) an application for a financial provision order under section 23 of the Matrimonial Causes Act 1973 or a property adjustment order under section 24 of that Act has not been made by the other party to that marriage, or

(b) such an application has been made but the proceedings thereon have not been determined at the time of the death of the deceased, then, if an application for an order under section 2 of this Act is made by that other party, the court shall, notwithstanding anything in section 1 or section 3 of this Act, have power, if it thinks it just to do so, to treat that party for the purposes of that application as if the decree of divorce or nullity of marriage had not been made absolute or the decree of judicial separation had not been granted, as the case may be.

(2) This section shall not apply in relation to a decree of judicial separation unless at the date of the death of the deceased the decree was in force and the separation was continuing.

14A Provision as to cases where no financial relief was granted in proceedings for the dissolution etc. of a civil partnership

(1) Subsection (2) below applies where—

(a) a dissolution order, nullity order, separation order or presumption of death order has been made under Chapter 2 of Part 2 of the Civil Partnership Act 2004 in relation to a civil partnership,

(b) one of the civil partners dies within twelve months from the date on which the order is made, and

(c) either—

(i) an application for a financial provision order under Part 1 of Schedule 5 to that Act or a property adjustment order under Part 2 of that Schedule has not been made by the other civil partner, or

(ii) such an application has been made but the proceedings on the application have not been determined at the time of the death of the deceased.

(2) If an application for an order under section 2 of this Act is made by the surviving civil partner, the court shall, notwithstanding anything in section 1 or section 3 of this Act, have power, if it thinks it just to do so, to treat the surviving civil partner as if the order mentioned in sub-section (1) (a) above had not been made.

(3) This section shall not apply in relation to a separation order unless at the date of the death of the deceased the separation order was in force and the separation was continuing.

15 Restriction imposed in divorce proceedings etc. on application under this Act.

(1) On the grant of a decree of divorce, a decree of nullity of marriage or a decree of judicial separation or at any time thereafter the court, if it considers it just to do so, may, on the application of either party to the marriage, order that the other party to the marriage shall not on the death of the applicant be entitled to apply for an order under section 2 of this Act. In this subsection "the court" means the High Court or the family court.

(2) In the case of a decreee of divorce or nullity of marriage an order may be made under subsection (1) above before or after the decree is made absolute, but if it is made before the decree is made absolute it shall not take effect unless the decree is made absolute.

(3) Where an order made under subsection (1) above on the grant of a decree of divorce or nullity of marriage has come into force with respect

to a party to a marriage, then, on the death of the other party to that marriage, the court shall not entertain any application for an order under section 2 of this Act made by the first-mentioned party.

(4) Where an order made under subsection (1) above on the grant of a decree of judicial separation has come into force with respect to any party to a marriage, then, if the other party to that marriage dies while the decree is in force and the separation is continuing, the court shall not entertain any application for an order under section 2 of this Act made by the first-mentioned party.

15ZA Restriction imposed in proceedings for the dissolution etc. of a civil partnership on application under this Act

(1) On making a dissolution order, nullity order, separation order or presumption of death order under Chapter 2 of Part 2 of the Civil Partnership Act 2004, or at any time after making such an order, the court, if it considers it just to do so, may, on the application of either of the civil partners, order that the other civil partner shall not on the death of the applicant be entitled to apply for an order under section 2 of this Act.

(2) In subsection (1) above "the court" means the High Court or the family court.

(3) In the case of a dissolution order, nullity order or presumption of death order ("the main order") an order may be made under subsection (1) above before (as well as after) the main order is made final, but if made before the main order is made final it shall not take effect unless the main order is made final.

(4) Where an order under subsection (1) above made in connection with a dissolution order, nullity order or presumption of death order has come into force with respect to a civil partner, then, on the death of the other civil partner, the court shall not entertain any application for an order under section 2 of this Act made by the surviving civil partner.

(5) Where an order under subsection (1) above made in connection with a separation order has come into force with respect to a civil partner, then, if the other civil partner dies while the separation order is in force and the separation is continuing, the court shall not entertain any application for an order under section 2 of this Act made by the surviving civil partner.

15A Restriction imposed in proceedings under Matrimonial and Family Proceedings Act 1984 on application under this Act.

(1) On making an order under section 17 of the Matrimonial and Family Proceedings Act 1984 (orders for financial provision and property adjustment following overseas divorces, etc.) the court, if it considers it just to do so, may, on the application of either party to the marriage, order that the other party to the marriage shall not on the death of the applicant be entitled to apply for an order under section 2 of this Act. In this subsection "the court" means the High Court or the family court.

(2) Where an order under subsection (1) above has been made with respect to a party to a marriage which has been dissolved or annulled, then, on the death of the other party to that marriage, the court shall not entertain an application under section 2 of this Act made by the first-mentioned party.

(3) Where an order under subsection (1) above has been made with respect to a party to a marriage the parties to which have been legally separated, then, if the other party to the marriage dies while the legal separation is in force, the court shall not entertain an application under section 2 of this Act made by the first-mentioned party.

15B Restriction imposed in proceedings under Schedule 7 to the Civil Partnership Act 2004 on application under this Act

(1) On making an order under paragraph 9 of Schedule 7 to the Civil Partnership Act 2004 (orders for financial provision, property adjustment and pension-sharing following overseas dissolution etc. of

civil partnership) the court, if it considers it just to do so, may, on the application of either of the civil partners, order that the other civil partner shall not on the death of the applicant be entitled to apply for an order under section 2 of this Act.

(2) In subsection (1) above "the court" means the High Court or the family court.

(3) Where an order under subsection (1) above has been made with respect to one of the civil partners in a case where a civil partnership has been dissolved or annulled, then, on the death of the other civil partner, the court shall not entertain an application under section 2 of this Act made by the surviving civil partner.

(4) Where an order under subsection (1) above has been made with respect to one of the civil partners in a case where civil partners have been legally separated, then, if the other civil partner dies while the legal separation is in force, the court shall not entertain an application under section 2 of this Act made by the surviving civil partner.

16 Variation and discharge of secured periodical payments orders made under Matrimonial Causes Act 1973.

(1) Where an application for an order under section 2 of this Act is made to the court by any person who was at the time of the death of the deceased entitled to payments from the deceased under a secured periodical payments order made under the Matrimonial Causes Act 1973 or Schedule 5 to the Civil Partnership Act 2004, then, in the proceedings on that application, the court shall have power, if an application is made under this section by that person or by the personal representative of the deceased, to vary or discharge that periodical payments order or to revive the operation of any provision thereof which has been suspended under section 31 of that Act of 1973 or Part 11 of that Schedule.

(2) In exercising the powers conferred by this section the court shall have regard to all the circumstances of the case, including any order which the court proposes to make under section 2 or section 5 of this

Act and any change (whether resulting from the death of the deceased or otherwise) in any of the matters to which the court was required to have regard when making the secured periodical payments order.

(3) The powers exercisable by the court under this section in relation to an order shall be exercisable also in relation to any instrument executed in pursuance of the order.

17 Variation and revocation of maintenance agreements.

(1) Where an application for an order under section 2 of this Act is made to the court by any person who was at the time of the death of the deceased entitled to payments from the deceased under a maintenance agreement which provided for the continuation of payments under the agreement after the death of the deceased, then, in the proceedings on that application, the court shall have power, if an application is made under this section by that person or by the personal representative of the deceased, to vary or revoke that agreement.

(2) In exercising the powers conferred by this section the court shall have regard to all the circumstances of the case, including any order which the court proposes to make under section 2 or section 5 of this Act and any change (whether resulting from the death of the deceased or otherwise) in any of the circumstances in the light of which the agreement was made.

(3) If a maintenance agreement is varied by the court under this section the like consequences shall ensue as if the variation had been made immediately before the death of the deceased by agreement between the parties and for valuable consideration.

(4) In this section "maintenance agreement", in relation to a deceased person, means any agreement made, whether in writing or not and whether before or after the commencement of this Act, by the deceased with any person with whom he formed a marriage or civil partnership, being an agreement which contained provisions governing the rights and liabilities towards one another when living separately of the parties to that marriage or of the civil partners(whether or not the marriage or

civil partnership has been dissolved or annulled) in respect of the making or securing of payments or the disposition or use of any property, including such rights and liabilities with respect to the maintenance or education of any child, whether or not a child of the deceased or a person who was treated by the deceased as a child of the family in relation to that marriage or civil partnership.

18 Availability of court's powers under this Act in applications under ss. 31 and 36 of the Matrimonial Causes Act 1973.

(1) Where—

(a) a person against whom a secured periodical payments order was made under the Matrimonial Causes Act 1973 has died and an application is made under section 31(6) of that Act for the variation or discharge of that order or for the revival of the operation of any provision thereof which has been suspended, or

(b) a party to a maintenance agreement within the meaning of section 34 of that Act has died, the agreement being one which provides for the continuation of payments thereunder after the death of one of the parties, and an application is made under section 36(1) of that Act for the alteration of the agreement under section 35 thereof, the court shall have power to direct that the application made under the said section 31(6) or 36(1) shall be deemed to have been accompanied by an application for an order under section 2 of this Act.

(2) Where the court gives a direction under subsection (1) above it shall have power, in the proceedings on the application under the said section 31(6) or 36(1), to make any order which the court would have had power to make under the provisions of this Act if the application under the said section 31(6) or 36(1), as the case may be, had been made jointly with an application for an order under the said section 2; and the court shall have power to give such consequential directions as may be necessary for enabling the court to exercise any of the powers available to the court under this Act in the case of an application for an order under section 2.

(3) Where an order made under section 15(1) of this Act is in force with respect to a party to a marriage, the court shall not give a direction under subsection (1) above with respect to any application made under the said section 31(6) or 36(1) by that party on the death of the other party.

18A Availability of court's powers under this Act in applications under paragraphs 60 and 73 of Schedule 5 to the Civil Partnership Act 2004

(1) Where—

(a) a person against whom a secured periodical payments order was made under Schedule 5 to the Civil Partnership Act 2004 has died and an application is made under paragraph 60 of that Schedule for the variation or discharge of that order or for the revival of the operation of any suspended provision of the order, or

(b) a party to a maintenance agreement within the meaning of Part 13 of that Schedule has died, the agreement being one which provides for the continuation of payments under the agreement after the death of one of the parties, and an application is made under paragraph 73 of that Schedule for the alteration of the agreement under paragraph 69 of that Schedule, the court shall have power to direct that the application made under paragraph 60 or 73 of that Schedule shall be deemed to have been accompanied by an application for an order under section 2 of this Act.

(2) Where the court gives a direction under subsection (1) above it shall have power, in the proceedings on the application under paragraph 60 or 73 of that Schedule, to make any order which the court would have had power to make under the provisions of this Act if the application under that paragraph had been made jointly with an application for an order under section 2 of this Act; and the court shall have power to give such consequential directions as may be necessary for enabling the court to exercise any of the powers available to the court under this Act in the case of an application for an order under section 2.

(3) Where an order made under section 15ZA(1) of this Act is in force with respect to a civil partner, the court shall not give a direction under subsection (1) above with respect to any application made under paragraph 60 or 73 of that Schedule by that civil partner on the death of the other civil partner.

Miscellaneous and supplementary provisions

19 Effect, duration and form of orders.

(1) Where an order is made under section 2 of this Act then for all purposes, including the purposes of the enactments relating to capital transfer tax, the will or the law relating to intestacy, or both the will and the law relating to intestacy, as the case may be, shall have effect and be deemed to have had effect as from the deceased's death subject to the provisions of the order.

(2) Any order made under section 2 or 5 of this Act in favour of—

(a) an applicant who was the former spouse or former civil partner of the deceased, or

(b) an applicant who was the husband or wife of the deceased in a case where the marriage with the deceased was the subject of a decree of judicial separation and at the date of death the decree was in force and the separation was continuing, or

(c) an applicant who was the civil partner of the deceased in a case where, at the date of death, a separation order under Chapter 2 of Part 2 of the Civil Partnership Act 2004 was in force in relation to their civil partnership and the separation was continuing, shall, in so far as it provides for the making of periodical payments, cease to have effect on the formation by the applicant of a subsequent marriage or civil partnership, except in relation to any arrears due under the order on the date of the formation of the subsequent marriage or civil partnership.

(3) A copy of every order made under this Act other than an order made under section 15(1) or 15ZA(1) of this Act shall be sent to the

principal registry of the Family Division for entry and filing, and a memorandum of the order shall be endorsed on, or permanently annexed to, the probate or letters of administration under which the estate is being administered.

20 Provisions as to personal representatives.

(1) The provisions of this Act shall not render the personal representative of a deceased person liable for having distributed any part of the estate of the deceased, after the end of the period of six months from the date on which representation with respect to the estate of the deceased is first taken out, on the ground that he ought to have taken into account the possibility—

(a) that the court might permit the making of an application for an order under section 2 of this Act after the end of that period, or

(b) that, where an order has been made under the said section 2, the court might exercise in relation thereto the powers conferred on it by section 6 of this Act, but this subsection shall not prejudice any power to recover, by reason of the making of an order under this Act, any part of the estate so distributed.

(2) Where the personal representative of a deceased person pays any sum directed by an order under section 5 of this Act to be paid out of the deceased's net estate, he shall not be under any liability by reason of that estate not being sufficient to make the payment, unless at the time of making the payment he has reasonable cause to believe that the estate is not sufficient.

(3) Where a deceased person entered into a contract by which he agreed to leave by his will any sum of money or other property to any person or by which he agreed that a sum of money or other property would be paid or transferred to any person out of his estate, then, if the personal representative of the deceased has reason to believe that the deceased entered into the contract with the intention of defeating an application for financial provision under this Act, he may, notwithstanding anything in that contract, postpone the payment of that sum of money or

the transfer of that property until the expiration of the period of six months from the date on which representation with respect to the estate of the deceased is first taken out or, if during that period an application is made for an order under section 2 of this Act, until the determination of the proceedings on that application.

21. . . . .

22. . . . .

23 Determination of date on which representation was first taken out

(1) The following are to be left out of account when considering for the purposes of this Act when representation with respect to the estate of a deceased person was first taken out—

(a) a grant limited to settled land or to trust property,

(b) any other grant that does not permit any of the estate to be distributed,

(c) a grant limited to real estate or to personal estate, unless a grant limited to the remainder of the estate has previously been made or is made at the same time,

(d) a grant, or its equivalent, made outside the United Kingdom (but see subsection (2) below).

(2) A grant sealed under section 2 of the Colonial Probates Act 1892 counts as a grant made in the United Kingdom for the purposes of this section, but is to be taken as dated on the date of sealing.

24 Effect of this Act on s. 46(1) (vi) of Administration of Estates Act 1925.

Section 46(1) (vi) of the Administration of Estates Act 1925, in so far as it provides for the devolution of property on the Crown, the Duchy of Lancaster or the Duke of Cornwall as bona vacantia, shall have effect subject to the provisions of this Act.

25 Interpretation.

(1) In this Act—

"beneficiary", in relation to the estate of a deceased person, means—

(a) a person who under the will of the deceased or under the law relating to intestacy is beneficially interested in the estate or would be so interested if an order had not been made under this Act, and

(b) a person who has received any sum of money or other property which by virtue of section 8(1) or 8(2) of this Act is treated as part of the net estate of the deceased or would have received that sum or other property if an order had not been made under this Act;

"child" includes an illegitimate child and a child en ventre sa mere at the death of the deceased;

"the court" means unless the context otherwise requires the High Court, or where the county court has jurisdiction by virtue of section 25 of the County Courts Act 1984, the county court;

"former civil partner" means a person whose civil partnership with the deceased was during the lifetime of the deceased either—

(a) dissolved or annulled by an order made under the law of any part of the British Islands, or

(b) dissolved or annulled in any country or territory outside the British Islands by a dissolution or annulment which is entitled to be recognised as valid by the law of England and Wales;

"former spouse" means a person whose marriage with the deceased was during the lifetime of the deceased either—

(a) dissolved or annulled by a decree of divorce or a decree of nullity of marriage granted under the law of any part of the British Islands, or

(b) dissolved or annulled in any country or territory outside the British Islands by a divorce or annulment which is entitled to be recognised as valid by the law of England and Wales;

"net estate", in relation to a deceased person, means:—

(a) all property of which the deceased had power to dispose by his will (otherwise than by virtue of a special power of appointment) less the amount of his funeral, testamentary and administration expenses, debts and liabilities, including any capital transfer tax payable out of his estate on his death;

(b) any property in respect of which the deceased held a general power of appointment (not being a power exercisable by will) which has not been exercised;

(c) any sum of money or other property which is treated for the purposes of this Act as part of the net estate of the deceased by virtue of section 8(1) or (2) of this Act;

(d) any property which is treated for the purposes of this Act as part of the net estate of the deceased by virtue of an order made under section 9 of the Act;

(e) any sum of money or other property which is, by reason of a disposition or contract made by the deceased, ordered under section 10 or 11 of this Act to be provided for the purpose of the making of financial provision under this Act;

"property" includes any chose in action;

"reasonable financial provision" has the meaning assigned to it by section 1 of this Act;

"valuable consideration" does not include marriage or a promise of marriage;

"will" includes codicil.

(2) For the purposes of paragraph (a) of the definition of "net estate" in subsection (1) above a person who is not of full age and capacity shall be treated as having power to dispose by will of all property of which he would have had power to dispose by will if he had been of full age and capacity.

(3) Any reference in this Act to provision out of the net estate of a deceased person includes a reference to provision extending to the whole of that estate.

(4) For the purposes of this Act any reference to a spouse, wife or husband shall be treated as including a reference to a person who in good faith entered into a void marriage with the deceased unless either —

(a) the marriage of the deceased and that person was dissolved or annulled during the lifetime of the deceased and the dissolution or annulment is recognised by the law of England and Wales, or

(b) that person has during the lifetime of the deceased formed a subsequent marriage or civil partnership.

(4A) For the purposes of this Act any reference to a civil partner shall be treated as including a reference to a person who in good faith formed a void civil partnership with the deceased unless either—

(a) the civil partnership between the deceased and that person was dissolved or annulled during the lifetime of the deceased and the dissolution or annulment is recognised by the law of England and Wales, or

(b) that person has during the lifetime of the deceased formed a subsequent civil partnership or marriage.

(5) Any reference in this Act to the formation of, or to a person who has formed, a subsequent marriage or civil partnership includes (as the case may be) a reference to the formation of, or to a person who has formed, a marriage or civil partnership which is by law void or voidable.

(5A) The formation of a marriage or civil partnership shall be treated for the purposes of this Act as the formation of a subsequent marriage or civil partnership, in relation to either of the spouses or civil partners, notwithstanding that the previous marriage or civil partnership of that spouse or civil partner was void or voidable.

(6) Any reference in this Act to an order or decree made under the Matrimonial Causes Act 1973 or under any section of that Act shall be construed as including a reference to an order or decree which is deemed to have been made under that Act or under that section thereof, as the case may be.

(6A) Any reference in this Act to an order made under, or under any provision of, the Civil Partnership Act 2004 shall be construed as including a reference to anything which is deemed to be an order made (as the case may be) under that Act or provision.

(7) Any reference in this Act to any enactment is a reference to that enactment as amended by or under any subsequent enactment.

26 Consequential amendments, repeals and transitional provisions.

(1) . . . .

(2) Subject to the provisions of this section, the enactments specified in the Schedule to this Act are hereby repealed to the extent specified in the third column of the Schedule; and in paragraph 5(2) of Schedule 2 to the Matrimonial Causes Act 1973 for the words "that Act" there shall be substituted the words "the Matrimonial Causes Act 1965."

(3) The repeal of the said enactments shall not affect their operation in relation to any application made thereunder (whether before or after the

commencement of this Act) with reference to the death of any person who died before the commencement of this Act.

(4) Without prejudice to the provisions of section 38 of the Interpretation Act 1889 (which relates to the effect of repeals) nothing in any repeal made by this Act shall affect any order made or direction given under any enactment repealed by this Act, and, subject to the provisions of this Act, every such order or direction (other than an order made under section 4A of the Inheritance Family Provision Act 1938 or section 28A of the Matrimonial Causes Act 1965) shall, if it is in force at the commencement of this Act or is made by virtue of subsection (3) above, continue in force as if it had been made under section 2(1) (a) of this Act, and for the purposes of section 6(7) of this Act the court in exercising its powers under that section in relation to an order continued in force by this subsection shall be required to have regard to any change in any of the circumstances to which the court would have been required to have regard when making that order if the order had been made with reference to the death of any person who died after the commencement of this Act.

27 Short title, commencement and extent.

(1) This Act may be cited as the Inheritance (Provision for Family and Dependants) Act 1975.

(2) This Act does not extend to Scotland or Northern Ireland.

(3) This Act shall come into force on 1st April 1976.

Source: https://www.legislation.gov.uk/ukpga/1975/63

APPENDIX II
INHERITANCE ACT INSTRUCTION FOR USE WITH FORM E: SECTION 1

This form can also be found online at:

http://familyproperty.org.uk/inheritance-act-book/instructions-form-download/

Client

1.1 Full name	
1.2 Date of birth	
1.3 Occupation	

Deceased Parent

1.4 Name	
1.5 Date and cause of death	
1.6 Place of death	
1.7 Death certificate? Y/N	
1.8 DP's age at death	
1.9 Will or intestacy?	

Estate

1.10 Gross value	
1.11 Net value	
1.12 Date of grant of probate	
1.13 Last issue date	

Contents of Estate

1.14.1 Land and real property	
1.14.2 Cash, savings, investments	
1.14.3 Beneficial interests (including discretionary trusts)	
1.14.4 Other	
1.14.5 Distribution of estate under Will/intestacy	

Supplementary information about AC

1.15 AC's interest under the Will/intestacy	
1.16 AC's state of health	
1.17 AC's current earning capacity	

Beneficiary/other claimant information – complete this section for any significant beneficiary or potential Inheritance Act claimant

1.18.1 Name	
1.18.2 Age	
1.18.3 General health	
1.18.4 Disabilities	
1.18.5 Relationship to DP	
1.18.6 Dependants	
1.18.7 If joint owner of property with DP, state property and approximate total value	
1.18.8 Gifts from DP during DP's lifetime	

DP's dependants

1.19.1 For each dependant: name, age, relationship	

APPENDIX III
FURTHER READING

Inheritance Act Practitioner Textbooks

Inheritance Act Claims Sidney Ross
London: Sweet & Maxwell, 4th Edition, 2017

Inheritance Act Claims: Law, Practice and Procedure Andrew Francis
London: LexisNexis Butterworths (Looseleaf)

A Practitioner's Guide to Inheritance Act Claims Nasreen Pearce
London: Wildy, Simmons & Hill 2017 (Third Edition)

Inheritance Act Claims: A Practical Guide Miranda Allardice, Tracey Angus, Paul Hewitt, Penelope Reed
London: Law Society Publishing 2017

Best Practice Negotiation and Communication

ACTAPS Code http://www.actaps.com/draft.cfm

Form E and Completion Guidance

Interactive Form E
https://formfinder.hmctsformfinder.justice.gov.uk/form-e1-eng.pdf

Form E Guidance Notes
https://formfinder.hmctsformfinder.justice.gov.uk/form-e-notes-eng.pdf

Budgeting Tools

MoneyAdvice Budget Planner
https://www.moneyadviceservice.org.uk/en/tools/budget-planner

Benefits Calculators

www.entitledto.co.uk/benefits-calculator/startcalc.aspx

https://benefits-calculator.turn2us.org.uk

https://www.gov.uk/benefits-calculators

DWP Decision Makers Guide: Capital

https://www.gov.uk/government/uploads/system/uploads/attachment_data/file/649901/dmgch29.pdf

Other Resources

Capitalisation of income needs in Inheritance Act claims: Duxbury or Ogden? Sidney Ross, Family Law Week, available online at: http://www.familylawweek.co.uk/site.aspx?i=ed33461

Charities and Litigation Guide
https://www.gov.uk/government/publications/charities-and-litigation-a-guide-for-trustees-cc38/charities-and-litigation-a-guide-for-trustees.

MORE BOOKS BY LAW BRIEF PUBLISHING

A selection of our other titles available now:

'A Practical Guide to Drone Law' by Rufus Ballaster, Andrew Firman, Eleanor Clot
'Practical Mediation: A Guide for Mediators, Advocates, Advisers, Lawyers, and Students in Civil, Commercial, Business, Property, Workplace, and Employment Cases' by Jonathan Dingle with John Sephton
'Practical Horse Law: A Guide for Owners and Riders' by Brenda Gilligan
'A Comparative Guide to Standard Form Construction and Engineering Contracts' by Jon Close
'A Practical Guide to Compliance for Personal Injury Firms Working With Claims Management Companies' by Paul Bennett
'A Practical Guide to the Landlord and Tenant Act 1954: Commercial Tenancies' by Richard Hayes & David Sawtell
'A Practical Guide to Personal Injury Claims Involving Animals' by Jonathan Hand
'A Practical Guide to Psychiatric Claims in Personal Injury' by Liam Ryan
'Introduction to the Law of Community Care in England and Wales' by Alan Robinson
'A Practical Guide to Dog Law for Owners and Others' by Andrea Pitt
'Ellis and Kevan on Credit Hire, 5th Edition' by Aidan Ellis & Tim Kevan
'RTA Allegations of Fraud in a Post-Jackson Era: The Handbook, 2nd Edition' by Andrew Mckie
'A Practical Guide to Holiday Sickness Claims' by Andrew Mckie & Ian Skeate
'RTA Personal Injury Claims: A Practical Guide Post-Jackson' by Andrew Mckie
'On Experts: CPR35 for Lawyers and Experts' by David Boyle
'An Introduction to Personal Injury Law' by David Boyle

Our books are also usually in stock at www.amazon.co.uk with free next day delivery for Prime members, and at good legal bookshops such as Hammicks and Wildy & Sons.

We are regularly launching new books in our series of practical day-to-day practitioners' guides. Visit our website and join our free newsletter to be kept informed and to receive special offers, free chapters, etc.

You can also follow us on Twitter at www.twitter.com/lawbriefpub.